What to Do…
What Not to Do…
and Where to Find an Expert When You Need One

It's a fact: Only one out of five new firms survives its first year. That's a distressing statistic for any would-be entrepreneur planning to reap the considerable financial and psychological benefits of being his or her own boss. But now Randy Baca Smith, a seasoned small-business expert with experience in advising thousands of real-life businesses, tells you how your firm can be the one in five that survives and prospers.

Many new ventures fail because their owners don't know the first thing about running a small business. Randy Baca Smith tells you the first thing and the second, with solid step-by-step advice on everything from advertising and PR to the nitty-gritty of negotiating credit and site selection. Cutting through the specialized details, she presents the essential information, necessary facts, and standard procedures that give you everything you need to know to successfully plan, establish, and operate your own business.

But more than this, *Setting Up Shop* provides critical insight into the many personal and financial pitfalls that you must watch for when you go into business for yourself—insight that can mean the difference between a solid business success and a near miss.

If you've ever contemplated starting your own business, *Setting Up Shop* is the one essential, straightforward book to tell you how you should—or why you shouldn't.

Setting Up Shop

The Do's and Don'ts
of Starting a Small Business

Randy Baca Smith

WARNER BOOKS

A Warner Communications Company

Warner Books Edition
Copyright © 1982 by McGraw-Hill, Inc.
All rights reserved.
This Warner Books edition is published by arrangement with
McGraw-Hill Book Company, 1221 Avenue of the Americas,
New York, NY 10020.
Warner Books, Inc., 666 Fifth Avenue, New York, NY 10103

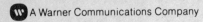 A Warner Communications Company

Printed in the United States of America
First Warner printing: May 1983
10 9 8 7 6 5 4 3 2 1

Library of Congress Cataloging in Publication Data

Smith, Randy Baca.
  Setting up shop.

  Bibliography: p.
  Includes index.
  1. New business enterprises—Management.   2. Small
business—Management.   I. Title.
HD62.5.S65   1983   658.1´141   82-20084
ISBN 0-446-37533-0 (USA)
ISBN 0-446-37550-0 (Can.)

TO BILL
With whom I share my joys, my sorrows, my life

Contents

Preface

Let's get something straight. You've obviously already bought or borrowed this book. I, therefore, have no further vested interest in these proceedings.

That's important, because what you are about to read is factual and you need to believe that. It may shock you, anger you, discourage you, appall you. It may also educate you, inform you, inspire you, and, perhaps, save you much time, grief, money, and heartache.

I've made my 27 cents on the deal; now it's your turn. I believe you'll get your money's worth.

The Great American Dream, contrary to popular opinion, is not "to grow up to be President." Not of the country, anyway.

No thinking person would consider that a reasonable or even desirable career goal these days. Rather, we seem to have a collective consciousness that makes about 97 percent of us long for the day we will own our own business; "be the boss," as it were. The other 3 percent of our population is relatively sane.

Advertising executives dream of owning chicken ranches; bank presidents imagine what unspeakable joy awaits them in running small gift shops in Providence, La Jolla, or Sante Fe; a bricklayer saves for years to open a restaurant; a teacher trades tenure for a real estate license and his or her own firm; a retired couple sells the family home and buys a motel, sight unseen, in Yuma, Arizona. And so it goes.

That's great, right? Right and wrong. It's great if you make it. And not at all great if you don't.

Of the thousands of new businesses started up this year in the United States, fully half will not be with us 12 months from now. Seventy-five percent of the rest will not survive their fifth anniversary sale. For these people, the Great American Dream will have become a nightmare.

Acknowledgments

I wish to thank the dedicated staff of the Arizona Small Business Association, the U.S. Small Business Administration, the National Economic Development Association, and my dear friend Anna Muller, area vice president of NEDA, for their advice and assistance. Without the help of these individuals and agencies this book could not have been written. To William R. Newton, senior editor at McGraw-Hill Book Company, "thank you" will never cover my gratitude and appreciation. Most especially, to Jeanne Provorse, secretary, proofreader, slavedriver, and friend; this is truly "our" book.

About the Author

Randy Baca Smith has been a disc jockey, advertising account executive, copy writer, public relations counselor, and small business owner. Her feature stories and articles have appeared in dozens of newspapers and periodicals ranging from *The New York Times* to *Holiday* magazine.

She became interested in the problems of small business owners while operating her own firm and soon entered into contracts with the U.S. Small Business Administration (SBA) and the National Economic Development Association (NEDA) to advise and assist small businesses experiencing problems throughout the country.

Her interest and expertise grew, leading to a two-year stint as executive director of the Arizona Small Business Association, a nonprofit business development and educational agency providing management and technical assistance to entrepreneurs. She has taught, trained, and counseled thousands of individual business owners.

Educated at the College of St. Joseph and the University of New Mexico, she lectures extensively throughout the country and serves as a curriculum and project development consultant to several institutions of higher learning.

Active in civic and political affairs, Ms. Baca Smith sits on numerous boards and commissions at the local, state, and national level. She and her husband, broadcasting executive William G. "Bill" Smith are the parents of five grown children. They make their home in Phoenix, Arizona.

1

Are You Sure You Want to Do This?

HELP WANTED: Combination manager-stock clerk to take full charge of new firm. Must like people and hard work. Duties include purchasing, books, payroll, marketing, personnel, shipping and receiving, customer complaints, government and public relations, janitorial, and sales. Must be available 24 hours daily, 7 days a week. Furnish own transportation. Salary depends on profits. Faiiure to meet goals may result in forfeiture of personal residence, repossession of car and furniture, destruction of credit rating. No vacation likely for a minimum of 2 years. Good opportunity for nervous breakdown and marital breakup. No previous experience necessary but all experience might be helpful. Apply in person. An equal opportunity employer.

If you read this ad in the classified section of your local newspaper, chances are you'd take it as a practical joker's wild attempt to identify the local loonies. Yet each year, thousands of reasonably sane, more-or-less mature men and women apply for just such a job.

As a matter of fact, they hock their homes and furniture, borrow from in-laws and friends, cash in life insurance policies, and sell the family jewels to pay for the privilege.

"Impossible!" you say? "Only a nut would even consider such a job offer!"

Well, I can't argue with that. Truth is, as they say, stranger than fiction. And the truth is that each year many thousands of men and women go into business for themselves.

The "help wanted" ad above very accurately describes the job these people create for themselves. Most of them don't know that is what they're doing, but know it or not, that is what they're doing.

These bright-eyed hopefuls scrape together a few hundred or a few thousand dollars and, armed with optimism and not much else, plunge headfirst into the mainstream of America's economy.

Not only do they not know how to swim in that mainstream, but the vast majority of them don't even own a pair of water wings.

There are exceptions to every generality. I am convinced that everyone thinks he or she will be that exception, whether regarding cigarette smoking, skiing, or the proliferation of small business.

People are lulled into the comfortable assumption that lung cancer, broken bones, and business failures are things that will happen to someone else, not to them. Does the shoe fit?

Look at it this way: Owning and operating your own business is very akin to slavery—except precious few slaves voluntarily take up their low-paying, benefitless existence. It's kicking and screaming all the way for them.

You think I'm kidding?

Just take a look at some of the fallacious reasons people give for wanting to own and operate their own businesses.

Dumb Reason Number 1:

"I'm tired of working for someone else!"

This one just blows me away! Whatever makes people think they won't get tired of working for themselves? You can, in fact, look forward to working harder than you've ever imagined working, once you open your own business. A conservative estimate is 60 to 75 hours per week for the first 18 to 36 months of operation. After that, if all goes extremely well, you may be able to cut back just a bit. Not much, mind you. But a bit.

Dumb Reason Number 2:

"I'll be able to do exactly what I please, when I please!"

Can you beat that? There are actually thousands of people who don't understand there's no such thing as a free lunch! As the owner of a small business, you'll have the privilege of doing exactly what everyone else in your employ doesn't get done. Because someone has to do it. Not when you please, either. When you have to. And that will usually be after-hours, weekends, Sundays, and holidays.

Dumb Reason Number 3:

"I don't like taking orders."

Now, that is priceless. Just try operating a business by not taking orders from every customer you manage to attract. You'll be out of business so fast it'll make you dizzy.

Dumb Reason Number 4:

"I'll be able to take time off whenever I want to play golf, gin rummy, etc., go skiing, chase women/men, go on vacation," or any of the other run-and-have-fun interests they—and you—can dream up.

Refer to numbers 1, 2, and 3 above. Add to these the fact that you probably won't have the money to do all your favorite things for some time to come. I've met small business owners who were rabid bridge players before opening their own firms. Haven't played in years. The same is true for golfers. When you're the "here" at which the buck stops, a lot of other things stop, too. Mainly the fun stuff.

Naturally. It's one part of your life that can most easily be rearranged. After all, you have to sleep a few hours each night or you'll eventually poop out. And that's not good for business.

I might also add it usually is rough on your sex life. For much the same reason. Ditto your family life. It is considered advisable to face this grim stuff with your spouse, mate, "significant other," children, and the rest of your family and friends, if the closeness of the relationships warrants it.

Getting their understanding, encouragement, support, and assistance during the rough months you'll be facing will help a lot. If you are not going to get this kind of backup, something's going to give. It may be a marriage, a friendship, a parental relationship, an affair. It may even be your business.

Face it right up front. When everyone involved understands it's going to be rough, they might just rise to the occasion. Then, if it's not as grim as I say, you'll be pleasantly surprised. And won't that be nice?

We could explore at least a dozen other dumb reasons. Enough is enough. There is, however, one right reason for going into business.

To make money.

Isn't that simple? And it is the only acceptable reason for facing this trauma, my friend. The profit motive is the *only* one for which risking so much might be considered justifiable.

I am not referring to the obvious monetary risks involved in private enterprise. There are other costs. Costs impossible to calculate.

Recognize that the hours you will miss with your children, for instance, can never be replaced. Place your own price tag on the strain your business will represent to family and friends.

There will be other very personal costs, as well—involving both your physical health and your emotional well-being.

You are the only person who can possibly assess whether the trade-off will be a good one, for the cost and the price you will pay are very individual things indeed.

These are value questions. Your values and mine probably differ. So any attempt on my part to come up with a bottom line figure for your more-than-money balance sheet would inevitably prove futile. But in the business world, the bottom line is all. Whatever the figure, you'll have to pay it—and live with it.

Forewarned, as they say, is forearmed.

DO YOU HAVE WHAT IT TAKES?

"Bull! You can't scare me!"

I know, I know, that's what you're thinking. And that's good. Because if you scare easily, you don't have one of the things it takes. Guts.

It takes a lot of other things, too. It takes you. A combination of your skills, your talents, your contacts. But maybe your abilities aren't enough. Then, perhaps, it takes two of you. Or more. Or what the business world refers to as a partnership. More on that later.

It takes money. Not just some money. Or a lot of money. It takes enough money.

And that's one of the things small business owners and potential entrepreneurs have a rough time determining. How much is enough?

Hang in there. This, too, shall come.

It also takes customers.

The whole process is very logical. Let's play a glorified game of "twenty questions" and find out if you have what it takes personally.

How about *you*? You already know it's not going to be a piece of cake. But what else do you have besides staying power? Have you worked in a business similar to the one you want to start? This can be a big bugger. Experience in the same or a closely related business can really tip the scales in your favor. If you have no related work experience, get some. Before you go into business.

This could mean moonlighting on evenings and weekends, or leaving your present job and investing 6 months or so in a similar business in order to give yourself practical working experience. Remember, there's a method to the madness of the boss's son or daughter working in the stockroom. The boss recognizes that the idiot kid is going to blow the whole deal unless he or she knows firsthand what Daddy's business is really all about.

You are going to need managerial skills. Ideally, you'll have working experience as a supervisor, manager, call it what you will. You will need to know how to manage other people. And experience is the best teacher.

Something else you will find crucial is some basic accounting training. If you haven't had it, get it—in night school, through workshops and seminars conducted by trade associations, community colleges, local chambers of commerce, and the like. If you have absolutely no bookkeeping acumen and no desire to acquire any, you'd better pay very strict attention to the information on CPAs coming up in Chapter 3. In addition, make sure your staff includes someone qualified and trustworthy to handle these record-keeping chores for you. Another option might be a spouse who knows what you don't about keeping books.

Last but not least, do you have any money? We'll spend lots of time on money: how much you need, where to get it, how to make it go as far as possible. But rest assured, if you have none of your own, you're not ready to go into business for yourself. For discussion purposes, you'll need a minimum of 20 percent of the total amount of the capital you anticipate as necessary for a successful new business start-up or existing business expansion before a loan officer will even consider your request. In addition, you better have collateral—your own, a partner's, your mother-in-law's, or somebody's. Banks are businesses too. And they don't lend money unless there's a darn good chance they're going to get it back—plus interest. A bank doesn't want to be an investor in your firm—just a lender.

To find out if you really have what it takes, make sure you can answer *yes* to all of the following questions:

Q: Are you a self-starter?

A: Absolutely! No one has to get me going.

Q: Are you a people person?

A: Love 'em! I can get along with just about everybody.

Q: Are you a leader?

A: That's me! All my life, I've been able to get people to do what I want and need them to do.

Q: Can you take responsibility?

A: Once I'm in charge, things get done.

Q: Are you a good organizer?

A: The best. I like to have a plan before I start something, and I see the plan through.

Q: Are you really a worker?

A: I've never minded working hard for something I want, and I keep going as long as I need to.

Q: Is your word "as good as gold"?

A: Put your trust in me. I always do exactly what I say.

Q: Can you really make decisions?

A: In a snap, especially when I have to. I'm usually right, too!

Q: Do you stick with it?

A: Once I make up my mind to do something, I don't let anything stop me.

Q: Is your health good?

A: No, it's excellent. I seldom get sick. When I do, I recover faster than anyone I know. I also have boundless energy, never seem to run out of gas.

If you can honestly and truly say all these answers describe the "real you," you probably have what it takes personally. And that's a big part of what it takes to successfully own and operate your own small business. If you're really being honest, your small business has a good chance of becoming a big business. Or at the very least, a profitable business.

Of course, there are many other considerations, and we'll go into each of them. But if you don't make it through this little quiz, forget it.

YOU'RE NEVER REALLY GOING TO BE THE BOSS

This is going to be short and not very sweet. Many people, places, and things are going to make significant demands on your time and talents as the owner-operator of a business. These include your customers, your employees, and the people to whom you owe money—and you will owe money. In a very special way, they all become your "bosses."

Take a good look at what "boss" really means: someone who has the right to make certain demands on your time and talents; someone who has the right to expect certain things of you, especially in the area of performance; the person in charge.

If and when you incorporate, there will likely be a board of directors, and possibly stockholders, to add to this list. Each will have a say in what you do, how you do it, when you do it, or if you do it at all.

In short, you'll trade one or two "bosses" for a whole string of them. As I said, you're really never going to be the boss.

On the positive side of the ledger, you will have a good deal more to say about the matter than possibly you currently have. To some, that's enough. To others, the idea of really forgetting the job when the whistle blows at closing time beats hands down carrying a sack of problems around with you big enough to make Santa Claus stagger, stumble, and fall from his sleigh.

Once again, no one can come up with a tally sheet but you. All you and I can do is take a realistic look at who really calls the shots. One thing's for sure. It ain't very often going to be you!

UNHEALTHY COMPETITION

Once in a great while, someone will come up with a "hot item." Something the world could get along very nicely without but decides it would rather do with. The hula hoop and pet rocks fall in this category.

Nobody really needed them, but a lot of people, millions to be precise, decided they wanted them anyway. They plunked down their money, the cash registers rang, and, voilà, we had a couple of new multimillionaires.

Be advised: It doesn't happen very often. So if this is what you are planning, good luck.

What does this have to do with unhealthy competition? Well, I would consider it fiscally unhealthy to have entered the marketplace 6 months after the hula hoop craze with a slender ring of plastic material called a "Hoop-T-Do," which you kept in motion by gyrating your hips, or to have tried to sell the world on the glories of owning a "pet brick" 2 months after the Christmas that everybody gave everybody their very own pet rock. The competition would definitely have been unhealthy.

By the same token, if your neighborhood, hamlet, village, town, city, state, or whatever already has enough of what you intend to offer, it's going to be unhealthy for someone. Probably you.

It never ceases to amaze me how many small business owners will decide what they are going to do and where they are going to do it without even a passing glance at the marketplace. Don't be one of them.

The goods and services people purchase or contract for are the result of want and/or need. So if they don't need you, they bloody well better want you—and what you have to sell.

A case in point: If you want to open a shoe repair shop, it would certainly behoove you to analyze whether another shoe repair shop is feasible. You'll be drawing from a finite number of people with a finite number of feet trudging along in a finite number of shoes—only a small percentage of which will be worthy of resoling.

If your potential customers are already being served by an adequate number of shoe repair shops, things don't look too good. You'll have to convince a substantial number of these folks that your service is better, your prices are lower, or your shop is more convenient, or else there's not much chance they are going to change already established patterns of use.

The competition can be unhealthy, indeed.

On the other hand, if your study of the market shows all those shoes have nowhere to go but your shop, things are looking healthier by the minute.

It is unlikely, at best, that your customers will drive by a half dozen or so similar businesses just for the privilege of helping your pocketbook. Example: a corner drugstore is a corner drugstore. If you are planning to open your area's fourth drugstore, healthy is to be the first drugstore people will pass, not the last. Healthy is to stay open longer, offer better prices, maybe make free home deliveries. Unhealthy is for the other three drugstores to beat you out in any or—God forbid!—all these areas.

Whatever business you are thinking of, assess the competitive situation thoroughly. Remember, honesty counts. You don't have to sell me! I'll believe anything you say. Just don't try to sell yourself a bill of goods. That could get very unhealthy.

In counseling small business owners, I'm appalled at the very small number of business owners who have physically visited their competitors' places of business. This should be the first thing you do, not the last. See what the scoundrels are up to. Otherwise, you will not know what you're up against until it's too late.

When you play "secret shopper," make sure you do so very thoroughly. First, check your competitor's advertising. There could be valuable information on how you can best counter the claims being made. Call the business on the phone. Then, make sure you and your staff are friendlier, more courteous, and infinitely more helpful, so that anyone calling both your business and your competitor's will come away with the strong feeling that yours is by far the better of the two.

Check out everything! Will you have more or less parking? How about signs? Will yours be more visible, more attractive?

Does your competitor's place of business look better than yours does as you approach the front door? It better not! And inside, study the traffic pattern. How can you improve on it? And how about displays? By the time you leave your competitor's premises, you should know the merchandise mix, pricing as it relates to yours, any customer services and benefits, and how "theirs" compares to "yours."

Yes, competition is healthy. Up to a point. But a little goes a long way.

Before your "Grand Opening" is the time to find out if anyone wants or needs you. Not after it. Too much of even a good thing is bad.

And unhealthy competition can give your business a terminal illness. Remember, the operation's not really a success if the patient dies.

EVERYBODY WANTS TO RUN A RESTAURANT

It ranks number 5 in a list of the ten worst small business ventures according to a poll conducted by *Money* magazine and published in their March 1978 edition. That means that, at least in the opinion of the experts, there are currently only four business categories with less of a chance to survive, all other things being equal. It also means there are a great many better places to put your money and your efforts!

Perhaps the attraction is that we all have to eat. And no matter what your skills and talents (or lack thereof), someone you know can cook. Please be advised that knowing how to cook (or having someone in your employ who knows how to cook) does not automatically qualify you to be a restauranteur.

Lest the paranoids start chasing you should you already own and operate a small restaurant, your fate is not necessarily sealed. Nor is it a foregone conclusion that all restaurants will fail. Just most of them.

In fact, the pros say growth potential in the restaurant business is fairly good; about 10 percent in 1978. Profits aren't all that bad either; about 3.5 percent in a successful operation. Still, according to a Small Business Administration official, for every one that succeeds, probably a dozen will fail, mostly for lack of management know-how. The odds aren't exactly with you, you must admit.

In a top-notch fast-food franchise operation like that of "golden arches" fame, you'll find management assistance a big part of the package and you'll find a substantially better success rate. However, keep in mind that a major fast-food franchise (if and when one is available) will require a cash investment up front of $85,000 to $250,000 or more. A less-than-top-notch franchise is usually a complete waste of money. You could do it for less on your own. So who needs them? Certainly not you.

Tops on the ten worst list is a local laundry and dry cleaning business. It makes sense: We live in a wash 'n' wear, do-it-yourself world and not too many of us like starch in our sheets.

Number 2 on the high-risk list is used car lots. There is a simple reason behind this one: Banks are peopled by people called bankers. Bankers are very conservative. Used cars, the people who sell them, and the people who buy them are not always associated with the more stable, conservative element in our society. The financing of used car dealers and their customers is, therefore, considered "high risk." Bankers don't like high-risk loans, so they're not making many.

Number 3 is gas stations. The experts say competition and thinning profits have dulled this once-glowing franchise opportunity. To clear a relatively modest $30,000 annually, a station would have to gross $1.8 million. That's a lot of gas.

Number 4 on the list of places not to put your money: local trucking firms. Combine high-priced union labor, ever-rising operating expenses, and overregulation by the government and you have a very risky enterprise indeed.

Number 5 is the everybody-wants-one restaurant.

Number 6 is infants' clothing stores. Blame this one on the pill if you will, but there just aren't as many babies being born as there used to be. Consequently, there just aren't as many baby clothes being purchased as there used to be. Logical deduction: not the greatest business opportunity around.

Number 7 on the worst-business list is the local bakery. You guys are being baked out of existence by superlarge, super-low-cost supermarket bakery departments. Make it good: You may have to eat your own cake.

Number 8 goes to machine shops. Talk about unhealthy competition, there are currently over 5000 independent machine shops. If all goes well, you'll produce an average $3000 in pre-tax profits from each $100,000 in sales your shop yields. That's not too good, folks.

Number 9 is grocery and meat stores. Unless you're planning to offer shop-by-phone and free delivery service in a neighborhood that can afford these luxuries, the big guys'll get you.

Last on the list of the ten worst is car washes. There are lots of reasons, say the experts: high turnover, strong competition, high capital investment. There is very likely an easier way to make a living.

Now for the good news. According to our experts, here are their current nominations for the ten best small business opportunities.

First are building materials stores. To the victor belong the spoils, and, in this case, increased residential construction and do-it-yourself repairs should boost sales by 10 to 15 percent a year with no downward trend in sight.

Second best may be good enough when it's an auto tire and accessory store. With runaway inflation making the purchase of a new car less attractive and less possible every month, today's auto owners are doing more and more repairs themselves. The outlook is for a growth rate of about 9.7 percent over the next year, with more of the same to come.

The number 3 slot goes to liquor stores. Maybe all these grim predictions are driving us all to drink. In any event, a hardworking retailer can expect 3 percent profit on each dollar of sales and a growth rate in excess of 11 percent a year.

Sports and recreation clubs get the nod for the fourth best small business. The growing interest in physical fitness and exercise is really the key here. However, it'll take money to make money—a club requires a substantial initial investment and annual membership fees of approximately $1 million to net $26,000 in profit.

Number 5 may not turn you on. The pros say funeral homes and crematories get the vote. Small firms average $9,200 profit on every $100,000 they take in. Despite a declining death rate, we still check out at a rate of approximately 1.9 million every year. The preponderance of senior citizens could bring the annual totals higher for a number of years to come. It may not be your thing; it requires special schooling and compliance with pertinent regulations, but dying makes for a pretty good business. Not lively, just profitable.

Number 6 on the best list is seed and garden stores. We're experiencing a nationwide surge in interest when it comes to making things grow. More homes mean more yards to be planted; higher food prices yield "inflation" gardens. The profit margin picture is comparable to sports and recreation clubs, and, for the next few years, the industry as a whole can expect 8 to 9 percent growth rates.

Number 7 is sporting goods manufacturing. We are fast becoming a nation of do-it-yourself recreation "nuts." Consequently, there's money to be made in making grown-up toys. Everything from golf balls to footballs look good. Depending on the product, growth estimates range from 8 percent per annum on bicycles and bicycle parts production to 19 percent for team sports equipment, and snow and water ski paraphernalia.

Number 8 on our list of likely business ventures is engineering, laboratory, and scientific equipment. According to the experts, the aeronautical industry is rebounding, and engineering equipment sales should grow about 12 percent a year. Those of you who manufacture scales and lab equipment can expect a growth rate of 11 percent.

Number 9 is hardware stores. Again, the increasing numbers of do-it-yourselfers make this a better-than-average risk. High profit margins mean hardware stores can produce a comfortable living for their owners with relatively low gross annual sales. Nationwide averages show this kind of firm will produce $30,000 profit from every $650,000 in gross sales. Not too shabby! And it's a great place to spend a Saturday morning.

Worst of the best, if you want to view it that way, is office supplies and equipment, which are remarkably resistant to recession and capable of turning substantial profits. Every $1 million in sales will net you approximately $40,000. The predicted growth rate is around 18 percent per annum. Not terribly exciting, perhaps, but a clean, tidy, pleasant way to make a buck.

Now don't go putting words in my typewriter. Nowhere in this section have I stated or implied that a business listed in the ten worst was doomed to failure. Nor have I allowed that choosing to open a firm listed in the ten best category would automatically lead to fame and fortune. All you have here is the collective thinking of a goodly number of business experts who ought to know a bit more about this sort of thing than most folks might. How's that for a hedge?

Your chances for success or failure in any of these twenty businesses (or two hundred others we could explore) will still depend on the same very important factors: your previous experience in the field; your expertise as a manager; the location you've chosen; how adequately your business is financed; your direct competition; the promotion and advertising you undertake to attract customers; how much time, energy, and talent you and the people you employ expend to ensure the success of your venture; and how adequately you comply with taxation and all other legal requirements for which your individual business is responsible, to name but a few. The list does get lengthy and includes everything from the weather to sheer blind luck.

Let your common sense be your guide: If you have a baker's dozen years' experience in the restaurant business, don't try to open a mortuary just because someone says restaurants are riskier than mortuaries. What you know best is most likely what you'll do best in business for yourself. And don't forget it.

HOW SMALL IS SMALL?

In all the years you've known about small business, has anyone ever tried to explain how small is small? Not likely. I personally cannot imagine why not, since the federal government has very specific guidelines we all follow, whether or not we agree with them. The Congress of the United States in 1953 established the Small Business Administration (SBA) to assist, counsel, and champion the millions of American small businesses, which are the essence and backbone of this country's competitive free-enterprise economy. If you don't believe me, just read the Small Business Administration pamphlet from which I lifted that sentence. It's called "SBA, What It Does." Isn't that original?

Before a bureaucrat (any bureaucrat) can function, he, she, or it must count and categorize everything in sight. When you're the Small Business Administration, that means you count and categorize small businesses.

They proceeded to do just that. By category. Which is to say, depending on what you need the Small Business Administration for, "small" can be very small or very "not small" (see the following chart).

There used to be a service area called surety bonds which listed about the same criteria as section A loans in the chart to the right. But the feds aren't into surety bonds right now, so forget it. They may start the program up again in the future. If it's an area that interests you, call your local Small Business Administration office. They're listed under U.S. Government, Small Business Administration.

So you see, according to the federal agency established to tell us how small a small business is, a small business can be small, or it can gross annual sales of $22 million, which in my bank book is not small. It can have one employee—you—or can employ 1500. It depends on what you're after—a loan or a contract; also on what you do, where you do it, and whom you compete against. It makes sense really. If your competition is ITT, IBM, or Summa Corp., you're small. Take my word for it. You're small.

If you're still in doubt, SBA further explains that a small business is one which is independently owned and operated, is not dominant in its field, and meets all the previously listed size criteria for SBA assistance programs. It usually has few employees. The owner is directly involved in the management as well as the operation of the business and may not have had much

Small Business Size Standards

	Annual receipts not exceeding	Average annual number of employees not exceeding
For Loans		
Service	$2–$8 million*	
Retail	$2–7.5 million*	
Wholesale	$9.5–$22 million*	
General construction	$9.5 million*	
Special trade construction	$5 million	
Farming and related activities	$275,000	
Manufacturing		250–1500*
For SBA help in winning government procurements contracts		
Service	$2–$9 million*	
General construction	$12 million	
Manufacturing		500–1500*
For small business investment company (SBIC) or 301(d) SBICs (formerly called MESBICs) assistance		
All industries		Assets not exceeding $9 million Net worth not exceeding $4 million Average net income (after taxes) not exceeding $400,000

*Varies by industry. Call your local SBA office for specific details. If your firm is located in what is deemed a labor surplus area, you may increase all above figures by 25 percent.

training or experience in accounting, taxes, finance, or business practices and procedures.

Now that's a very polite way of telling you most small business owners haven't the foggiest notion of what the devil they're doing. But we're going to fool them! You've stuck with me this far; by the time we finish Chapter 15, you'll know a lot more about operating a small business than most of the "experts" who work for SBA. Of course, that may not be too difficult. After all, if they knew so much, they'd all own their own successful businesses. Anything is preferable to being a bureaucrat.

2

OK, First Things First

DO YOU WANT TO MAKE A LIVING, OR A FORTUNE?

That may sound like a strange question, but the answer you come up with will have significant impact on how you go about setting up your firm. It may, in fact, have a decisive part to play in what kind of business you establish.

Few fortunes are made in small business. That's not to say that individual small business owners have not and will not become rich beyond anything they might have imagined. But they usually accomplish this through other investments, not as a direct result of the firm they own and operate.

If your planned business involves manufacturing and/or marketing an item or product you invented and on which you hold a patent, or if your service or retail business is one you could foreseeably franchise in the future, your chances of becoming a tycoon are slim, but alive.

Most of us settle rather happily for earning a "comfortable" income. That translates into a home with a roof that doesn't leak and a mortgage that doesn't pinch too much, orthodontia and college for the kids (in that order), membership in a club of some sort, an annual trip somewhere we sort of want to go, and a few bucks tucked away for the decade of our dotage.

If you really want to be rich, my suggestions are to pick your parents more carefully next time around, marry well, steal lots of money and get away with it, win the Irish Sweepstakes, or spend less than you make and invest the difference very wisely. The last being the most likely.

I guess the only group of potential entrepreneurs I have a small problem with is that which is simply creating a job for the owner because he or she can't get one anywhere else.

Granted, it's the fastest way to become president. But there's got to be a better solution to unemployment than business ownership.

If you're such a loser no one will hire you, the chances of your having all the skills and talents necessary to make a success of your own firm are pretty slim. And I'm being generous.

There are several notable exceptions to the above, the most notable being those very bright, energetic folks whom existing firms aren't smart enough to hire. Very specifically, this group most often includes those over 40 (or some other equally arbitrary chronological cutoff past which some personnel departments automatically write an applicant off) and that vast army of displaced homemakers who have successfully managed everything but staying married (most often through no fault of their own since the good guys die and the bad guys aren't worth hanging on to).

These folks, usually female, are really up against it in the work force since they have no "marketable" skills and precious little (if any) recent experience in an out-of-the-home job.

Now, here's a gathering of potential entrepreneurs I can really work with. Their major problem stems from a lack of cash and self-confidence; members of either group (and often the same person fits into both categories) can and should seriously explore the potential which owning and operating their own business might afford.

For heaven's sake, I've worked with groups of welfare mothers who've joined forces and opened everything from day-care facilities to catering services. And there's a unique program currently operating in Hawaii that turns disadvantaged, unemployed, CETA-eligible people into entrepreneurs within 1 year, giving them nothing but technical assistance and encouragement in the process.

No, what I'm not too thrilled with are the real losers, the lazy so-and-sos who think opening a business is a quick and dirty way to wealth without work. The person enterprising enough to turn a lawn mower and a few garden tools into a small lawn service business earns my respect—and my only wish is that the grass grows fast and the business grows faster.

There is also the very real possibility that a really small small business can supplement your regular income, pay your way through college, or help tide your family over some rough times. Just keep in mind that the same rules and regulations vis-à-vis taxes, permits, zoning, etc., will most likely apply to the one-person enterprise you're running out of the spare bedroom as apply to the firm employing 20—or 200.

As a matter of fact, quite a number of firms today grossing upwards of $1 million annually started out as one- or two-person "hip pocket" businesses. The formula remains constant: the right service or product at the right time, the right price, and the right place. Add a lot of work and luck, and (the good Lord willin') you're on your way.

WHAT KIND OF BUSINESS?

A number of factors must be considered carefully in deciding what business you will open. These include the amount of capital you have or can accumulate and the specific needs of the community in which you will locate your firm, but, most of all, the skills and talents you personally possess.

If you've been a house painter all your working life, you'll most likely be best equipped to open and operate your own house painting business. Likewise, a watchmaker will do well to explore the possibilities available in the area of watch repair shop ownership. That might sound simplistic to you, but the number of watchmakers trying to start scuba diving schools or laundromats far outnumbers the sensible few who want to open watch repair shops.

Your direct working experience may very well be the deciding factor in obtaining financing. It makes sense, really. You can hire people to do some of what needs doing, but the boss better know the real meat and potatoes stuff. If nothing else, you'll be able to adequately supervise your staff to ensure they do the job correctly.

Keep in mind that you'll probably do less of what you do best after opening your own shop than you ever dreamed possible. And that should be both carefully considered and understood prior to opening day.

Say, for example, you're a shoe salesperson. You are a very good shoe salesperson. You've saved a few thousand bucks, can borrow a bit more from your in-laws or your life insurance policy, there's a great location available, and your contacts in the shoe business are both substantial and willing to extend you a line of credit. Everything looks hunky-dory.

You hire a part-time sales clerk, stock the shelves, run a little advertising, and open your doors for business (an oversimplified view of what our intrepid entrepreneur actually goes through, but you get the picture). After a few months, you're spending 70 percent of your time dealing with books, paperwork, stock ordering, advertising salespeople, and customer complaints, as well as your banker, insurance representative, and accountant.

The business is going well, you're holding up surprisingly well under the demands of a 70-hour work week, the kids still remember who you are, but you spend precious little time on the sales floor fitting shoes, the thing you do best.

Mind you, this is typical.

A most successful young woman advertising executive told me not long ago that the one thing she absolutely hated about owning her own agency was she had no time to do creative work anymore. It was what she did best, what she enjoyed doing most, and what she did least nowadays. Her schedule was crammed full of employee problem-solving sessions, assigning work to others that she really wanted to do herself, and hustling for new business— all of which would be handled by someone else.

"They get to write and produce commercials," she moaned, waving toward the other offices in her chrome and glass kingdom, "while I get to review last month's billing.

"I haven't had time to do the fun stuff, the creative part of advertising I love so dearly, in months. Sometimes I wonder what in the heck I'm doing this for. Maybe I ought to sell this stupid place and get a job working for someone else again where I'll be free to create. Then, again, I look around sometimes and think, 'This is mine, I made it happen!' and I know I'd never be happy working for anyone else, ever again."

Somehow, I doubt my friend will ever punch anyone's time clock. She'll come to complete grips with the demands of business ownership and continue spending most of her time "administering," and doing precious little creating.

Keep in mind the same thing will likely happen to you. You can minimize this now that you're aware of it, but no business owner I've ever come into contact with has ever totally managed to eliminate the problem.

The choice of a business is yours completely. You should, however, make an honest inventory of what your work experiences have been. Many small businesses have also been successfully launched by turning a hobby or a vocation into a full-time enterprise.

This accounts for the few scuba diving schools owned and operated by folks who used to repair watches.

A specific skill or talent can be parlayed into a thriving little firm. Antiques, needlepoint, furniture refinishing, dog grooming all have been transformed from a hobby into a business by hustlers just like you.

Probably the worst way to decide what business to go into is to buy an existing business about which you know absolutely nothing. The only thing that could possibly make this situation riskier is to buy said business in a strange new town.

This is a double mistake made by many retirees and should be avoided at all costs 'cause it'll cost you dearly if you don't.

Purchasing an existing business is tricky, at best. It's downright suicidal when you don't bring firsthand knowledge to the deal, and nothing short of loony when the business is miles away from everything familiar in your life. Little things like finding city hall (so you can apply for a permit or license to operate) or locating a reasonably competent accountant or bookkeeping service become monumental gambles when you're new to the area.

You'll also find banks a bit more reluctant than usual to lend to newcomers. They're testy enough. Don't add to the problem.

You'll also not be able to call on family and friends to buy your wares if they're back where you should be instead of where you are.

If you must make a move, make it a minimum of 6 months before you sign a purchase agreement on a business. This will at least allow you time to familiarize yourself with whether or not a freeway is about to be built right through your parking lot or a giant chain store is building just up the street. Such minor details could result in your "going out of business" sale following their "grand opening" by a matter of weeks.

Events such as those mentioned above are often the real reason behind the "for sale" sign. Let someone else be the sucker.

Now that you've decided upon just exactly what sort of business you'd like to open, we begin in earnest.

WHERE—LOCATION AND REALTOR-AGENT PITFALLS

Probably the second-most critical decision you have to make (after what kind) is where.

Where, exactly, will you locate your firm?

There are basically four types of businesses you may choose from: retail, wholesale, service, or manufacturing (which would include construction). Under those four come dozens of subdivisions, but for our purposes here, just determine under which of the four your individual business will fall.

Now put your common sense in gear. Local zoning ordinances will dictate some of the decisions. As part of their police power, cities and towns are empowered to enact and enforce zoning ordinances which are designed to regulate the size of structures, density of population, proximity to the street, parking requirements, the percent of a lot which may be occupied by buildings, and the use to which those buildings may lawfully be put. Zoning ordinances may also affect the size and/or shape of signs allowable on or adjacent to your business.

When in doubt, head for the city or county planning and zoning department. If zoning isn't quite right and you feel strongly enough about the location, you can attempt to get the zoning changed. Your local planning and zoning department can advise you of the procedure. A lawyer would also come in handy.

Assuming that the zoning is proper, the first rule of thumb is that retail and service businesses need better locations than wholesale and manufacturing firms.

Keep in mind that when the customer will have to come to you, you'd better be easy to find, not too far away, and served by mass transit and adequate parking.

When you have to go to the customer, as in wholesale and manufacturing, as long as you can get there from where you are, *mochts nichts*.

If you're opening a manufacturing plant or wholesale business, keep in mind that your need for a work force may be adversely affected if you choose a location deep in the heart of the low-rent district. Your decision must be made with your labor force, transportation, raw materials, and available buildings each being carefully considered.

To further define the deal, retail is the most location-dependent of all businesses.

But think, please. You don't want even the best location in town if you're planning to open a day-care center in a retirement community. Those old folks just don't have a lot of toddlers in need of care. While we'll cover this sort of madness in Chapter 4, Don't Sell Ice Cubes to Eskimos, you should at least be conscious of what kind of clientele your business will need to survive when you look at locations.

In retail, many experts think the top three reasons for failure are (1) location, (2) location, and (3) location. It's that important.

Different stores have different locational requirements. What you sell, the customers you serve, the things they buy, the way they can reach your store, adjacent and similar businesses, the neighborhood, all these factors must be carefully considered. Should you locate in a shopping center? If so, what kind? A small neighborhood strip center, a community center, or a major regional shopping center?

Let's take a look at a couple of statistical approaches to locating your store. Each would be part of a feasibility study, if you had the money to have one done. What we're aiming for here is to give you the ability to do your own feasibility study.

The number 1 data bank is the U.S. Census. Taken every 10 years, this massive count includes valuable information you should tap before deciding where to locate.

In addition to the nationwide statistics that the census is designed to tabulate, each community of 50,000 or more inhabitants is divided into census tracts. Each of these tracts represents some 4000 residents. And the information you can glean from census tract data includes how many persons or families reside in the area and how this has changed over the past 10 or 20 years; where these people work; how many old people, young people, children, and teens live in the tract; how many families there are, including one-person families and families with children or teenagers living in the home; what the family income is; what the wage earners do for a living; how many rent or own their homes; what the total value of the home is; what monthly rent the family pays; what the age and quality of the home is; whether or not the homes are air-conditioned and what other appliances families own; even the number of families there are with one or more automobiles.

Now even the most devout dummy could manage to extract a lot of extremely valuable information about the possible success ratio of any given business when presented with all these facts.

Every business has a trading area—that is to say, an imaginary geographic boundary within which will reside (or work) the vast majority of the customers and prospective customers of the business.

Don't locate your store where it doesn't belong just because you found a vacant building and the rent's not out of sight. Make sure the census tract information strongly indicates that your particular kind of business has a reasonable chance for success there.

The next bit of data you'll want to analyze carefully is traffic count information. As a matter of fact, many retail locations are leased on the basis of traffic count: the higher the traffic count, the higher the rent.

There are two things normally counted: cars and people. If you can best envision your customers driving up to your shop in their automobiles, look for a traffic count based on cars. If you're interested in a shopping center, downtown, regional, or anything in between, get the pedestrian count for your specific location.

This data is readily available, by the way. Census tract information can be obtained from the U.S. Office of the Census (contact your local federal building switchboard for the telephone number and location); also, the public library can usually help you, and your city's planning department will certainly have what you're looking for. You'll likely find some poor little worker in the archives section of city hall who'll be just tickled pink that someone finally wants to see what he or she's got to offer.

Information on traffic count results can be found in the traffic engineering department at city hall, the county or state highway department, or your local billboard company (check the yellow pages under advertising, outdoor).

Pedestrian traffic count data is found in pretty much the same place as automobile data, except in the case of shopping center counts. There, you're often at the mercy of the shopping center leasing agent. Double check what you're told with existing shop owners. They'll give you a practical and (usually) honest account of how much humanity trucks by the place daily.

If all else fails, call the nearest university and ask for the bureau of business research. Every major campus in America has one (under some similar name—the operator will be able to connect you) as part of their college of business. These folks are very up on business statistics, and I've always found them most willing to help. As a matter of fact, I've had several offer to do specific feasibility studies for my clients, at little or no cost, as a way of giving their graduate students practical experience.

When shopping for your location, keep these additional factors in mind:

- The quantity and quality of competitive businesses
- The location of competitive stores

- Availability of access routes to your location
- Direction of the area's expansion
- General appearance of the area

When one or two specific sites tweak your interest, take a careful look at:

- Adequacy of parking
- Total traffic passing the site
- Ability of the site to intercept traffic en route from one place to another
- Availability of turn lanes and mass transit
- The complementary nature of adjacent stores and businesses
- The types of goods they sell
- Vulnerability of the site to unfriendly competition

It's not enough simply to know how many people will be passing your location on a given day. Your next step is to determine why they're passing your store. Then, you must further define and analyze the characteristics of the passing traffic.

For counting purposes, divide the traffic into classifications according to the typical customer who would patronize your type of business. For a drugstore, you're probably interested in the total volume of passing traffic. If you're going to open a men's store, your primary interest is obviously in males. Depending on the kind of men's store yours will be, you'll want to further define their ages and income levels. In other words, if there are 100 people passing your potential location each day, perhaps 53 of them are male, between the ages of 16 and 65. If your men's store will be catering to the jeans-wearing, 16-to-30 age group, probably only fifteen or twenty are potential customers.

By the same token, if you're opening an exclusive women's store, the same 100 passersby would yield 47 women, perhaps 7 of whom would have the income necessary to patronize your shop.

Another serious consideration is why these people are passing. The time of day at which individuals go by is often an indication of their purpose. If traffic is clustered in the early morning and late afternoon hours, you can pretty much assume the majority of people passing your potential location are on the way to and from work. This traffic pattern might indicate that your potential site would be good for convenience-oriented shopping. One major chain store is only interested in the number of potential women customers. They only consider the total number of women passing a potential site between 10:00 A.M. and 5:00 P.M. to be serious shoppers for them.

Pay careful attention to which direction traffic is headed mornings and afternoons. This can be very valuable information if what you've got to sell is what potential buyers will need on their way home from work, for instance. You could be in big trouble just by locating your store on the wrong side of the street.

Since location is so important, it's not a bad idea to conduct your own minisurvey of pedestrian traffic passing your potential site. Ask them where they're going, what the stores are they plan to shop at, and whether their trip is oriented for business, pleasure, or shopping.

The season, month, week, day, and hour all have an effect upon any kind of traffic survey and analyses. During the hot summer season there is usually an increased flow of traffic on the shady side of the street. During holiday shopping times, such as the month before Christmas or the week before Easter, traffic is likely to be much denser than it is regularly. Shopping patterns vary by day of the week, too. Shopping traffic usually increases toward the latter part of a week. In some cities, you must take into consideration the local major employers' paydays and days when Social Security checks arrive.

As much as possible, you'll want your survey information taken on the day of the week and time of the day which represent the most normal traffic flow. It's usually wise to survey and study traffic patterns on several days of the week and at several hours of the day. Depending on the hours of operation you are planning for your store, pick 3 days of the week and survey at least a half hour in the morning, during the noon hour, in the afternoon, and in the evening if you plan to stay open late. Then, average the numbers to give yourself an accurate "average" day.

If this all seems like a lot of trouble, let me show you how valuable it can be. Data from this kind of traffic survey can give you information on whether the site you're considering will generate a profitable volume for your store.

You can actually estimate the total volume of sales from accurate traffic count data. Once you've determined how many people pass and what percentage of that total are potential customers for you, all you have to do is estimate what percentage of those potential customers you might be able to attract. If out of 1000 people passing each day 5 percent enter your store and each person spends an average of $8, your store at that site, opened 300 days a year, would have an annual sales volume of $120,000.

This is exactly the kind of information you need to assess your chance for success, and it'll really come in handy when you're looking for financing. Any banker in town would feel a lot more comfortable lending money to you when provided with this kind of information.

It also helps a bunch if, instead of $120,000, you really need to generate sales of $175,000 in order to make it.

This kind of careful traffic analysis is in order, whether your location is a free-standing building or part of a shopping center. Speaking of which, let's take a quick look at shopping centers.

Most retailers want a shopping center location. Like every other decision in small business, it can be a good one or a bad one.

The first thing to consider is what kind of center you are talking about. Shopping centers generally fall into three types: the neighborhood center, the community center, and the regional center.

The neighborhood center generally serves 7500 to 20,000 people living within a 6- to 10-minute drive from the center. The major store (and the prime traffic generator) in the center is almost always a supermarket. The other stores in the center may include a drugstore, hardware store, bakery, and beauty shop. The best location is obviously adjacent to the supermarket.

The community center usually serves 20,000 to 100,000 people living within a 10- to 20-minute drive. The lead store is usually a small department store or a large variety store. The majority of the stores carry shopping goods such as clothing and appliances. There are also a number of stores offering convenience items (as in the neighborhood center). Again, the prime location is as near the dominant store as possible. If you are planning on locating in a community center, carefully assess your hours of operation and the available parking, among other things. If you're planning on opening a drugstore, your best site is probably a location at one end of the center. This is so that adjacent parking is more readily available. The end site nearest a major thoroughfare is also your most desirable pick. Drugstores tend to be open longer hours than the other stores, and this will give you the most easily accessible location. It's also not surrounded by a number of dark stores at night. The same reasoning would hold true of a liquor store. If you're planning on opening a service-oriented establishment such as a dry cleaning store or barbershop, you're looking for rapid turnover in traffic. Your prime consideration is a location where there is always available parking.

The regional shopping center serves 100,000 to 200,000 people or more within a 20- to 40-minute drive from the center. One or more major department stores would be the lead traffic draws. Often, this type of center features an enclosed mall with a large department store at each end. Locating your store between the two "biggies" will usually let you take advantage of the best traffic flow. Stores handling convenience goods and services should generally be located at the edge of the center or near the entrance to the mall where there is easily accessible parking and quick in-and-out service for the customer.

Especially in the case of a regional shopping center location, wishing does not necessarily make it so. Center management will be very picky about the people they lease to. Just being able to plunk down the rent won't usually be good enough.

These centers have a very distinct client mix in mind and are almost always unreceptive to new and untried businesses.

They are also not going to permit too many similar and competing businesses in the center. The lead or major stores do most of the traffic generating, but the center administration staff are always on the lookout for the kinds of shops which will add to that traffic draw.

Keep in mind, major shopping center locations are very expensive, and their management usually dictate your hours of operation, among other things. Make sure you completely understand the merchant association rules and regulations and can comply with them without undue cost to your shop.

In addition to your rent, there are almost always assessments of individual stores for an advertising fund.

In short, here's what you're facing: You're a new, untried business, the new kid on the block, and they probably don't want to rent to you anyway. If they do, you'll be charged rent based on the number of square feet you will physically occupy. Some of the "common areas" may very well be included in this rent-assessment formula. You'll also most likely be assessed a percentage of your gross sales as part of the rent and either a flat fee or a percentage based on gross sales or square footage to be used by the merchants' association to fund both its operations and a general center advertising effort. You can see how this can get very expensive.

The first time you contact a realtor or shopping center agent, you'll be treated like the long-lost prodigal son. Very soon, you'll discover one of two things: They want to rent space and don't particularly care about you and your problems, or they don't want to rent space to you at all.

This always comes as a shock to the individual interested in renting. After all, you're trying to buy something (space for your business) and he or she (the rental agent or realtor) is trying to sell something (space). Therefore, it only stands to reason that the realtor or agent should be absolutely ecstatic at your willingness to sign on the dotted line, right? Wrong.

You must keep in mind that the rental agent has two mandates: first, naturally, to rent space and second—and usually the uppermost priority—to rent space only to those individuals or companies who will operate successfully in the location and, in the process, add prestige and/or "pull" to the location. This is especially important to community or regional shopping center locations. In most neighborhood centers, they'll rent to anyone with the rent and a pulse.

The realtor presents a slightly different set of problems. Here, keep in mind that this person is out to make a sale. That means renting or leasing a location to you. That does not mean renting or leasing the right location to you. The average realtor or agent could care less what happens to you next year, or the year after. He or she will likely be long gone by then, unlike the shopping center representative who will probably be your "landlord." So caveat emptor, one more time. What's presented to you as the best location in town, the lowest price per square foot in the county, or whatever should still be subjected to your close and careful consideration. These folks aren't all bad; just most of them.

To be absolutely fair, I should add that realtors and rental agents are not business-development experts; they're realtors and rental agents. Even those who would give you the straight scoop seldom have access to it. You must become the expert in locating your location.

It is often helpful to contact two or three realtors and compare the facts and figures provided by each. This composite will sometimes prove closer to accurate than any single information source.

If you've really done your homework, decided on a location, say, in a major regional shopping center, and the rental agent won't budge from the polite but firm "sorry, you're just not experienced enough," or "don't fit our client mix"—or whatever—your banker, lawyer, accountant, or a business consultant can sometimes intervene on your behalf.

I've often been able to engage in candid conversation with shopping center managers reluctant to sign a lease with one of my clients and have been able to get them to change their position by offering my view of the business's potential. There's always a bit of added credibility to hearing nice things about your firm's future from someone other than you. You're expected to think positive. Hearing it from a reputable banker, attorney, etc., might carry enough weight to swing things your way.

If nothing else, a third party intervention can often get the real reason behind a center's reluctance (i.e., "we're waiting to hear from a similar business," or "we never lease to people with less than 5 years of successful operation behind them"). Obviously, some of the reasons can be overcome. Other rules are stonewall-fixed and you'll have to keep on hunting.

A rough rule of thumb: A realtor will rent you anything—even the wrong thing—a shopping center rental agent will oftentimes not rent you anything, even the perfect thing.

Something else to keep in mind when choosing your location is size. You need to determine how big a physical space you'll need to successfully operate your shop.

Your needs might include showroom or selling space, an office area, storage for inventory and equipment, and possibly a shipping and receiving area.

While you don't want to pay for more space than you'll need in most instances, keep in mind that too much is better than not enough. Give yourself a bit of growing room if at all possible. And remember, in retail, space translates into gross sales. You must have enough merchandise on hand to generate a set sales volume. And you must have enough space to accommodate that inventory, or you just won't make it.

It can become a physical impossibility to stock and sell enough goods to generate the sales volume you'll need to turn a profit. In this situation you have three choices: change your merchandise mix to provide for higher-priced merchandise that will take the same or less space; move the business to a larger location; do nothing until you're bankrupt. Obviously the third choice is not a good one.

A careful analysis of some firms may suggest that a more adequate physical location would boost sales—and profits—substantially. Sometimes the deciding factor prompting relocation is the availability of new technology, new equipment that can do more work for less money. Your existing location just might not be adequate to accommodate such an expansion. In cases like this, a move is more than suggested, it's mandated.

Also remember that you don't have to use all the space from day 1: It's perfectly acceptable to partition off a chunk of your facility and leave it until you need it. The only time this becomes a no-no is when the rent per square foot is prohibitive.

The last thing you'll want to consider doing if you're just starting a new business is buying. As a matter of fact, the U.S. Small Business Administration won't even consider lending money to purchase land or buildings for the first 3 years a firm's in operation. Most other lenders feel exactly the same way.

It is best to prove you can make it before buying an expensive chunk of real estate.

The same holds true of equipment: The general rule is lease first, buy later (if at all). This really does make sense. Along with the reduced drain on your borrowing ability (since leases don't cut into your creditworthiness), you'll have the opportunity to test each place or thing you lease to ensure that it's really what you want or need. There's also such an explosion in technology that what might be available in a few months from now will likely be better than what you're using today. You're in a real mess if you own the obsolete. It's much better to upgrade by renegotiating your lease agreement.

Let me give you one final peek at how critically important location can be. Not long ago, I had a most enterprising young client come to me for help. He had opened a combination delicatessen and convenience food store a few months prior. He was operating 24 hours a day, 7 days a week. The major problem: He picked the wrong location.

His was the only business open those hours on a street where traffic was absolutely nonexistent past 8 P.M. He was also located in a residential area, very suburban, where everybody was in bed by 11:00 P.M.

It didn't take him many months to realize he had made a costly mistake, so he moved his business.

His second location was absolutely perfect, the only problem being that by then he was so deeply in debt and in trouble that no amount of help from me or anyone else could make it right.

Needless to say, he's no longer in business.

This almost-tycoon made several fatal mistakes. But the most deadly was his choice of a location.

WHEN—YELLOW PAGES AND OTHER
SEASONAL THINGS

Comedian Steve Martin had us rolling in the aisles as he ran around yelling, "The new phone books are here, the new phone books are here!"

You'll probably feel like doing the same bit the first time that that ultimate advertising vehicle hits the homes in your area with your shop's name, location, and telephone number included.

For survival's sake, keep in mind that Ma Bell only publishes the phone book once a year. This may not seem important to you now, but, believe me, if you open a store 11 months before the new phone book will be printed and circulated, you're going to have a long dry spell.

Whether you're opening your first store, expanding services, or adding an additional location, it's more than a good idea to plan your move to coincide with the Yellow Pages dates and deadlines. It's critical.

For many, if not most, small businesses the Yellow Pages will be the primary source of advertising and, therefore, customers. If you must open a location between directories, plan to spend adequate sums of money in other advertising media to get the word out about your store.

Keep in mind that the deadline for insertion of telephone directory ads and listings is several months before the book appears. For complete information on deadlines, prices, and copy requirements, check the Yellow Pages (where else?) at the very front of the book for yellow page services. We'll deal with advertising later, but the dates and deadlines should be a prime consideration in deciding when you'll make your move.

Deadline and publication dates for other directories might well impact on your business. If, for instance, you're going into the mobile home–park business, there are a number of directories published annually and semiannually that could be a source of customers for you.

Honestly assess the "seasonality" of your goods or services. If you're going to open an income tax service, it simply makes good sense to plan your opening 3 or 4 months prior to nasty old April 15. By the same token, if 30 percent of your business can be expected during the pre-Christmas peak in retail, don't open the doors January 15.

Every business has its peaks and valleys. Make sure you understand where yours will occur and plan your opening or expansion to coincide with one of the peaks—not one of the valleys.

If you don't know the seasonal patterns of the business you are about to embark on, check with a trade association or the owners of a similar business to try to establish them. Your local chamber of commerce might also be a source of data.

Believe me, you'll be far better off in the pocketbook department if you delay your business start-up for a few months in order to be able to take advantage of a peak selling season. The alternative is to open your doors and wait it out.

While this is possible, most small businesses simply do not have the capital to play the waiting game. Cash flow management is pretty tough when there's no cash flowing.

HOW—MONEY IN BRIEF (MORE TO COME)

Before I can help you determine where to go for money, you've got to determine how much money you need to go for. Step number 1 is work sheet no. 1 (Figure 1).

Fill in the blanks as completely and honestly as possible. Don't start playing games: The only loser will be you if your figures are inaccurate.

To help you fill in the section of work sheet no. 1 headed Starting Costs You Only Have to Pay Once, complete work sheet no. 2 (Figure 2). Then transfer the totals to work sheet no. 1, and you can really get to work.

If you've followed the work sheet instructions carefully and completely, you now have the magic number: the estimated total cash you need to start your business. A quick look at your bank balance will let you know the difference between what you have and what you need.

Now, let's take a look at where you might look for the money you need and don't have.

You have three basic sources of finance available to you: (1) self-investment, (2) the sale of stock in your business, or (3) borrowing.

Since you've already established the fact that there's a difference between what you have in the bank and what you need, the first option might seem unlikely. But let's look further. Take a careful inventory of what you own. You may well find you have assets that can be made liquid fairly easily. These can include the sale of real estate, stocks or bonds, jewelry, your coin collection, art, or other items of value. If you're currently employed by someone else, take a look at severance pay and pension benefits you may be entitled to as you leave to open your shop.

Your second option is the sale of stock in your business. This has a couple of advantages:

1. You avoid a drain on your cash flow to meet interest payments.

2. You avoid monthly payments on principal.

3. Your stockholders may be an asset in your business, providing expertise

in a specific area or a source of clients or customers from their circle of friends and family.

WORKSHEET NO.1			
ESTIMATED MONTHLY EXPENSES			
Item	Your estimate of monthly expenses based on sales of $_____ per year	Your estimate of how much cash you need to start your business (See column 3.)	What to put in column 2 (These figures are typical for one kind of business. you will have to decide how many months to allow for in your business.)
	Column 1	Column 2	Column 3
Salary of owner-manager	$	$	2 times column 1
All other salaries and wages			3 times column 1
Rent			3 times column 1
Advertising			3 times column 1
Delivery expense			3 times column 1
Supplies			3 times column 1
Telephone and telegraph			3 times column 1
Other utilities			3 times column 1
Insurance			Payment required by insurance company
Taxes, including Social Security			4 times column 1
Interest			3 times column 1
Maintenance			3 times column 1
Legal and other professional fees			3 times column 1
Miscellaneous			3 times column 1
STARTING COSTS YOU ONLY HAVE TO PAY ONCE			Leave column 2 blank
Fixtures and equipment			Fill in worksheet 2 and put the total here
Decorating and remodeling			Talk it over with a contractor
Installation of fixtures and equipment			Talk to suppliers from whom you buy these
Starting inventory			Suppliers will probably help you estimate this
Deposits with public utilities			Find out from utilities companies
Legal and other professional fees			Lawyer, accountant, and so on
Licenses and permits			Find out from city offices what you have to have
Advertising and promotion for opening			Estimate what you'll use
Accounts receivable			What you need to buy more stock until credit customers pay
Cash			For unexpected expenses or losses, special purchases, etc.
Other			Make a separate list and enter total
TOTAL ESTIMATED CASH YOU NEED TO START WITH		$	Add up all the numbers in column 2

Figure 1   New business start-up cost estimate work sheet. How much is enough? By filling in this work sheet, you'll have a pretty fair idea of the amount of money necessary to start your new business. To help you estimate the necessary furniture, fixtures, and equipment and the total to insert on that line (starting costs you only have to pay once), fill in work sheet no. 2 on the following page. (Courtesy of U.S. Small Business Administration.)

Carefully weigh these advantages against the disadvantage of giving up a portion of ownership in your firm to the other stockholders. The sale of stock will mandate the incorporation of your firm. This will have tax consequences, among other things, and should be considered carefully in the light of professional advice from a good lawyer. Don't enter into any stock agreement or partnership situation without legal advice. Ever.

The third possible source of money is borrowing. It's probably the most realistic option for the small business owner. If you're the type who just can't sleep nights if you owe someone money, you've got a problem. There is absolutely no possibility that you can run a successful business without at some point owing somebody something. In most cases, you'll owe money before you open the doors.

There are a number of ways to borrow for your business:

1. You can get a personal loan, secured by your personal assets. This could include a second mortgage on your home, borrowing against your life insurance, or a chattel mortgage on your furniture.

2. You might possibly be able to arrange a loan from a member of your family, a friend, or the employees of your business.

3. Sometimes, you can get cash advances from your customers.

4. Loans (either outright or as lines of credit) can sometimes be arranged from suppliers or equipment manufacturers with a vested interest in getting you and your firm going.

5. You can borrow from a financial institution. Depending on the size of

WORKSHEET NO. 2					
LIST OF FURNITURE, FIXTURES, AND EQUIPMENT					
Leave out or add items to suit your business. Use separate sheets to list exactly what you need for each of the items below.	If you plan to pay cash in full, enter the full amount below and in the last column.	If you are going to pay by installments, fill out the columns below. Enter in the last column your down payment plus at least one installment.			Estimate of the cash you need for furniture, fixtures, and equipment.
		Price	Down payment	Amount of each installment	
Counters	$	$	$	$	$
Storage shelves, cabinets					
Display stands, shelves, tables					
Cash register					
Safe					
Window display fixtures					
Special lighting					
Outside sign					
Delivery equipment if needed					
TOTAL FURNITURE, FIXTURES, AND EQUIPMENT (Enter this figure also in worksheet 1 under "Starting Costs You Only Have To Pay Once".)					$

Figure 2   Furniture and equipment cost estimate work sheet. One-time costs of furniture, fixtures, and equipment: Complete this work sheet and enter the total figure on work sheet no. 1 under "Starting Costs You Only Have to Pay Once." (Courtesy of U.S. Small Business Administration.)

the loan, your personal financial situation, and the economic climate, this may be made by a bank or other lending institution all by itself or from a governmental agency such as the Small Business Administration. Most usually, a small business loan is a combination of the two, involving a local bank as the lender and the SBA as a guarantor on the note.

If you do borrow money, your first choice should be arranging a "line of credit" instead of borrowing the full amount needed at one time. With a line of credit, you can borrow money as you need it and pay principal and interest only on the actual amount in use.

Option 3 listed above (advances from your customers) might sound like a pipe dream. Keep in mind, however, that many large businesses are under the governmental gun to purchase goods and services from small firms. Sometimes the only way for them to meet these mandates is to "grow their own" small suppliers. If you are a potential solution to a large customer's problems in this area, you may have a good chance to obtain financial support from them. In any event, it doesn't hurt to try.

PERMITS, PATIENCE, AND PERSISTENCE

A number of people representing a number of entities will have to give their permission for you to risk the family fortune in the business arena. Unfortunately, they're all located in different locations. To further muddy the water, the permit requirements vary from state to state, county to county, city to city.

One thing's for sure, the first folks you gotta deal with are the feds. You must have a federal identification number or you're headed for big trouble. Contact the Internal Revenue Service nearest you for the necessary forms and information on how to obtain your federal I.D. number.

Next in line will be the state in which your business will be located. Some states don't want to know about you until and unless you have paid employees. Others have permit requirements from day 1. Contact the state tax forms and publication division of your state tax commission office for specifics on what hoops you must jump through for the state.

In addition, the county and the municipality have some claims to make on you and your business. Contact the county and city tax assessor's office for the particulars. At the very least, you will probably need what is termed a "privilege license," which means they grant you the privilege of collecting taxes for them.

Other units of government have some really off-the-wall requirements. A nice little lady I counseled some time ago was very nearly shut down when an inspector from the state horticulture department discovered she didn't have a horticulture license. Of course, she was in the gift shop business and came under the jurisdiction of this governing authority only because a couple of her pots for plants were being sold with plants already in them. Some of the permits and licenses are free; others carry a price tag.

Try to cover all possible bets and give complete information on the kind of business you will be operating. Remember the little lady just mentioned and list everything you intend to offer for sale.

There are also specific state and local requirements for certain kinds of businesses; for example, food and beverage services require health department inspection and approval; most professions have their own licensing requirements in addition to all the foregoing ones.

Your local chamber of commerce may well be a source of valuable advice regarding your local licensing rules and regs. An attorney who's up on this sort of thing can't hurt, either.

The rule to remember is when in doubt, ask and/or apply.

Meet Four VIPs

There are four people who can have an extremely important bearing on your business. As a matter of fact, they can help make you or break you.

There are two common failings in the average small business owner with regard to these four individuals. Failing number 1 is the failure to utilize their services. Failing number 2 is equally common: using some, if not all, of these people, but using them incorrectly or incompletely.

The smart business owner (and that surely includes you!) knows who they are, what they can do, and how to get them to do it.

We seem to have some psychological excess baggage when it comes to dealing with all four. The first three, your lawyer, banker, and accountant, will most usually fill your heart with fear. They are part of the mysterious, secret, godlike group headed by doctors. We all tend to think these men and women are so special, so brilliant, that we dare not ask a question.

We also tend to accept their grunts and mumbles as gospel and to believe that the mere notion of asking "how much is all of this going to cost" is an almost-mortal sin. The fourth specialty on the list is the insurance specialist. This poor soul is one we tend to avoid like the plague.

Try diligently to erase all these erroneous and ineffectual reactions. The four specialists we are about to deal with are critical to your success, and you should keep that uppermost in your mind. It is also meet and just to remember that they are working for you and that you have a perfect right to expect both answers and explanations.

Let's take a look at them one at a time. Even more important, we'll explore how you can best work with each of these VIPs.

LAWYER

Anytime you're operating a business—large or small—you're going to be involved in legal principles regarding the rights of buyers and sellers, landlords and tenants, creditors and debtors, employers and employees, to name but a few. The number and complexity of all these various laws and legal situations make it nigh onto impossible for small business owners to know all their rights and responsibilities, never mind their opportunities.

There is an obvious need for someone who can sort it all out for you, namely, a lawyer you can turn to for advice on everything from routine to major decisions.

Many (if not most) owners of small firms use such legal services only in dire emergencies. That's a very dumb way to go.

If you wait to seek legal services until you're in trouble, you'll usually have just that—trouble. A lot of legal trouble can be reduced or avoided by good planning and continuing consultation with a good attorney. Your lawyer can and should give you advice and suggestions on how to operate your business that will help prevent those very costly and time-consuming problems.

Keep in mind that a lawyer's job, properly done, is to see that you—the client—adhere to the law and avoid inadvertent violations and near-violations. What can and should your lawyer do for you? Four words sum it all up: checking, advising, guiding, and representing.

Your lawyer can check your past actions to determine if you've unintentionally failed to comply with some regulations or law. You might have, for example, failed to get a necessary license or permit for a new product you're now carrying. Your lawyer can also turn up facts to be used to improve your firm's operation. For example, your lawyer's examination of your balance sheet might suggest that another form of business organization would be better financially for you and your family.

In advising you, the lawyer can and should explain the legal principles involved in the various courses of action open to you under the law. Making up your mind is easy when the law only allows one action. It gets a little tougher when the law allows you several possible courses of action, and a good attorney won't make those choices for you. Instead, he or she will give you all the options and alternatives, a complete look at the pros and cons, and you'll be the judge.

Here's where your lawyer's guidance can be valuable. While the ultimate decision must always be yours, your lawyer can help evaluate the courses of action open to you and be a big help as you make those difficult decisions ahead.

In the area of representing you, your attorney speaks as one specialist to another specialist. He or she knows and speaks the language of licensing boards, regulatory bodies, and other governmental agencies. Of equal importance is the representation your lawyer will provide you in negotiating and drawing up contracts. This will ensure that your interests are protected.

When "your" lawyer sits down with "their" lawyer to negotiate a lease, for instance, you can rest a lot easier knowing you are protected from unknowingly entering an agreement which might place restrictions on, say, future expansion of your shop or from unwittingly agreeing to pay for a leaky roof.

Your first contact with your lawyer will likely be as you form your new business and turn to a member of the legal profession to help you to incorporate or to draw up partnership papers. Unfortunately, this is usually the last contact most small business owners have with legal counsel for months and even years.

There are three basic forms of business operation generally available to you—sole proprietorship, a partnership involving two or more individuals, or a corporation. Each form has its own rules and regulations regarding taxation, management, the liabilities of the owner(s), and how profits are to be divided. Only after learning a lot about you and your personal situation can your attorney advise you of the pluses and pitfalls of each of the various forms. Then, you can make a halfway intelligent decision as to which form is most suitable to you.

Legal services are an absolute necessity when the choice of organization is partnership or corporation. These require contracts, agreements, or the filing of certificates that must be handled by a member of the bar. Keep in mind that there are many municipal and state legal requirements attached to the start-up of any new business. Meeting these requirements fully can only be assured with sound legal advice. So take my advice and don't try to go it alone.

Even after your business is well-established legally, periodic checks should be made as the business progresses. Particularly from a tax standpoint. For instance, sole proprietorship may have been the best way for you to go in the early years when losses were incurred or profits were minimal and this situation could be used to offset your other income sources. As a firm grows and profits are shown, the owner-manager may find distinct tax advantages available through incorporation. There is also some reduction in personal liability available in operating as a corporation.

You might, for instance, start as a sole proprietorship and find that you wish to add a partner or two either to help carry the load or to inject new capital into the business to assist in its growth. Or you may want to sell shares in your firm to the public. A lawyer who's really on your team can guide you safely through this legal maze.

Your lawyer can earn an honest fee when it's time for you to purchase property—either real estate or merchandise.

In the case of real property, your first concern with real estate is usually through a landlord. You'll rent the space in which to operate your business, and, in such cases, your lawyer should always check the provisions of the lease or rental agreement. Some of the more important considerations which you'll want your attorney to check before you sign a lease are title to and cost of any improvements to be made in the property, ownership of these improvements when the lease ends or is terminated, renewal provisions, any restrictions on your business operation by the landlord or others, compensation provisions for subletting or assignment of property, and the specific means of determining and measuring your sales—an important item when your rent will depend on a percentage of sales.

If you buy a building in which to operate your business, the services of a lawyer are essential. In those states where title companies are not in operation, your lawyer can examine the certified title to the real estate to ensure that you really own what you're paying for. Your lawyer can also explain the meaning of the fine print in any mortgage or other loan instrument involved in financing such a purchase.

If you buy merchandise from another business, your lawyer can make sure that you're in compliance with the applicable provisions of the uniform commercial code or the bulk sales law of the state in which both you and the seller are located. These laws require that the creditors or the seller be protected in any outright sale of the seller's stock to another (that means you). Your title to the inventory may be in jeopardy if you are in noncompliance with these laws. Your lawyer should be called on to ensure that you'll have proper title before you close the deal.

You just can't run a retail business without an inventory. Very seldom is inventory obtained through a cash purchase. Some form of inventory financing is almost essential. If you're borrowing against inventory, you should consult your lawyer to make sure the contracts and security documents are all in order and to help you understand what commitments you're making.

Basically, in inventory financing the seller doesn't turn the goods completely loose. Some form of security or other interest in the property is held by the seller until the merchandise is sold and/or paid for. You need your lawyer to make sure that any security restrictions in which you're involving yourself are fully understood so that the fine print of financing doesn't unnecessarily or unduly hamper your business operation.

There are lots of other ways to borrow money. Most of them will include the possibility of imposed restrictions on how you can and will operate your business—up to and including how much you can pay yourself. That ought to get your attention. Legal advice is a must, especially when you're assigning your accounts receivable as collateral or involving yourself in equity financing, that is, when you raise funds by selling a part of your business to another person, bringing that poor lost soul in as a part owner. If you do this by offering stock to the general public, your lawyer has to make sure that you're meeting all the requirements set by the Securities and Exchange Commission and by the state regulatory body that might be involved in such a transaction. It's all sticky stuff and why beg trouble? A good lawyer can keep you clean.

I'll bet when you hear "antitrust" you think "huge" and "conglomerate." Most small business owners do. But keep in mind that small as well as big businesses are subject to these same laws and regulations. Your lawyer can help you to be aware of the federal antitrust laws and how they impact your operation.

You should definitely check with your lawyer before you enter into any form of franchise or dealer arrangement with a manufacturer, wholesaler, or supplier. When pricing your merchandise, you must keep in mind the impact of any fair-trade laws applicable in your state. Your legal beagle can keep you advised as to the meaning and impact on you of federal laws relating to resale price-fixing and -maintaining.

In addition, many states have some form of localized unfair-competition laws that might influence your day-to-day operations. Never enter into any agreement regarding price or the division of territories for competitive purposes without checking it out with your lawyer. If you join a trade association, make sure that legal counsel attends the same meetings you do. It doesn't have to be *your* legal counsel; the trade association should have its own lawyer to keep you all collectively out of the soup.

There's a whole batch of laws affecting employees and how you must deal with them. For example, your lawyer can point out and help you observe all the requirements which federal and state laws set on wages, employees' hours, workman's compensation, unemployment compensation, and on-the-job safety.

Another whole batch of law pertaining to equal employment opportunities must be dealt with. Once again, look to the lawyers.

If and when your employees are represented by a labor union, your lawyer will be an essential member of any collective bargaining and contract negotiations team.

When the happy day comes that you can provide profit sharing and retirement plans for your employees, your lawyer earns a fee yet another time.

Naturally, you'll use your lawyer to defend you and your firm if someone should sue it or you or if you have to sue someone. It'll probably happen sooner or later, and it's the pits. A good array of legal services can help you avoid this kind of crisis situation. Good preventative law can keep your business out of the courtroom. And this means a saving in time and money to you.

Litigation is also damaging to your business's image and reputation. Having your firm's name frequently listed in the court news is not exactly the ideal way to attract new customers.

In spite of both our best efforts, you may someday find yourself unable to pay your debts. If things haven't gone too far downhill, your lawyer may be able to work out arrangements with your creditors which will enable you to pay your business debts on a custom-made installment plan out of current income over an extended period of time. In other situations, your attorney may be able to reorganize your business's financial structure so that your creditors can receive a reasonable amount and still permit the business to operate. If worse comes to worst, your attorney can guide you through receivership or bankruptcy and minimize its impact on your personal finances.

Buying or selling a business is another situation that absolutely mandates legal counsel. For heaven's sake, don't try to do it alone.

We'll dig into taxes a bit. Suffice it to say, a lawyer well-versed in small business law can be very helpful in saving you money and keeping you out of trouble with the IRS.

The ideal lawyer is one who knows and enjoys small business law and whom you can talk to. It also helps if he or she can talk to your accountant. These two getting together can really work miracles for a small firm.

Not all lawyers are good lawyers and not all good lawyers are good small business lawyers. Do a little shopping around. Ask your trade association and possibly a couple of business friends whom they would recommend. This might be the time to make your first contact with your friendly neighborhood banker and solicit suggestions for a good attorney.

When you call a lawyer in order to make an appointment, find out how much your initial consultation will cost. If the firm won't give you that information, forget it. Keep in mind, you're buying a service and you have a perfect right to ask and receive a firm quote for your initial consultation. With the new, relaxed advertising code in effect, most law firms are becoming human enough to tell you what their services will cost. If your's won't, get one that will.

I would suggest very strongly that you make a list. That's right, write down all the questions you have to which you want answers. If you don't, you'll forget 75 percent of what you need to know and you'll waste both time and money in the process. Go in armed for bear: Be ready to outline as much as possible about your business plans and projections. This preparation will enable you and your lawyer to educate each other in a minimum amount of time. And with lawyers, time is money. Those folks charge by the minute.

If you haven't decided on a certified public accounting firm, you might ask the lawyer at your initial visit to suggest one. It will very definitely be to your advantage to have a legal firm and an accounting firm that communicate. It can also save you a lot of money, since one won't have to reproduce the other's work, or, as is often the case, have you pay for its learning process (they call it "research").

BANKER

One of the best friends you, as a business owner, will have is your banker. Not only can a warm and comfortable relationship with this individual, one built on mutual admiration, trust, and respect, make your business life a lot simpler—it can literally save your business.

There are at least three very good reasons why a strong relationship with your bank and your banker is to your advantage: (1) You and your firm will receive faster and better service from a banker familiar with you and your business; (2) suggestions for keeping your business financially healthy are much more readily given by a bank and a banker informed about your particular business; and (3) you can avoid costly and harrowing crisis-type borrowing when you plan for your financial needs in a businesslike and timely fashion.

The "typical" small business owner does everything wrong when it comes to banking. He or she doesn't know anyone in the bank on a first-name basis, never mind being one of the manager's buddies. Mr. or Ms. Business Owner has never taken the time or trouble to meet the branch manager or the loan officer, or even been sensible enough to try to use the same teller window each time deposits or withdrawals were made.

Most small business owners send someone else to the bank to make routine deposits and conduct the day-to-day banking business of the firm. Instead they should be taking this opportunity to become a recognized and valued customer by handling this chore personally at least several times a month.

Again, the average business owner only approaches the bank when it is necessary to borrow money. And that's the very worst way to approach a bank for the first time.

Let's take a look at the right way to build strong banking relationships. First off, you have to pick the right bank. Up until now, chances are your banking needs have been limited to a checking account, a savings account (possibly), maybe a safe deposit box, and, perhaps, a personal loan for money used to purchase your automobile. For this sort of service, you're in good hands just about anyplace you go. Business banking requires considerably more than this.

Some banks may be too big, and your small needs will get lost in the vast world of high finance. By the same token, others might be too small and unable to meet your soon-to-grow fiscal needs. That's not to say that a big bank is categorically wrong for a small business or that a small bank can't serve even very large financial needs by drawing on the resources of a larger bank with which it has a working agreement. Certainly you have no size problem if you are doing business in a state with branch banking. In this situation, your friendly neighborhood corner bank has access to the same financial resources as the main branch. Notice that I said financial resources: The right bank has much more to offer you than just money.

Some new business owners open a checking account in their firm's name at the same bank which they've been using for personal banking. In many cases, that works out just fine. It can be an advantage if you already personally know one or more of the bank's officers. In other cases, however, your personal bank may not offer the services and expertise needed by your business.

If you are really lucky, an alert banker may have already learned of your business plans. He or she may have visited you to explain the services the bank could offer and to solicit your account. In this case, you would have learned that the bank can provide (1) credit references on your customers or potential customers; (2) financial, investment, and estate advisory services; (3) the loan needed to establish or expand your business; (4) discounting of customers' accounts and notes payable; (5) check certification; (6) safe deposit boxes for valuable papers, etc.; (7) night depositories; (8) collection of remittances (lock boxes); (9) payment of freight invoices; (10) check reconciliation services; and (11) payroll and other accounting services.

If you aren't already familiar with them, your first step in building really strong relationships with your bank is to find out the kinds of services offered there. If there's something you need not currently being offered, don't hesitate to mention it to your banker. Banks are in a highly competitive business. If the one with whom you are negotiating can't or won't meet all your needs, find one that can—and will.

Whether you're evaluating your present bank or are shopping around for a new one, you'll want to look at five areas: (1) geographic convenience, (2) size of the bank, (3) its requirements for loans, (4) the bank's knowledge of your business and/or its interest in your account, and (5) whether many of your customers use that particular bank.

If at all possible, your bank should be in a location geographically convenient to you—either your business or your home. If it is near your place of business, you'll reduce the risks involved in carrying cash receipts to the bank.

Some small business owners find it convenient to bank near their homes. If this is true in your case, keep in mind that carrying large cash receipts is always a risky practice. Ask your banker's advice on how you can minimize the risks involved.

Unless you need really large loans, the bank's size may not be important to your business. Even then, a small, efficient bank can draw on the resources of a larger bank with which it has a working arrangement. Keep in mind that all branch banks and their loan officers and managers have limits on their lending capacity. What does this mean? It means that in some cases the guy or gal you'll be doing business with can only make loans up to, say, $5000 without getting someone else's approval. In other instances, the individual banker's loan limits might be $50,000 or more. It stands to reason that the higher your personal banker's lending limits, the less delays and red tape will be involved when you need a loan.

All banks have set procedures regarding the lending limits an officer or a specific branch can reach before the loan request will have to be sent "upstairs." For really large sums of money, a loan committee made up of senior officers and members of the board of directors will have to pass judgment on whether the loan will be approved or denied.

Before you open an account, and certainly before you need to borrow money, find out the bank's requirements on loans. Almost all businesses need to borrow money sooner or later. And before you need to borrow is the best time to find out what your bank's collateral requirements are. The only way to find out is to ask. So ask questions such as: Is collateral required on various kinds of loans? How much collateral? How long does it take to have a loan approved? Does the bank have limitations on the number or type of small business loans that it will make? What are the repayment terms? What reports or supporting information do borrowers have to provide? Will the bank give you a "line of credit"? Is it necessary for a borrower to maintain certain balances before the loan can be considered?

If at all possible, find a bank that is somewhat familiar with your type of business. At the very least, find a bank and a banker with no negative feelings about your type of business. There are, for instance, bankers who wouldn't lend money to a car wash operator if the alternative were driving a dirty car for the rest of their natural lives. Others wouldn't lend to a restaurant if the loan were collateralized five times over. Usually, a banker with this kind of prejudice has been "burned" a time or two by some bad loans to similar firms.

If your banker has this sort of negative attitude against your type of operation, you're dead before you start. Again, the only way to find out is to ask. Sometimes the answer will lie between the lines. But surely you're astute enough to be able to determine how your banker really feels about you and your business.

If it's at all practical, it's usually a pretty good idea to use the bank which the majority of your customers or potential customers use. This can be helpful to you because (1) the "float" is minimized, that is, your customers' checks clear the bank more quickly, and money is credited to your account faster; and (2) you'll find that credit information on your customers will be more readily available to you.

A good way to find out about where your customers bank is to note the bank and branches on the checks your customers present to you as payment. Again, another good way is simply to ask them where they bank.

You can also ask other local merchants about the bank with which they do business. Your trade association, or members thereof located around your business, could very well be another source of information about where the good guys are located.

Now, pay attention. Here's how you go about building a profitable and productive working relationship with your banker.

First off, call the bank and make an appointment with the branch manager if it's a small neighborhood bank or with a vice president in the commercial banking department if it's a larger bank. Arrive at the bank on time, dressed in a neat, conservative businesslike fashion. Introduce yourself to the banker, shake hands warmly and firmly, and immediately begin to explain the kinds of services you think you will need from the bank, including any feelings you might have regarding how the bank can best service your account. Ask for advice about other bank services that you might not know about which may be helpful. Have a pad and pen with you; write down the answers to your questions.

Be concise and candid and give the banker as much information on your business plans as (1) you're comfortable disclosing, (2) time permits, (3) he or she seems willing or able to absorb on this first visit. You'll want to repeat this process at a couple of different banks, maybe even more. After comparing your notes on and reactions to each bank and banker, decide on where you want to place your account.

Again, call for an appointment. At this visit, advise the banker that you have shopped around and consider his or her bank to be the very best possible choice for your needs. A little flattery never hurt anyone, and, contrary to popular opinion, bankers are just as human as the rest of us. Since you happen, in this case, to be telling the truth, so much the better.

Tell your new banker that you would like to apprise the bank of your business progress, and ask if you might send monthly (or, at the minimum, quarterly) profit and loss statements for its files. Also ask your new banker to give you input after receiving the statements. There is a very distinct motive behind all this; when and if you need to apply for a loan, the banker will know a great deal about both your business and you and will be much more likely to respond quickly and positively to your request for funding.

You want to establish this kind of good working relationship *before* you need to borrow money, not *when* you need to borrow money. The worst possible time to try to get to know your banker is when you desperately need something that only the bank can provide. In addition, often when you need to borrow money, you are least able to pay it back. Doing all this groundwork before the fact can really pay off.

At this stage in getting to know your banker, mention that you would like very much for him or her to visit your place of business in the very near future. If at all possible, set up a time when your banker will find such a visit desirable. You might suggest planning a quick lunch in conjunction with such a visit.

At this point, your banker will probably introduce you to a new accounts representative or head teller. Make a big point of shaking hands and finding out the names of these various people. Ask if you may call them if you have any questions. The answer will obviously be yes, and they will be flattered that you view them as capable of making a positive contribution to your business.

As you conduct your routine banking, try to make it a point to go to the same teller window. Your aim here is to get on a first-name basis with the teller. A teller can also prove extremely helpful to you. By the same token, each time you pop into the bank to make a deposit, make it a point to smile and wave or say a quick "hello" to your friendly loan officer and/or branch manager. All these activities are calculated to make your banker feel that you are a valued customer to the bank. Involve the bank in every possible way in your business to the point where said banker would much rather say "yes" than "no" to your requests.

In getting to know your banker, you are trying to develop a real friend at the bank—someone who knows you and the problems of your business, someone in whom you can confide and from whom you can receive advice.

In addition to regularly sending financial statements to your banker, make it a point to include newspaper clippings or copies of articles that pertain to your business from trade journals or general-interest publications. Again, your aim is to familiarize your banker with your business. This kind of personalized contact, in addition to keeping your banker informed about business trends affecting your particular kind of business, will serve to reinforce the fact that you are a real go-getter. And everybody, most of all bankers, loves a winner.

Keep in mind that a good banker really has a finger on the total pulse of any community. Bankers can give you valid advice on the strengths and weaknesses of, say, a location you're considering. Your banker might very well know about some large firm about to move into the area or about the expansion of an existing firm that might impact on your business. Your banker may also often be in a position to recommend your firm to other firms or individuals seeking the goods or services you are capable of providing. Your banker could be a trustworthy source of referrals that will lead you to good legal and accounting services. The rule of thumb is ask. You might get some valuable input. At the very least, your banker will feel warm and huggy because his or her counsel was valuable enough to you for you to seek it.

Always show good faith in dealing with your banker. Keep your word just as you expect your banker to keep his or hers. Always observe the bank's policies. Don't ever try to pull a fast one on your banker. If things are bad, be honest. If you've really done your homework, your banker can help see you through those bad times.

If, for instance, you have a note with a bank—obviously you're going to make payments on time. If for any reason a payment is going to be late (even a day or two late), call your banker and explain why. Too many times, the small business owner who is unable to meet obligations tries to duck the issue. In most cases, this is worse than the actual condition warrants. Telling it like it is, in a businesslike manner, can avoid getting your banker buddy into an embarrassing situation at the bank. And that banker buddy of yours very likely has the authority to grant you an extension on the note, let you pay only the interest and defer payment of principal until a later time, or pull the account entirely and hold it for a few days. Insofar as it is possible, give your bank enough volume to make you a profitable customer. Banking is a business, too. And banks are interested in and keep fairly close tabs on the average checking account balances carried by their business customers. An active and profitable bank account helps create goodwill at the bank just as an active customer account does at your place of business.

I've already said you'll want to provide financial data on a regular basis to your banker. Make sure this financial data is accurate. If at all possible, make sure the financial statements are prepared by an independent outside service such as a firm of certified public accountants. This kind of factual information on your firm's finances will help to build your reputation for integrity with your banker. Any loan officer will be suspicious of statements which are either padded or too scanty. If anything, stay on the conservative side with projections.

When your banker physically visits your place of business, really show off your operation. Advise your banker of your sources of supply; show how you receive and maintain your stock. If you have any special merchandising techniques which give you an edge over your competition, talk them up. Also point out any methods you might have come up with for reducing operating expenses.

During the visit, introduce your banker to your staff. If it's a big staff, keep the introductions down to your immediate assistant and/or the person in charge of your bookkeeping records. It's just got to make your banker feel better to know that there are other warm bodies capable of keeping the show on the road if you catch the flu.

A banker who knows about your plans for the future is a banker better-equipped to understand what your financial needs will be. Your goal is to involve the bank in helping to plan for those future needs. A time to make this happen is considerably before the date you actually need your banker's financial help.

It's just one heck of a lot easier to borrow money to cover a period with a cash flow problem when you have anticipated it, your banker has anticipated it, and you have made the necessary arrangmeents for a line of credit or a loan considerably in advance. The alternative is waiting until you're about to be overdrawn and pleading with a banker who (1) doesn't know you, (2) doesn't know your business, and (3) is presented with a financial picture that looks less than glowing. A "yes" under such circumstances is a bloody miracle, and rightly so.

Bankers generally prefer dealing with business owners who plan their financial needs. Such business people are usually considered very good credit risks because they know what to expect and when to expect it, and they prepare accordingly.

Basically, financial planning involves four things: (1) estimating as nearly as possible the amount of sales for a fixed future period—3, 6, or 12 months; (2) estimating as nearly as possible the expenses connected with those sales; (3) determining whether or not your business will need cash, in addition to that brought in by sales, to pay its bills on time; and (4) if a loan will be needed, determining how your business can repay it.

This kind of planning can help you and your banker to reduce the cost of financing. Knowing what your needs will be beforehand gives you time to build your case for the money and to shop around for it, if necessary. Really progressive small business owners also plan for the long range. They try to estimate and project their financial situation for the next 2, 3, or even 5 years. By covering these plans with your banker, you strengthen your relationship further.

In making these financial plans, you will have certain data. You can develop it, or it can be developed for you. For example, you can have your accountant work up financial analyses such as cash flow forecasts, income and expense budgets, and capital budgets. Your accountant should also prepare financial statements such as profit and loss and balance sheets, and should work up financial ratios to show your business expenses in relation to sales, your break-even point and margin of safety, and inventory turnover.

When armed with this sort of hard data, any banker worthy of the name is going to feel a lot more comfortable about saying yes. If nothing else, he or she will get the very distinct feeling that you know what you're doing. And you will.

I've already mentioned some of the things a full-service bank has to offer you and your business. Here are a few more for you to explore with your buddy the banker.

Agency Services

A bank may act as agent in many important and complex ways. For the average small business owner, the bank's use as an agent for collection and disbursement services of various kinds would likely be of most interest. Check it out.

Trust Services

Almost any bank has a trust department. Some of the smaller branch offices may not offer this service on the premises but can refer you to the main office and provide introductions to a trust officer. This department, among other things, handles the financial affairs of people who want it to manage their investments or hold them and collect income and make payments from it as agreed upon. Some folks buy this kind of service during their lifetime; many more name the bank as executor of their will so that the bank's trust department takes charge of the estate's assets when an individual dies. As you become successful in your business operation, it very well might behoove you to explore the trust services of your bank.

Safe Deposit Boxes

Most banks provide safe deposit box services. Boxes are available in several sizes, and the cost depends on the size of the safe deposit box. This service is a simple one, minimal cost is involved, and a safe deposit box is an ideal place to keep various corporate records, leases, stock certificates, anything of real value.

Credit Advice

Every bank of any size has a credit department which handles credit problems daily. Such a department could be extremely helpful to you in providing information on credit references and the like, and can steer you to bank card and check guarantee services.

Special Services

The major banks also employ engineering and management experts who are made available to clients and who can offer some pretty worthwhile suggestions and guidance. Almost all the big banks also have research departments that can be veritable gold mines of statistical information and business forecasts. Most of these big kids publish some reasonably readable documents on a regular basis. Ask your buddy the banker if your bank has such a service. It's almost always free of charge and all you have to do is ask. As a matter of fact, such a department will sometimes do special little bits of research at your banker's request to come up with specific information you might need in your business.

A few of the really major banks even publish regular reports of special interest to small business owners. An excellent example of this kind of special service is the Small Business Reporter, published by Bank of America. This ongoing series of publications is absolutely first-rate. Next time you find yourself in sunny California, stop in at a Bank of America branch and ask them to place you on the mailing list for this series.

You know what you have to do. Now, go do it. Join the "take a banker to lunch" bunch.

CPA

Let me set the record straight. You don't have to have a CPA. But you probably should.

The various services and functions that your certified public accounting firm can and most likely should perform for you can be done by someone other than a CPA, such as a bookkeeper or accountant. These functions include setting up and keeping an accounting system adequate to record your business's cash receipts, disbursements, sales, and operating expenses; with regularity (and in a timely fashion) preparing your balance sheet, income statement, statement of accounts payable and receivable, and other such financial information that you may need to operate your firm; preparing your state and federal income tax forms, social security, withholding, personal property, and other tax returns; and providing you with estimates about future prospects that might be needed by banks or other lenders if and when you apply for loans.

Any or all of these functions can be performed by a competent bookkeeper. And in some instances, it might be more feasible—financially or otherwise—for a bookkeeping service or a staff bookkeeper to do so.

A good certified public accountant is a good deal more than a glorified bookkeeper. But first you gotta find a good one. Second, you have to learn how to work with this professional so as to use him or her to your very best advantage.

We'll deal with the first problem situation first. A couple of good places to start happen to be with the first two VIPs you just met, namely, your lawyer and your banker. Between the two of them, you'll probably end up with four or five possibilities. Then it's up to you. You'll be looking for (1) someone you like and can relate to, (2) someone who knows small business and its problems, and (3) someone who wants your business.

This last comment isn't as farfetched as it might seem. Many large accounting firms don't want to handle small clients. They just don't find us little guys and gals very profitable. There is, however, a growing appreciation of small businesses among the so called "big eight" accounting firms. (These are the really big guys like Price Waterhouse, Arthur Anderson, Deloitte Haskins & Sells, et al.) Some of these monstrous firms are starting small business departments that actively (as actively as certified public accounting firms can) solicit new small business accounts. The staff assigned to these small business divisions are people who enjoy working with small firms and are, in fact, specializing in this area of public accounting. You may still feel more comfortable placing your account with a smaller local firm. Go with what feels right for you.

It doesn't hurt to ask other small business people which CPA firm they're utilizing and what their honest evaluation of the service provided happens to be.

The CPAs, like doctors and lawyers, tend to turn normally self-assured, forceful individuals such as you and me into quivering, quaking, jelly-kneed idiots incapable of asking a reasonable question. You've gotta get over that. And fast.

Square your shoulders, stick out your chin, and keep repeating to yourself, "They're working for me. They're working for me."

And that's the truth. They are working for you. You pay for their service, you have a right to expect good service, and since you'll be conducting yourself like a good client, I think you'll get it.

A good accountant is part historian, part futurist. It is important to keep records. In many instances, you are legally required to do so. And proper records can be critical in assisting you in planning, organizing, and controlling your business. From an historical perspective, your records will help you answer the question, "How am I doing?" From these same records, you and your accountant can determine, "Where am I going?"

This last futuristic activity is absolutely critical to lending institutions, obviously, who are all-concerned with whether you'll be able to pay back any money you might be seeking to borrow. But this look into tomorrow will also assist you in determining whether to hire additional staff, expand physical space, add a new store or plant, drop a particular line of merchandise or add another, in short, all the many activities that will influence how your business will do a month, a year, or a decade from now.

It's a toss-up as to whether, once you decide that you are going to open a business, you should consult with a lawyer first and an accountant second, or whether the order should be accountant first, lawyer second. One thing's for sure, you should consult with both these professionals prior to making any significant moves toward opening day.

A primary necessity is finding a CPA that you can personally relate to. You'll be telling this individual a great deal about yourself, your family situation, your plans, hopes, dreams for the future, and it only stands to reason that it should be someone you are comfortable talking with. It is also most helpful, as stated earlier, to have a CPA who can relate well to your attorney (and vice versa). The ideal situation is having one who can also communicate effectively with your banker. The absolutely ideal situation is all the above plus an accountant who really views him- or herself as an integral, ongoing member of your management team, a person involved in all major decision making.

Someone must perform the following functions:

1. Start and keep an accounting system for the accurate and timely recording of your company's cash receipts, disbursements, sales, and operating expenses

2. Periodically prepare the following:
   a. Statement of assets and liabilities as of a given date (commonly referred to as a balance sheet)
   b. Statement of results of operation for a given period of time (commonly referred to as an income statement)
   c. Statement of changes in financial position
   d. A list of customers owing you money as of a given date and those firms and individuals to whom you owe money (accounts receivable/payable)
   e. Such other financial information as may be needed in your own individual business situation

3. Prepare state and federal income tax returns

4. Prepare social security, withholding, personal property, and other tax returns

5. Make estimates about future prospects that may be requested by banks and other lenders from whom loans are requested

6. Maintain the necessary checking accounts to disburse payroll payments to employees, and payment of the firm's operating expenses in a timely fashion

7. Prepare and send out statements to those customers of your firm doing business on a credit basis with you (billing)

Notice that I said "someone" has to perform all these functions. You can do them yourself. You can have a staff bookkeeper, accountant, comptroller, or combination of these folks on your payroll performing all these tasks. You can hire an outside bookkeeping service. Some of them—if not all—could be performed by your bank if you're doing business with a major bank. Most of the big guys do offer computerized accounting services. This started with payroll and check-writing services and now extends to cover a full range of record-keeping services. You can also have a certified public accounting firm perform all these many chores. But that can get expensive. Your best bet will likely be a combination of service deliverers.

Certainly, your CPA should set up the accounting system under which your firm will operate. A staff bookkeeper (maybe your spouse or an in-law) can handle most of the other functions, with your CPA overseeing the process.

I would suggest that your CPA balance your books a minimum of semiannually; quarterly would be even better. At such time, all your current books and records will be turned over to your CPA, and for a period of anything from a few days to a few weeks, he or she will either physically reside at your place of business or move all your books and records to the CPA office. The CPA will check everything over to make sure that all entries have been made correctly and will prepare any combination of the periodic reports just outlined in number 2. Keep in mind, this is not an audit of your books. But even with the disclaimers he or she will add, having a CPA sign your balance sheet will give it considerably more weight with investors, lenders, etc.

At this time, it is wise to plan regular sessions with your CPA to discuss estimates about your business prospects for the future and to present any problems or projects that you've been mulling over since your last get-together for input and comment. In between these quarterly or semiannual business reviews, you might also seriously consider running any major business moves by your CPA before you make them. This might include hiring of a new staff member, purchase of a new piece of equipment, implementing a profit sharing or retirement plan for your staff.

From time to time, the services of a certified public accountant will be absolutely mandated. So even if you decide not to use a CPA on an ongoing basis, the day will probably come in your business life when you will be required to seek out such a professional. Some folks still wonder what a CPA is. In a nutshell, it's an individual who has proven proficiency in accounting, auditing, tax law, and a complex collection of business-oriented problems by passing a truly exhaustive written examination prepared by the American Institute of Certified Public Accountants and who has thereby received a state license for the public practice of accountancy. After passing the test, the individual must also serve a 2-year apprenticeship under the supervision of an already certified CPA. In contrast, anyone can be a bookkeeper or announce to the gullible world that he or she is an accountant. The CPA designation is kind of the Good Housekeeping Seal of Approval—it's the best guarantee you have that the individual you're considering working with is competent. The CPAs are also bound by a rigid code of ethics. The profession demands a respect for client confidentiality, scrupulous honesty, and continuing education to keep the CPA current on new legislation and the like. A CPA not living up to the profession's high standards can be given the boot by the state association.

As I implied earlier, some situations will demand the services of a CPA. Such instances could include your contracting with the federal government. Almost all federal contracts mandate an audit by a certified public accountant. Likewise, firms offering stock for sale to the general public are mandated by the Securities and Exchange Commission to have their books and records regularly audited by a certified public accountant.

In the case of your small business, more than likely your CPA will be called upon to audit your accounting records and prepare certified financial statements, prepare your tax returns and help you with estate planning, and consult with you vis-à-vis your future moves in your business.

In the first instance, that of certified financial statements and records, most lenders (such as banks and the Small Business Administration) will require certified audits both before a loan is granted and at regular intervals during the period that the loan is outstanding.

Far more than simply preparing your tax return, your certified public accountant should help you through the maze of tax laws so that you pay the lowest possible present tax liabilities and should help you plan your business life (and often your personal life) in such a way as to minimize future tax consequences.

Your CPA may be able to assist you in cost reduction, the improvement of reports and reporting systems, installation or upgrading of your accounting system, budgeting and forecasting, financial analysis, production control, quality control, compensation of your personnel, inventory control and pricing, and proper records management.

In addition to all the above, your CPA may also perform special studies and investigate suspected fraud.

As you can see, your CPA can—and should—be one of the best friends your business can have. I also mentioned earlier that you will conduct yourself as a good client should. That includes a lot of things, not the least of which is to pay your CPA's bills promptly. These rules on how to be a good client include:

1. Pay your bills promptly. (It's important enough to state twice!)

2. Play it straight. Give your CPA the most honest information you have access to. Save the embellishments and poetry for your golfing buddies and your hairdresser. You won't fool a pro for long, and the subterfuge will cost you money in more ways than one.

3. It's your system—but it won't work without you. Make sure that once your CPA has installed a record-keeping system in your firm, you and your staff make all the entries, fill out all the forms and reports, and generally do what you're supposed to do so that your CPA can perform efficiently. If you don't, keep in mind that the only person it will cost will be you. CPAs charge by the hour, and the more hours it takes to get to the bottom of your mess, the more it will cost you.

4. Ask and ye shall receive. Your CPA is not a gypsy fortune-teller or mind reader and can't know what you're thinking, dreaming, scheming, or needing unless you speak up.

5. You're paying for professional advice. Take it. If you don't agree with the

advice on a relatively regular basis, maybe it's time to change CPAs. But it strikes me as less than wise to pay for advice and then absolutely ignore it.

6. Last but not least, make sure that you understand the information your CPA is providing you. If you don't understand how to read a balance sheet, say so. The best service your CPA could provide you in that case is to teach you how to read the thing. By the same token, if your accountant is generating more data than you have time, energy, or inclination to absorb—say so! Perhaps a summary can be provided which will give you the most pertinent points in a nutshell. Or maybe the report really isn't necessary, and you can save yourself money as well as time by eliminating it.

By now, I think you have the general gist of how to work with the first three VIPs on our list. Now let me give you a specific example of how two young businesswomen did everything right. I've protected the privacy of everyone involved by changing their names, but the situation is God's own truth.

Several years ago, while I was executive director of the Arizona Small Business Association (ASBA), a young woman (let's call her Lynn) attended a small business management seminar sponsored by the association. The ASBA is a private nonprofit organization which provides educational seminars and workshops, management and technical assistance, and loan proposal assistance (among other things) to small or aspiring entrepreneurs.

In conversation before and after class, I learned that Lynn and her partner had just started a medical laboratory service. They both had had extensive background as laboratory technicians, and, after carefully studying the business climate and the need for such a service, they had formed their own firm and were set up to provide an extensive array of medical laboratory services to doctors, clinics, hospitals, and other health care professionals. Their service was unique in that the two young women had equipped a large motor home, which one of them owned, as a mobile laboratory. In this manner, they could take laboratory facilities to the doctor when this unique "at your door" service was to the patient's and/or doctor's benefit.

Two of the guest instructors with whom Lynn came into contact were Geof Smith, a senior partner in the law firm of Smith and Gray, and Mike Shuster, a CPA and partner in the firm of Ladd and Ladd. Both professional firms had nonfinancial agreements to provide services at reduced rates to association clients and members.

Among many of the things Lynn learned about small business management during the 6-week course was that she really needed professional help in the area of law and accounting. I also learned that Lynn and her partner were in need of capital with which to operate and to purchase much-needed additional laboratory equipment and supplies.

Lynn made an appointment to consult with me privately. After reviewing their situation, I called a third professional (you've got it, a banker!), namely, Sandy Bishop, a vice-president at First National Bank. At the time, Ms. Bishop was working in commercial lending, and I had had great success in obtaining funding for various ASBA clients through her and her fine bank.

I briefly explained the situation as I viewed it to Sandy on the telephone and made an appointment for Lynn and her partner to see her regarding their money needs.

Lynn also made an appointment with Geof Smith and another with Mike Shuster. Smith suggested incorporation and took care of all the legal details. He and Mike Shuster worked together to minimize the firm's tax liabilities and to keep everything nice and legal.

Mike Shuster worked with Lynn and her partner to set up easy-to-keep books and instructed them until both principals in the firm were completely comfortable with all their record-keeping responsibilities.

Sandy Bishop called me a few days later to advise me that she was most impressed with the two young businesswomen and that she had established a line of credit at the bank for them. This seemed the best route to go after an analysis of their immediate capital needs.

A year or so later, Mike Shuster mentioned to me that he had just advised Lynn and her partner to add two more mobile laboratory vans to their fleet and to expand services throughout the state. Geof Smith continues to keep them legal; Shuster—through his advice, counsel, and creative accounting— has assisted their firm through a rapid, yet planned and orderly, growth period; and Sandy Bishop and the nice folks at First National Bank have continued to provide the necessary financing that is fast turning these two industrious and enterprising young women into budding tycoons.

I've heard nothing but the highest praise from all three professionals about these two fine young women. The women have nothing but glowing reports for the attorney, CPA, and banker who made it all possible, and I have every confidence that what started out as a small two-person laboratory three years ago will very soon be grossing a million bucks a year.

To recap what Lynn and her partner did right:

1. They had experience in the business they were starting.

2. They had carefully and accurately determined the need for their services.

3. At least one of the principals obtained additional training in how to operate a small business.

4. They sought and heeded the best professional advice available to them.

5. They found a professional or trade association that could be of help to them in many ways.

6. They took advantage of personal introductions to establish good relationships with their banker and other professional advisors.

7. They picked professionals who could work with them and with each other.

8. They acted on the advice they were paying for.

9. Take my word for it—they did excellent work for their clients.

10. They worked their heads off.

Lynn's story isn't unique. I can't honestly say it's commonplace, either. I hope that it illustrates very clearly how using the right professional assistance in the right way can put your business on the right track and keep it there.

CLU

Pity the poor insurance peddler! Too often, an insurance salesperson is the last person you want to see on a busy day. He or she seems a harbinger of doom, the bearer of unpleasant tidings—specifically, that "from dust thou art and unto dust thou shalt return."

Insurance ain't fun. The way it works, some joker's betting that you won't die and you're betting that you will. Or the same clown says no one's going to rob your home or bash into your car, and you keep repeating, via your monthly payments, that they will. It's kinda like putting your money on the don't-pass line at the dice table when you have the dice. And somehow it seems less than reassuring to bet against oneself.

Reasonable sentiments, all. Now you have to overcome them because an insurance professional is the fourth and final member of your VIP team.

Now, it may not take much training or talent to simply take orders for insurance policies. But it takes a great deal of training and talent to be a competent, first-rate insurance adviser. And that's why the designation CLU is used: to remind you to seek out a true professional.

For the uninformed, CLU stands for certified life underwriter. It means the insurance salesperson using these initials after his or her name has successfully completed certain training requirements and passed certain tests of proficiency (very much as a CPA has). There are a number of other professional milestones, and the appropriate letter designations thereof you may find trailing your insurance counselor's name. One of these might be CFP— certified financial planner. When in doubt, once again, ask. If initials are trailing after a person's given and family names, that person must be proud of them and will jump at the chance to tell you what they mean.

What you want to find is someone who doesn't just sell insurance but, rather, who can advise you of how to use the minimum amount of insurance to give you the maximum amount of protection, who won't make you "insurance-poor" but by the same token will make sure that you have adequate coverage in all aspects of your business.

Your best bet will probably be to find an independent agent who specializes in business insurance. Again, find someone you like—someone you can talk to, relate to, trust, and communicate with. Someone who seems interested in you and your needs, not just a quick sale and a quicker getaway.

Since you now have at least three good sources of referrals, namely, your attorney, your banker, and your CPA—ask them who they'd recommend to serve your insurance needs. But before you talk to your potential insurance representative, let's talk about what some of your insurance needs might conceivably be.

Four kinds of insurance are essential in almost every business: fire insurance, liability insurance, automobile insurance, and workmen's compensation insurance. In addition, special circumstances will sometimes mandate specific insurance coverage. An example might be a lease that mandates a specific kind and amount of insurance coverage, or a loan granted under conditions mandating specific amounts and types of insurance coverage for either the debtor or whatever the loan proceeds were used to purchase (such as a building, merchandise, or equipment).

Fire insurance can cover a building, including part or all of the contents therein. Most fire insurance policies can also cover other perils such as windstorm, hail, smoke, explosion, vandalism, and malicious mischief at a relatively small additional cost.

Your best bet is to discuss your business plans and procedures thoroughly with your insurance counselor. When he or she really understands how you operate and what your future plans include, you'll be much more likely to get the very best suggestions on how to protect both your dreams and your realities.

Keep in mind, you can insure property you don't own. You must, however, have a proveable financial interest to make such property insurable by you. For instance, a shoe repair shop or dry cleaning plant may carry insurance on customers' property while it is in the shop.

Depending on the kind of business you operate, you may want special protection other than the standard fire policy to cover loss by fire or water damage of account records, bills, currency, deeds, evidences of death, and money and securities. Remember, this takes special protection. Most standard fire insurance policies don't cover these items. But you and your insurance counselor should assess the cost to your business of the loss of any or all these bits and pieces of important paper.

Given today's legal maze, it is absolutely critical that you carry adequate liability insurance. You may find yourself and your firm liable for injury to not just employees and/or customers but even trespassers under certain conditions. Most liability policies, in addition to bodily injuries, may now cover personal injuries such as libel and slander charges against you and/or your firm.

Automobile insurance is another must. When an employee or subcontractor uses a car on your behalf, you can be legally liable even if you don't own a car or truck yourself.

Keep in mind that personal property stored in an automobile and not attached to it (for example, merchandise samples or merchandise being delivered) is not usually covered under an automobile policy. If this is a situation that might occur in your business, mention it to your insurance counselor. Special coverage can and should be provided to protect you in these instances.

Most states now mandate workers' compensation insurance. Common law requires that an employer provide employees a safe place in which to work, that the employer hire competent fellow employees, provide the worker with safe tools, and warn all employees of any known existing dangers. Workmen's compensation provides insurance to the employee in the event of an accident on the job. The rates for such insurance vary widely depending on how dangerous the employee's occupation is perceived to be. You can also lessen the financial impact by keeping a safe place in which your employees will work and by maintaining a sterling safety record. If you reduce the accident rate, you may reduce the premium.

There's a lot more business-related insurance you should at least explore. Included in this big bag of tricks is business interruption insurance. This would cover your fixed expenses if, say, a fire were to shut down your business. The insurance premiums would cover salaries to your employees, taxes, interest, depreciation, utilities, as well as the profits you lose. Coverage can also be obtained if an insured peril seriously disrupts business while not actually closing it totally down. Business interruption can even be written to cover you and your firm in case there is a failure or interruption of the supply of power, light, heat, gas or water furnished by a public utility company.

The chances are, if it can happen, it can be insured against. Crime is big business, and small business can be protected against it. There are now comprehensive crime policies just for small business owners offered by most major carriers. In addition to burglary and robbery, these policies cover other types of loss by theft, destruction, and disappearance of money and securities. It even covers thefts by your employees. Perish the thought, but sometimes this kind of stuff happens.

If you're in a high-risk area with excessive crime rates and cannot get insurance through normal channels without paying through the nose, you may be able to get help through the Federal Crime Insurance Plan. Your insurance agent or state insurance commissioner can tell you where to get information about these special programs.

You can purchase glass insurance policies that cover all risk to plate-glass windows, glass signs, motion picture screens, glass brick, glass doors, showcases, countertops, and insulated glass panels. If it gets broken, you get paid. These glass insurance policies cover not only the glass itself but also the

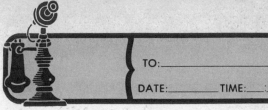

TO:_____

DATE:_____ TIME:____:____ ☐ A.M. ☐ P.M.

M_____

OF_____

AREA CODE

CALL BACK PHONE NO _____/_____

1 ☐ TELEPHONED   4 ☐ WILL CALL AGAIN

2 ☐ RETURNED YOUR CALL   5 ☐ WANTS TO SEE YOU

3 ☐ PLEASE CALL HIM   6 ☐ CALLED TO SEE YOU

Message: *Keyboard*
University Sign

CALL TAKEN BY:_____

lettering and ornamentation thereon (if they are specifically insured) and the cost of putting up either temporary glass panes or boards, if this is necessary in order to secure the premises.

Another novel kind of insurance can be written to cover your rent payments in case fire, flood, or other insured perils should interrupt your business while the lease keeps right on truckin'. My advice is (1) try to get your attorney to negotiate these clauses out of any lease before it's signed and (2) insure against its occurrence if you can't get it out of the lease.

Another area to be explored with your insurance agent is the bonding of employees who might have access to cash or other negotiable securities or valuable merchandise.

Insurance coverages can be used to provide employee benefits including group life insurance, group health insurance, disability insurance, and re-tirement income. Key-person insurance can protect your company against financial loss caused by the death or disability of a valuable employee or partner.

These employee benefits can help you attract and keep good people and can save you a ton of money. A case in point: Imagine a small staff; you're on a personal and very friendly basis with all of them. One of them becomes seriously ill for an extended period of time. You have a choice: You can terminate the employee and let the welfare system take over; you can continue to pay at least a portion of the employee's wages at great cost to your firm both because the employee is no longer productive and because the financial drain of the partial salary leaves you unable to replace the employee with a new staff member; or you can do the smart thing and provide insurance coverage that kicks in, say, 2 to 4 weeks after the employee is disabled. This takes care of everyone. The employee continues to receive an income, the firm is free to hire at least temporary help to replace the disabled staff member, and your conscience is clear without clearing out your checkbook.

If you operate a sole proprietorship, you might very well want to look into an individual retirement account (IRA). And there can be some income tax deductions available to your firm for plans of insurance or annuities approved for use under the Employees Retirement Income Security Act of 1974 (ERISA). Here again, your insurance agent is the best source of infor-mation on such plans.

One of the most serious setbacks your business can suffer is the loss of a key staff member. Key-person insurance provides both life insurance and disability insurance to your company. It's paid for and payable to the firm. The proceeds of a key-person policy are not subject to income tax, but premiums are not a deductible business expense. The cash value of such key-person insurance, which accumulates as an asset of your business, can be borrowed against, and the interest and dividends are not subject to income tax for as long as the policy remains in force.

A sound insurance protection plan is just as important to the success of your business as good financing, proper marketing strategies, personnel management, or any other important business function. And like the other functions, good risk and insurance management is not achieved by accident (no pun intended!), but by careful organization and planning.

A lifetime of work and dreams can be lost in a few minutes if you are inadequately insured. To make sure you're covered, take the following actions:

1. Recognize—through careful assessment—the various ways you can suffer.
2. Get professional advice.
3. With this professional advice, organize your insurance management program.
4. Once adequate insurance is arranged for, make sure you periodically reassess your insurance needs and update your insurance coverage as needed.

And by "periodically," I don't mean once every 5 years. I mean each time there is a significant change in your business or its operation. This could mean following a growth period when you've got significantly more to lose than you have insured or, perhaps, when you hire additional staff—especially in key areas. At a minimum, review your insurance program each year to make sure that coverage keeps pace with inflation.

Saying an occasional prayer or taking an it-can't-happen-to-me attitude will not lessen or remove the possibility that something might happen to your business. To help keep insurance costs down, be sure to cover the following points with your insurance counselor:

1. Decide what perils to insure against and how much loss you might suffer from each.
2. Cover your largest loss exposure first.
3. Use as high a deductible as you can afford.
4. Avoid duplication in insurance.
5. Buy your insurance in as large a unit as possible. Many of the so-called package policies are very suitable for the types of small businesses they are designed to serve. Often they're the only way a small business can get really adequate protection. If one of these fits, wear it.
6. Review your insurance program periodically to make sure your coverage is adequate and your premiums as low as possible, consistent with sound protection.

Finally, here are some dos and don'ts in dealing with your insurance agent.

Do write down a clear statement of what you expect insurance coverage to do for your firm.

Do select only one agent to handle your insurance. Having more than one may spread and weaken responsibility, confuse the issue, add unnecessary duplication that will cost you money, and leave you with insurance gaps where no protection is provided.

Do make sure, if an employee or partner is going to be responsible for your firm's insurance program, that he or she fully understands the responsibilities of the position.

Do everything possible to prevent losses and to keep those that do occur as low as possible. Running a safe business with few—or no—claims will reduce the cost of coverage. And that's money in your pocket instead of the insurance company's.

Don't withhold information from your insurance agent. If it relates to your business and its exposure to loss, play it straight. Failure to do so could result in a coverage gap.

Don't try to save money by underinsuring or by not covering what could cause very costly losses. If the probability of loss is really small, the premium will also be small. The lack of insurance could totally wipe you out. The premiums won't.

Do keep accurate records of your insurance policies, including premiums paid, losses, and loss recoveries. These records should be kept in an absolutely safe place—preferably a safe deposit box or a safe impervious to fire and flood.

Do have your business property appraised periodically by an independent appraiser. This will help you keep your insurance coverage adequate.

And above all, do get professional advice about your insurance. Insurance is a complex and detailed subject. Professionally qualified agents, brokers, or consultants earn their fees many times over. And the business they save might be yours.

It's a Great Location, But Don't Sign Anything Yet!

Well, you found it. A vacant corner of God's green earth that seems to fill the bill. It's got four walls, the roof doesn't leak, and, best of all, you can afford the rent. You've got butterflies in your stomach, and the last time you were this excited was just before the junior or senior prom.

You can't sleep, can't eat, don't want to talk about anything but this physical facility in which you will build your future and your fortune. I know. I understand. I've been there. But the wrong move now could blow the whole deal.

So contain yourself, keep on reading, and don't sign anything yet.

RENT VERSUS ADVERTISING DOLLARS

If the rent's low, your advertising costs will be high. That theorem can almost always be reversed. High rent usually reduces the advertising budget you will need.

Why is this so? We touched on this briefly in Chapter 2. But let's take a thorough look at the rent/advertising−budget ratio.

There is almost always a direct relationship between the amount of rent charged for a business location and the traffic count, either foot or vehicular, passing by the place every day. The higher the traffic count, the higher the rent.

If you're looking in the low-rent district, one or more of the following are probably true statements: (1) The space is located in an area with few people; (2) there may be lots of people, but none of them has very much money to spend in your shop or anyone else's; or (3) the area is physically or psychologically what could be termed a "bummer." Maybe it's near a sewage treatment plant or a packing house. Maybe it's in a neighborhood noted for a high crime rate.

You can sometimes overcome the first situation by expending enough dollars in an advertising and/or public relations effort to draw people to your location. In the second instance, lots of luck. Unless you're planning to operate a thrift store or some similar sort of business that would appeal to a low-income clientele, you've got problems. In the third instance, forget it. There ain't enough money in your loan application to lure the locals into an area where the stench more than clears your sinus problem or the muggers outnumber the victims.

Sometimes, however, the trade-offs are very realistic in instance number 1.

Now's the time to realistically assess what I like to call the "real rent" will be in your chosen location. Imagine for a moment that you have found a perfect location for $1000 a month rent. A second location is not nearly so "perfect," but the rent for this place is "only" $500 per month. Any budget-minded businessperson could tell at a glance that the second location is by far the most cost-efficient. But hold your horses. Let's further imagine your number 1 location is in a high traffic count area with many hundreds— perhaps even thousands—of potential customers passing the place daily. For purposes of discussion, let's assume that your advertising costs for a modest newspaper ad and a half dozen radio spots weekly will run $500. Are you with me?

Let's continue with this hypothetical situation and assume that the prime location will require only 2 weeks of advertising per month to keep a consistent flow of customers streaming through your front door. That means that your advertising budget will run $1000 per month. Got that?

Now let's imagine that the second, less-than-perfect location will require the same media support, only you'll have to spend that $500 every single week to keep the customers coming. That means that location number 2, the $500 a month rent jobbie, will need a $2000 per month advertising budget to succeed.

A little basic arithmetic, if you please. Rent of $1000 a month plus $1000 for the 2-week advertising campaign on the prime location comes to $2000 monthly for rent and advertising. Rent of $500 a month for the "cheap" location plus $2000 a month advertising support to compensate for the turkey location adds up to $2500 per month in rent and advertising. Thus, the first location at $1000 per month will *save* $500 per month in fixed overhead costs.

Add to this the fact that a really choice location can go a long way toward ensuring the profitability of your new venture, and I'm sure you get the message. There are some very false economies that can cost you dearly.

That's not to say that some businesses—maybe even yours—would not do splendidly in a low-rent district. Just be aware of what you're getting into before you get into it.

A good rule of thumb here is that if the customer must find you, be easy to find. If you must go to the customer, just make sure you can get there from here.

And carefully assess what it will cost you to inform, educate, and motivate your customers to get from where they are to where you are. When you view that cost as part of the rent, you may find it beneficial to pay a little more to the landlord and a little less to your media salesperson.

DON'T SELL ICE CUBES TO ESKIMOS

Before you legalize the lease, it's also time to come firmly to grips with the demographic realiites of the location that's about to be yours. To a great extent, in business, where you are is what you are. We've touched very briefly on the lunacy inherent in locating a maternity or infant's-wear shop in a retirement community. We've also alluded to the fact that it might not be terribly wise to establish an expensive women's apparel shop in the heart of a slum neighborhood.

While some boo-boos are pretty obvious, others are very subtle.

A case in point: A couple which I'll call Mary and Walter Madrid. The Madrids came up to me after a lecture I had given and asked if they might have a few minutes of my time. Mr. Madrid explained that they had a marketing problem with their business and wanted my advice. We headed for the hotel's coffee shop, and over steaming cups of coffee Walter Madrid outlined the situation.

Walter and Mary operated a corner bar and restaurant in a blue-collar residential area of the city. The neighborhood was predominately Hispanic, and their place, El Toro, specialized in authentic Mexican food.

Monday through Thursday, El Toro was a classic example of the "work-ingman's" bar; enough food was served to keep the kitchen profitable, while the bar poured a lot more Coors than Chívas Regal. By 11:00 P.M. on weeknights, the place was deserted.

On weekends, Walter booked in live Mariachi music and the place was jammed until 2:00 A.M.

"Sounds pretty good," I said. "Are you making money?"

Walter assured me that he and Mary were netting about $55,000 per year.

"So what's the problem?" I asked.

Walter and Mary, at times stepping on one another's words, explained that they wanted to learn how to change their clientele—by changing the image of El Toro—from the working-stiff, blue-collar bunch which they were currently attracting to the white-collar, upper-middle-class professional from the other side of town.

Rather than talking off the top of my head, I accepted Walter and Mary's kind invitation to visit their humble establishment for dinner the next evening. The situation was exactly as they had described: clean, attractive—but a long way from posh—with almost every seat at the bar and booth in the restaurant area filled. The crowd was predominately male, almost exclusively blue-collar workers (if clothing and similar externals can be trusted), and the food was fantastic.

After comfortably (no, now that I come to think of it—uncomfortably!) stuffing myself on beef tacos, fidello, and other assorted south-of-the-border delicacies, all washed down by ice cold beer (when in Rome!), I was joined by Walter and Mary and we continued our conversation. While we did explore some possible ways to attract a few more folks from the other side of town, my final advice to this very nice couple was to enjoy their good fortune. They were doing extremely well in a high-risk business. The influx of folks from a different socioeconomic group might very well cause more problems than benefits. And why mess with a good thing?

My final advice was to take their hard-earned profits, open a posh place on the other side of town if that was their hearts' desire, and let El Toro pay for such folly.

There was absolutely no need to change the market position of this going concern. There was also little chance that such an effort would really succeed. The biggest drawback was the reluctance—justified or not—for a potential customer to travel to an "alien" neighborhood to rub shoulders with the unknown "other half."

Walter and Mary seemed disappointed; in their case, apparently the desire to operate a "class" supper club–type operation was taking precedence over all else. Luckily, it was a temporary lapse of judgment. When I last heard, Walter and Mary were still making a much-better-than-average living serving some of the best food north of the border and pouring a heck of a lot of beer.

The moral of this story is pretty simple: Besides not selling ice cubes to eskimos, when you're selling the eskimos what they want to buy, don't muck around with the winning formula.

THE TRUTH ABOUT RENTAL AGENTS

Rental agents are there to do a job. The only problem is that many times their job is to do a job on you.

A rental agent has one mandate—to rent space at a profit. Second on their list of "must dos" is often to rent to a certain kind of business. This special firm must (1) be successful, (2) fit into the overall plan of the center, and (3) enhance the prestige and, thereby, the traffic flow of the center.

I say "center" because most rental agents represent one or more shopping centers.

Now the *numero uno* mandate to yourself is also to make a profit. But keep uppermost in your mind that you know a heck of a lot more about what you need and want than does your rental agent.

The ugly truth is that the agent is not in this to help you (the exception proves the rule!). He or she is in this to make money and keep a job. These motivating factors will very often lead an intrinsically honest individual to tell a few lies or, at the very least, omit a few truths.

If you're starting a brand-new business, chances are exceptionally good that a rental agent representing a really choice location will avoid at all costs renting to you and, if the location is significantly less-than-choice, will do everything in his or her power to entice you to sign on the dotted line.

Your best defense is (1) to have a dear and trusted friend or relation who happens to be a rental agent for a choice property or two and (2) to arm yourself with as much hard data as possible on what space you need and where you need it. If you can't have both, very definitely aim for the hard data.

THE SCIENTIFIC APPROACH

Before we explore how to do it right, let's take a look at how to do it wrong. This is how too many small business owners choose a location. And sometimes this negative approach will help you to remember how to do it right.

The wrong way to choose a location is simply to find an empty storefront reasonably close to your home and, based on the landlord's willingness to lease and the not-too-exorbitant price tag, sign a 5-year lease which makes it all yours. It happens all the time. And I guess somewhere, someone has done it that way and everything has worked out hunky-dory. I just haven't heard where such a miraculous occurrence has taken place. What's wrong with this approach? Let me count the ways. The new entrepreneur has not committed to paper any of the following:

1. A precise word picture of exactly what kind of business our budding tycoon is about to establish.

2. A composite picture of the "ideal" customer of such a firm and how many of these rare creatures reside within a reasonable geographic area surrounding the store.

3. How much money the store will have to gross annually to break even (and, one would hope, make a small profit).

4. How much merchandise will have to be turned and at what rate to generate this sales volume. In a nutshell, what I mean by this is simply that if you're planning a standard 50 percent markup on merchandise to be offered and you have determined that you'll need gross sales annually of $100,000 to break even, then you must determine at what rate similar types of stores turn their merchandise. In most retail establishments, it's four times per year. It would then follow that the minimum merchandise required to generate $100,000 in sales volume annually would be $12,500. This $12,500 at wholesale would translate into $25,000 retail, turned four times for a grand total of $100,000. (Keep in mind that this simplistic approach in no way addresses the need to "mark down" some merchandise, the fact of pilferage, and other such events.)

5. Our entrepreneur obviously has not determined number 4 so he or she could not possibly have determined how much space would be necessary at a bare minimum to accommodate this amount of merchandise. The logical deduction is that either too much or too little space will be leased. Either situation can be disastrous. The one may be unnecessarily costly; the other makes it physically impossible to carry enough merchandise to generate the necessary sales volume. The end result—disaster.

6. Since our dumb bunny hasn't done any of the above, it is equally obvious that he or she has not utilized traffic studies, census data, or even the educated "guesstimates" of a 2- or 3-year projection of income and expenses for the proposed business itself. This kind of peek into the future, referred to as a pro forma statement, might very well show that any location to be considered should include room for expansion in the near future. As has already been stated, moving is a costly and traumatic undertaking. It is often much more feasible to arrange for projected space needs at the time the initial lease is negotiated. As a matter of fact, you can sometimes pay for what you need now and write into your lease the option for additional space at a prearranged price tag.

7. Our resident "yo-yo" obviously has also neglected consideration of what size promotional budget will be needed to entice customers—assuming they are enticeable.

8. In all probability, our lessee has not bothered to check zoning requirements that might affect the business in question. This should very definitely include any sign ordinances that might inhibit or prohibit the size or placement of signs, banners, etc.

9. And who cares about parking or easy access, right? Likewise, this approach to locating the location precludes the need to check public transit

schedules. As a matter of fact, this approach assumes that customers will simply appear by magic at the appropriate time and in the required numbers.

10. Last, but certainly not least, our about-to-be-in-trouble entrepreneur would never dream of presenting the lease itself to the firm's lawyer and certified public accountant for their review, comment, and concurrence.

I could add several more failings to this list of atrocities, but these are the biggies. Now, how do you do it right? Obviously, by doing the exact opposite of how to do it wrong.

FANCY PHONES AND OTHER COSTLY MISTAKES

If you are getting the feeling that most of the people who say that they want to help you are really trying to help themselves to a chunk of whatever working capital you may possess, you're right. High on the list of these "helpful" folks is your friendly Ma Bell service representative. This charming man or woman (usually woman) is hired and trained to do just one thing: to sell you telephone equipment and service. Granted, there is a place where your needs and the telephone company's meet. You do need phone service. You do need a phone. You may even need a telephone system. But your aim should be to contract for the minimum you will need, and their aim is to sell you the maximum.

Some years ago, a business I was helping to establish was visited by a friendly telephone installer. He (they are still mainly men) made a sage— albeit not very scientific—comment. He said, "This place is gonna make it."

When I asked on what he based his positive assessment of the business's potential, he stated simply, "I've been installing business lines for 18 years. When I put in a lot of fancy equipment, the chances are very good I'll be back in a few months to take part—if not all—of it out. This place is installing what they need—no more, no less. That, to me, is a very good sign."

This wise fellow had a good point. And it's one you should keep in mind. Exotic intercom and paging systems, things that go dingdong instead of ring, music piped into the hold line, the fanciest, most exotic-looking telephone receivers, they're all available. And each is touted to cost just "a few pennies a month" that can conveniently be added to your bill. The choice is simple: You can have basic, adequate business telephone service for, say, $40 to $80 monthly, or you can have all sorts of gadgets and playthings that can run the same service as high as $500 to $600 monthly.

Carefully assess your phone needs. If you truly find that a specific device will be cost-efficient, by all means order it. If you can do without, do so.

Your friendly phone installer can always be called back to add to your system. And overkill can kill you.

Add $200 to $400 monthly to your phone bill, and you might very well be using up your first year's profit—or even worse, condemning your new enterprise to lose money for longer than might be necessary.

There are other potential danger areas of which you should be aware. These include printing. It's downright appalling how many new firms will spend three, four, maybe five times what they need to spend on letterheads, calling cards, and even paper bags.

Studies indicate that people have a negative response to printed material that is obviously of extremely low quality. They likewise have an adverse reaction to printed matter that they perceive as having cost a great deal to produce. Today's consumers are not dumb. They fully understand that the cost of every phase of doing business must be passed down to the customer. Cheap, shoddy printing gives your place of business a "shlock" reputation, sight unseen. By the same token, printed matter perceived as costly warns the consumer that the price will be higher than it might be elsewhere.

Decor, showcases, office furnishings, business equipment, these are all areas where too many new firms overspend. Probably the second-most over-equipped area of small business (next to the telephone system) is copying equipment. Xerox, IBM, Savin, and their colleagues have a lot more money than you do. And they're going to try to keep it that way. Again, the rule is to order what you need. No more, no less.

If you really want to impress people, run a successful (translation: prof-itable) business. Better yet, run two or three or four successful businesses. Impressive telephone systems, duplicating equipment, and the like can have a very depressing effect on your bank account, your balance sheet, and your state of mind.

WHAT ARE YOU REALLY RENTING
(LEASEHOLD IMPROVEMENTS
AND OTHER COSTS)

"I'm renting," you say, "my store (or office, or plant, or whatever). I'm renting a location in which to set up shop."

Maybe. And maybe you're not renting all that you think you are. Maybe what you're really renting are four walls, a floor, and a roof that doesn't leak—if you're lucky.

"What more is there?" you ask.

The answer is "plenty." Are the walls finished? Is the floor covered? Is the roof free of leaks? And if not, who gets the pleasure of paying to have it finished, covered, or repaired—you or the lessor (that's the guy or gal who owns the place)?

Add to that the really obvious stuff such as who pays the utilities. Who's responsible for insuring the place—in part or totally? If and when the place needs painting, who's to do it? If it's you, may you do it in the color that you choose or must your shop remain a vanilla-colored domain?

Some locations (and this includes shopping center sites) are let under what might be termed bare leases: The walls are bare, the floors are bare, the ceiling is unfinished, the darn place doesn't even have light fixtures. As a matter of fact, sometimes the storefront isn't even part of the deal. So you're only leasing three walls. And you're responsible for erecting the fourth, supposedly to "suit your individual needs." This "storefront" wall could cost thousands of unplanned bucks.

There may be a need for drapes or other window coverings, heating and air-conditioning equipment, or special plumbing to suit your business needs or code requirements. If so, you need to find out who will pay—you or "them."

In addition, you will most likely have to count on significant expense to furnish the place to fill whatever your individual business requirements might dictate. Make sure you clearly understand (and the lease clearly states) who will ultimately end up owning all this stuff. Many—if not most—leases state in not-always-clear terms that anything attached to floors, ceilings, or walls becomes the property of the lessor. And that means them—not you.

This means you can spend many thousands of dollars for shelves, fixtures, carpet and draperies, even equipment that must be bolted to the floor, that instantly become and remain the property of the landlord.

If you intend to do extensive remodeling to a building, explore the possibility of a reduction in rent with your landlord. It may not fly, but it's worth a try. At the very least, know fully and completely who's responsible for what and exactly what your monthly rent really covers.

It all boils down to this: It's a great location, but don't sign anything yet. When all your questions are answered, all your homework done, and all your plans and projections as complete as you can make them, your last step is to have the lease reviewed by your lawyer. When he or she says it's OK to sign, then and only then close the deal.

Legal Junk and Stuff

You have 3½ choices. You may elect to operate your business as a sole proprietorship—that's number 1; as a partnership, that's number 2; as a corporation, that's 3; or you can incorporate under subchapter S (IRC §§ 1371–1379), that's choice number 3½.

Everyone knows about the "world's oldest profession." That particular occupation is probably the purest (or should I say impurest?) form of sole proprietorship.

The sole proprietorship can be defined as a business which is owned and operated by one person. To establish a sole proprietorship, you need only obtain the licenses applicable to your type of firm and begin operations. Many new business owners select the sole proprietorship as their form to start with. Later, if the businesses succeed and the owners feel the need, they can form either partnerships or corporations.

The uniform partnership act, common to many states, defines a partnership as "an association of two or more persons to carry on as co-owners of a business for profit." Though the act does not mandate them, written articles of partnership are a good way to go. Such articles outline the contribution by each of the partners into the business, specify whether those contributions are monetary or managerial, and clearly outline the role each partner in the business relationship will play. Operating a partnership on a handshake closely resembles playing Russian roulette.

If you are considering the partnership as the form of business under which you will operate, do yourself a favor. Each of you get a lawyer and commit your business relationship to paper—a legal, binding document that will help keep you from coming to blows and/or grief in the future. And please don't tell me that your partner is your best friend; or your brother-in-law or cousin; or even your spouse, lover—or both. As a matter of fact, if this be the case,

73

it is all the more reason why you should have a written partnership agreement. You want to keep your relationship intact.

Typically, your articles of partnership should contain the following:

1. The name by which the business will be known, its purpose for existence, and where it will be physically located.

2. The duration of the partnership agreement.

3. The exact performance expected of each partner.

4. The character of each partner (general or limited, active or silent).

5. The specific contribution of each partner at the inception of the business and at a later date, should the contribution be anticipated to change.

6. How the partnership will handle business expenses.

7. The authority you will grant each individual partner in the conduct of the business.

8. How the partnership will separate debt.

9. The method of accounting to be used and what books and records are to be kept. It's also advisable to state which partner, if any, will be responsible for these accounting functions or if the business will employ an outside firm.

10. How profits and losses are to be divided among the partners.

11. Draws and/or salaries; expense accounts and any other "perks" that any or all partners might be entitled to.

12. Rights of continuing partner.

13. What will transpire upon the death of a partner (dissolution and winding up).

14. Employee management.

15. Release of debt.

16. The sale of partnership interests.

17. Arbitration between partners should a disagreement or misunderstanding arise.

18. A method by which additions, alterations, or modifications of the partnership agreement may be made.

19. How disputes are to be settled.

20. Any required or prohibited acts.

21. How you will deal with the absence and/or disability of a partner.

While this list is by no means all-inclusive, thinking and talking through each of the above points and committing what you agree to to paper will go a long way toward avoiding disaster in the future. Your own particular partnership situation may very well suggest other areas to be clarified.

Please don't assume anything. As a matter of fact, remember that "to *assume* makes an *ass* out of *u* and *me*."

And assumptions will kill you if you don't watch out. Love has a way of turning to hate, friendships sour, relationships change, stuff happens. While it may seem cold-blooded and in some ways "not nice" to admit the need to settle this sort of stuff in such a formal manner, business must be business. And your partnership will have a much better chance of not only surviving but also thriving if you candidly and realistically outline exactly what each partner's responsibilities and authorities will be. While there are but two forms of partnership, formal or informal, there are many kinds of partners. And a partnership can consist of any or all of these various kinds.

- Ostensible partner: Is active and known as a partner.
- Active partner: May or may not be ostensible as well.
- Secret partner: Active but not known or held out publicly as a partner.
- Dormant partner: Inactive and not known or held out publicly as a partner.
- Silent partner: Inactive and may or may not be known publicly as a partner.
- Nominal partner (partner by estoppel): Not a true partner in any sense since not really a party to the partnership agreement. However, the nominal partner holds him- or herself out as a partner, or permits others to make such representation by the use of his or her name or otherwise. Therefore, the nominal partner is liable, as though a partner, to third persons who have given credit to the actual or supposed firm in reliance on the truth of such representation.
- Subpartner: One who, while not being a member of the partnership, contracts with one or more of the partners in reference to participation in the interest of such a partner or partners in the firm's business and profits.
- Limited or special partner: Assuming that the partnership is in compliance with the statutory formalities, the limited partner risks only his or her agreed-upon investment in the firm. The limited partner is generally not subject to the same extent to the firm's liability as is a general partner, so long as he or she does not participate in the management and control of the business nor in its ongoing conduct.

Some of this stuff sounds confusing and it is. And the best advice here is ask your lawyer.

You'll notice that a way back I suggested that each partner should get a lawyer. I meant just that. Each of you should ensure that your own personal interests are protected. And that cannot be accomplished by a single attorney. When you try that, it's akin to one lawyer representing both parties in a divorce proceeding. Somebody's very apt to get taken.

So for the very few bucks it will cost you, seek individual legal counsel. You might even use this as a means of testing a couple of different law firms to decide which will represent the business on an ongoing basis. So it could be money well-spent in a couple of areas.

The corporation is by far the most complex of the forms of business available to you. Of necessity, we'll deal here with generalities. For the specifics and intricacies—again, see your lawyer.

Chief Justice Marshall in a famous 1819 decision defined a corporation as "an artificial being, invisible, intangible, and existing only in contemplation of the law." In words you and I can relate to, a corporation is a distinct legal entity, separate and apart from the individual or individuals who own it. Unlike the sole proprietorship or partnership, a corporation survives the person or persons who started it, own it, operate it.

A corporation is usually formed by the authority of some state government. Corporations which do business in more than one state must comply with federal laws regarding interstate commerce and with the state laws (which may vary considerably) in each state in which the corporation operates.

The majority of small businesses, especially those whose trade is local in nature, will find it advisable to charter their corporation in the state in which the greatest portion of their business is conducted. Out-of-state, or "foreign," incorporation can often result in additional tax liabilities and fees in another jurisdiction. In addition, some state laws subject a foreign corporation to less-favorable treatment, especially in the area of attachment of corporate assets. On the other hand, there just might be benefits to be gained from incorporation in another state. Such factors as state taxes, restrictions on corporate powers, lines of business in which a company may engage, capital requirements, restrictions upon foreign corporations in your state, and so forth should all be taken into consideration in selecting the state of incorporation. Some states require that a foreign corporation obtain a certification to do business in their state. Without such certification the corporation, among other things, may be deprived of the right to sue in those states.

Obviously, these complexities should be explored with a competent attorney.

Generally speaking, small and medium-size businesses do obtain their charters from the state in which they are geographically located. The fee or organization tax charged for incorporation varies greatly from state to state.

If you turn this task over to an attorney (and you should!), incorporation is really a very simple procedure. First, subscriptions to capital stock are taken and a tentative organization created. Then, approval is obtained from the secretary of state in the state in which the corporation is to be formed. This approval is in the form of a charter for the corporation stating its power and limitations.

Most states used to require that the certificate of incorporation be prepared by three or more legally qualified persons; the trend today is to require only one incorporator. An incorporator may, but not necessarily must, be an individual who will ultimately own stock in the corporation.

Many states have a standard certificate of incorporation form which may be used by small businesses. The information usually required includes the corporate name of the company; the purpose for which the corporation is being formed; the length of time for which the corporation is being formed; the names and addresses of the incorporators; the location of the registered office of the corporation; the maximum amount and type of capital stock which the corporation seeks authorization to issue; the capital required at time of incorporation; the provision for preemptive rights, if any, to be granted to the stockholders and restrictions, if any, on the transfer of shares; provisions for regulations of the internal affairs of the corporation; the names and addresses of persons who will serve as directors until the first stockholders' meeting or until their successors are elected and qualify; and the right to amend, alter, or repeal any provision contained in this certificate of incorporation. This right is generally statutory, reserved to a majority or two-thirds vote of the stockholders. Still, it is customary to make it clear in the certificate.

If, like me, you enjoy understanding why the devil all this stuff is required, here are a few answers:

When you name your company, the law generally requires that the name chosen not be so similar to the name of any other corporation authorized to do business in your state as to lead to confusion and that the name chosen not be deceptive so as to mislead the public. What will usually happen is that you'll pick a name, your attorney will conduct a search, sometimes through a service company specializing in such things, and (assuming that there is no conflict) you've just passed through hurdle number 1. In some states, there is a procedure for reserving a name. You might also want to register your name or trademark if your business is to use one.

When you state the purpose for which your corporation is formed, some states permit very broad language, such as "the purpose of the corporation is to engage in any lawful act or activity for which corporations may be organized." Very informative, right? Most states more wisely require fairly specific language in setting forth the purposes of the corporation. Even where law doesn't mandate it, the better practice is to employ a "specific object" clause. This spells out in broad descriptive terms the projected business enterprise while at the same time taking care to allow for the possibility of territorial, market, or product expansion. In other words, the language here should be broad enough to allow for expansion, yet specific enough to paint a pretty clear picture of the projected enterprise.

This is advisable for several reasons. It will convey to financial institutions, potential investors, and interested others a clearer picture of the corporate enterprise and will help prevent problems in qualifying the corporation to do business in other states.

The length of time for which the corporation is being formed can vary from a period of years to perpetuity. You, your stockholders, your creditors, and other firms with which you will do business have a right to know for how long the corporation is intended to exist.

The need to state the names and addresses of the incorporators is pretty self-explanatory. Keep in mind that certain states demand that one or more of the incorporators be a legal resident of the state within which the corporation is being organized.

The location of the registered office of the corporation must be in the state of incorporation. If you decide to obtain your charter from another state, you will be required to have an office there. You may, however, appoint an agent to act for you. That agent is usually your attorney and is required only to represent the corporation, to maintain a duplicate list of stockholders, and to receive or reply to suits brought against the corporation in the state of incorporation.

In spelling out the amount and type of capital stock which the corporation seeks authorization to issue, you should set forth the proposed capital structure of the corporation, including the number and classification of shares and the rights, preferences, and limitations of each class of shares.

Some states require that a specified percentage of the par value of the capital stock be paid in cash and banked to the credit of the corporation before the certificate of incorporation is submitted to the designated state official for approval. Don't give yourself a migraine worrying about how much common and preferred stock is right for your corporate structure or what the par value of capital stock should or could be. Leave it to your lawyer.

If the designated state official determines that the name of your proposed corporation is satisfactory, that the certificate contains all the necessary information and has been properly filed, and that there is nothing in the deal that violates state law or public policy, the charter will be issued.

Next, the stockholders must meet to complete the incorporation process. This meeting is extremely important. It is almost always conducted by an attorney or someone familiar with corporate organizational procedure.

At this meeting, your corporate bylaws are adopted and a board of directors is elected. The board of directors in turn will elect the officers who will actually have charge of the operations of the corporation. These might well include a president, secretary, and treasurer. In small corporations, members of the board of directors frequently also serve as officers of the corporation.

The board of directors and legal counsel will develop bylaws for the corporation. The bylaws may repeat some of the provisions of the charter and state statutes but usually spell out in much greater detail such items as the following:

1. The location of the principal office and other offices of the corporation.

2. The time, place, and required notice of annual and special meetings of stockholders. The bylaws should also spell out the necessary quorum and voting privileges of stockholders.

3. The number of directors, their compensation (if any), their term of office, the method of electing them, and the method of creating or filling vacancies in the board of directors.

4. The time and place of the regular and special directors' meetings as well as the notice and quorum requirements for such meetings.

5. The method of selecting officers, their titles, duties, terms of office, and salaries (if any).

6. The issuance and form of stock certificates and transfers and their control in the company books.

7. Dividends: when and by whom they may be declared.

8. The fiscal year under which the corporation will operate, the corporate seal, who will have the authority to sign checks, and the procedure under which annual statements will be prepared.

9. Like all good bylaws, yours should include procedures for amending the bylaws.

Now let's look briefly at choice number 3½—subchapter S.

At the time of the first meeting of your board of directors—prior to the issuance of any shares—it's time to consider the possible benefits of adopting a plan under the section of the Internal Revenue Code (IRC § 1244) that grants ordinary rather than capital treatment to losses on certain "small business stock."

Among the requirements and qualifications as "section 1244 stock" are (1) that the stock must be common stock, (2) the stock must be issued by the corporation for money or other property pursuant to a written plan containing several limitations, and (3) the amount of contribution received for the stock in equity capital of the corporation must not exceed prescribed maximum dollar limits.

True subchapter S status (IRC §§ 1371–1379) permits a "small business corporation" to elect to have its income taxed to the shareholders as if the corporation were a partnership. One of the major benefitis of this subchapter S option is that it overcomes the double-tax feature of the present system of taxation of corporate income. It also permits the shareholders to have the benefit of offsetting business losses incurred by the corporation against the income of the shareholders.

To be able to elect and maintain subchapter S eligibility, your corporation can have no more than ten shareholders, there can be no nonresident, or "alien," shareholders, the corporation must have only one class of outstanding stock, all shareholders must consent to the election, and a specified portion of the corporation receipts must be derived from actual business activity rather than from passive investment. No limit is placed on the size of the corporation's income or assets.

There can be some real financial benefits to small business under subchapter S. Even if you decide it's not for you, I would suggest that you explore it with your attorney.

If you decide to operate as either a sole proprietorship or a partnership for the moment and at some time in the future elect to incorporate the firm, you will need to secure a new taxpayer identification number and unemployment insurance account. You should also find out in advance whether the licenses and leases under which you operate will be transferable to the new corporate entity which your business will become. Some may need to be reapplied for or renegotiated.

PITFALLS AND PLUSES

Any of the legal forms of business available to you comes complete with assets and liabilities. While the idiosyncrasies of your own particular situation should be carefully weighed, and while—most important—this is by no means an all-inclusive gathering of the pros and cons, let's take a look at each business form. I'll give you the good news first.

Sole proprietorship pluses: It's easy to form a sole proprietorship. There are less formality and far fewer legal restrictions involved in establishing this type of business entity. You'll need little or no governmental approval, and it's usually less expensive than a partnership or corporation.

You, and you alone, own the profits. You will not be required to share profits with anyone. This, of course, presumes that there will be profits.

With the possible exception of your spouse, there are no co-owners or partners to consult when making decisions. You maintain complete control.

A sole proprietorship also affords you great flexibility. Constrained only by applicable law and good sense, you'll be able to respond very quickly to business needs as they arise. The sole proprietorship also enjoys relative freedom from government control and special taxation.

Now for the bad news. At the top of the list is unlimited liability. The sole proprietor is responsible for the full amount of business debts, which may very well exceed the owner's total investment. This liability involves all your assets, such as your home and car, furnishings, jewelry and artwork, even your pet poodle. If a customer slips on a banana peel in front of your store or your delivery truck creams somebody's car, the sole proprietor is liable as an individual. By the same token, if you or your spouse is sued, the assets of the business can—and probably will—be involved. In short, your business and personal life become one big bowl of mush.

And speaking of business life, it's pretty unstable. All you have to be is disabled or dead, and the business suffers the same fate.

There is usually less available capital to operate a sole proprietorship since your own personal assets are all the business has to call upon. Along these same lines, the sole proprietor faces relatively more difficulty in obtaining long-term financing.

It may not be a fatal flaw, but also keep in mind that a sole proprietorship will always be relatively limited in viewpoint and experience. Your knowledge, expertise, talents, and skills are all the firm really has to call upon. While you may certainly hire employees, the entire burden is really on you.

Some entrepreneurs welcome that solitude. One thing's for sure: A sole proprietorship is really your business—sometimes to a fault.

One thing you might keep in mind: Many small businesses are begun as sole proprietorships. Later, as the business prospers and the owner feels the need, a partnership or corporation is formed. If this should happen to be your case, be sure to discuss the tax consequences of switching from a sole proprietorship to a corporation with your accountant and your lawyer before proceeding. Neglecting to do so could cost you pretty dearly come next April 15, even if no actual money changes hands during such a legal maneuver.

Now, what's good about a partnership? Well, you'll enjoy the same ease of formation offered by a sole proprietorship. Because there are two or more of you sharing the profits, it's reasonable to assume (asinine though assumptions are!) that there will be two or more of you to split the work.

By the same token, it is also assumable that you'll have more capital and more credit since there are more than one of you to ante up. If two heads are truly better than one, a partnership might well expand the skills, talents, and abilities upon which the firm can draw.

Like the sole proprietorship, the partnership enjoys relative freedom from government control and special taxation.

Partnership pitfalls have to be headed by the issue of unlimited liability. As with the sole proprietorship, the personal and professional become one in a partnership. In addition, don't forget that the actions of one partner are binding on all. That simply means that if you have a screwball partner who goes on a binge and charges stuff all over the country, the other partners and the business might very well be held responsible. Along these same gruesome lines, if your partner plays very bad poker, in one evening he or she could lose the business you've spent years building. Regarding the issue of unlimited liability for both the sole proprietorship and the partnership forms of business, your insurance agent can be of great help in minimizing the obvious risks involved.

A partnership has a most unstable life. Elimination of any partner constitutes the automatic dissolution of the partnership. If you live in a community-property state, the whole deal would be blown sky-high by the death of the spouse of one of the partners or the divorce of any of the partners. Your attorney might possibly be able to include a clause in the partnership agreement covering the right of survivorship and the creation of a new partnership. You should very definitely consider partnership insurance which can provide the bucks necessary to pay off a surviving or departing spouse and, possibly, give the poor foundering business a financial shot in the arm to weather the storm.

The partnership will also likely encounter some difficulty in obtaining large amounts of capital. This will be particularly true in the case of long-term financing. As partners, you will probably be better off than a sole proprietorship, however, since your joint assets are likely to be greater than those of a single individual.

There is considerably less freedom involved in decision making in a partnership. This can really get sticky if you've got an "odd couple" situation where, say, one partner is a real gambler and wants to expand and the other is a fiscal conservative who is scared witless of both risk and debt.

There's also the very difficult situation you face in disposing of partnership interests. The buying out of a partnership can be difficult, to say the least, unless you specifically arrange for such an eventuality in your written partnership agreement. You don't know how horrible it is until you've tried to run a business with a partner or partners you can no longer tolerate. If you can't agree on how to best operate the business, it's very unreasonable to assume that you'll be able to agree on who will buy out whom and for how much. Face it up front when, presumably, things are still friendly.

Probably the two key issues to be considered in both the sole proprietorship and the partnership forms of business are those of liability and taxation. Either form, as has already been stated, can be converted to a corporate status if and when the time is right.

Operating as a corporation can be pretty advantageous. High on the "good stuff" list is the limit-of-liability issue. If you are a stockholder in a corporate structure, your liability—the amount of money you have to lose—is limited to a fixed amount, usually the amount of your investment. While this certainly does not erase the need for adequate liability insurance, it does help one sleep better at night to know that the personal and professional are distinctly and forever separate.

Because a corporation is a separate legal entity, what's yours is yours, what's the corporation's is the corporation's. This extends far beyond the issue of liability. It provides relative permanence of existence. For example, if a stockholder or officer in the corporation dies, the corporation doesn't. It continues to exist and do business. That's not to say that the loss won't be felt. It is to say that the corporation does not cease to exist as does a sole proprietorship or partnership in a similar circumstance.

This relative stability also comes in handy when you seek to obtain capital. Lending institutions seem to feel a little more secure when dealing with a corporation. They will, however, often require that the personal assets of stockholders and principals be pledged as collateral until or unless the corporation has adequate assets of its own to cover the loan.

This is commonly referred to as "stepping outside the corporate shield." In this situation, you would be personally liable for the debt in question, but the liability would be limited to just that individual situation.

In a corporation, ownership is readily transferable. This is also helpful in raising additional capital. All you have to do is issue stock or bonds and find some idiot gullible enough to purchase them.

The corporation has the ability to draw on the skills and expertise of more than one individual. Every silver lining must have a cloud. Here are but a few of the corporate pitfalls awaiting you:

The corporation's activities will be limited by its charter and by numerous and various laws. Some states do allow very broad charters, but the corporation certainly will not enjoy the wheeler-dealer freedom of, say, the sole proprietorship.

Then there's the potential for manipulation. Minority stockholders are sometimes badly exploited. You might even find yourself voted right out the door one day.

And then there's Uncle Sam. Extensive government regulations and often burdensome local, state, and federal reports are mandated for corporations. There are numerous and sometimes excessive taxes to be paid. Also, there's the sometimes-considerable expense involved in forming the corporation in the first place.

However, incorporating does not have to be a terribly costly process. And attorneys have been known to take stock in lieu of cash for some—if not all—of the fees involved. It's worth a try, if you're interested.

Subchapter S can provide you with considerable tax relief if it's a viable alternative in your case.

Compare the pluses with the pitfalls, carefully assess your own situation, and discuss in detail the options and alternatives with both your accountant and lawyer. You could look at it this way: There's no perfect choice, so it's hard to make a really wrong decision.

CONSIDER THESE, PLEASE:
MATES, FAMILY PARTNERS, DEATH,
DIVORCE, AND TAXES

If you're married and you operate a business, you have a partner automatically. In a community property state, this is a legal reality. In the rest of the world, it's simply a reality.

It makes pretty fair sense, therefore, to take steps to ensure that the partnership will be a positive rather than a negative.

Also keep in mind that if you have a partner in your business and each of you has a mate, you really have four partners involved in the deal. Now the cheese becomes a bit more binding. I would suggest that you look over your partner's mate as carefully as you look over your partner. Things could get very unpleasant if you pool your life's savings and a lot of sweat and blood with a partner or two, only to discover that you absolutely detest one or more of the spouses involved in the arrangement. Especially in a community property state, the marriage partners of your business partners are your partners. The whole thing gets very incestuous and can get very uncomfortable.

It might help somewhat to have a clear-cut understanding of how spouses fit in or out of the business picture. Do be advised, however, you can't really do a lot to keep an irate, meddlesome, or downright unpleasant spouse totally out of the picture.

And if either death or divorce rears its unpleasant head, you've really got problems.

If, for instance, the spouse of your partner dies and has left a big chunk of his or her estate to someone other than your partner, your partner may find it essential to liquidate holdings in your business to satisfy the demands of the estate. Likewise, estate taxes could put an incredible crimp in everybody's style. If it's the partner who kicks the bucket, the partnership is, of course, terminated too. To make that very bad situation, potentially, even worse, you may find it necessary to liquidate the entire assets of the firm at a significant loss to satisfy the surviving spouse's interests. That's a not uncommon occurrence, as a matter of fact. Most small businesses don't have the liquid assets usually requried to satisfy the demands of a partner's estate and still reorganize the firm to avoid extinction for the business as well.

Right of survivorship clauses in partnership agreements and adequate insurance to provide the cash necessary to settle such matters are your best hope. Take a good strong look at your mate, your partner's mate, and the unpleasant but extremely possible possibility of divorce. Obviously, it is also highly recommended that you take a thorough look at how the unpleasant but unavoidable prospect of death will affect your business. And for heaven's sake—and yours—seek legal advice, accounting advice, and insurance advice to minimize the potentially drastic impact any or all of these forces can and probably will have on your firm.

With regard to family partners, my off-the-cuff suggestion is don't. The same is equally true of forming business relationships with bosom buddies. They work once in a while simply to prove that exceptions to the rule do exist.

To be absolutely honest, I do know of a number of family relationships that have survived business relationships. I can say the same for friendships that have survived business partnerships. They do exist. And yours might be one of them. But if it's not, keep in mind that you'll stand to lose a lot more than money if the deal sours.

It is especially important, if you persist and insist on doing business with family or friends as your business partners, that you explore all the grim possibilities in advance. Somehow, most folks seem to think it's less than familial to clarify rights, responsibilities, and remuneration when entering a business relationship with a member of the family or a close friend. I've already said I don't encourage such liaisons. Suffice it to say, if you can't discuss unpleasantness in the abstract, you certainly shouldn't go into business together.

I've a lot more to say about taxes in Chapter 7. Here, let me make just two points: First, pay them. Before they're due if possible, but certainly on time at the very least.

Secondly, don't pay more of them than you have to. Since this should be your patriotic goal in business life, enlist the full support of your accountant and your lawyer to that end.

The form of business under which you operate will have a significant influence on the amount of taxes which you pay. If your gross profits are less than $25,000 annually, you're probably just as well-off operating as a sole proprietorship or partnership. Since you are taxed as an individual under these two forms of business, unless you have significant other income sources, odds are in favor of the status quo.

A partnership files a separate information return from which the taxable amounts are reported by each partner on his or her individual return. All your income is taxed at individual rates which, as you very well know, vary with the amount of income and deductions.

A corporation, on the other hand, pays taxes based on *its* net income—not *your* net income. Dividends paid to the corporation's shareholders out of such earnings are taxed again to its shareholders when received. Here's the double taxation I referred to a while back. The feds sock it to corporate structures pretty heavily: You're taxed at approximately 20 percent of the first $25,000 of taxable income and approximately 48 percent on the remainder. This can, however, be a lighter bite than a sole proprietorship where the proprietor has an inordinately high annual income for an individual.

Again, subchapter S may very well be the way to go. One thing's for sure, better the bucks stay in your pocket than in Uncle Sam's.

GET IT IN WRITING

I come from a very large family. In this whole huge tribe, there was one grandparent whose handshake was good as gold. The rest are charming, delightful, lovely people who can be trusted in infinitely varying degrees dependent on the importance of the matter or situation at hand.

Mine is a very normal (translation: average) family. Yours is very likely the same.

I mention this to stress the importance of written contractual relationships in business. Cut the illusion about "needing nothing but a handshake" to conduct business. I've also heard that there's a bridge for sale somewhere along the Hudson River. I'm not interested in either fable.

If it's important, that is, if it involves money—or potentially involves money—it simply makes sense to commit the details to paper.

Spelling out who is to do what, where it is to be done, by when it is to be completed, and how much—if anything—you will be paid and under what conditions is simple, clean, sensible, and essential. Whether your agreement is financial or nonfinancial, reach a consensus on all the terms, fix them firmly on the requisite pieces of paper, and get the involved and interested parties to sign and a couple of trustworthy folks to witness the deal.

Instead of being appalled at the idea of this cold, calculating, "businesslike" approach to everything, train yourself to think of your signature as the handshake of those long-lost "good old days." Get it in writing, or forget it.

6

KISS Record Keeping
(Keep It Simple, Stupid)

There's an old adage that says, "If you don't know where you're going, you'll probably end up somewhere else." The small business owner could expand that to state, "If you don't know where you've been and where you're going, you'll probably end up broke."

The books and records you keep for your business tell you where you've been. Using this information will help you make decisions on how to get where you want to go. Unless you are terminally 'round the bend, I will assume that where you want to go is not broke. Therefore, I will presume that you at least superficially concur that accurate record keeping is vital to your business.

Adequate records are necessary to prepare various tax returns. They are required by financial institutions and suppliers you may deal with on a credit basis. Your books will assist you in making good, sound business decisions if you're smart enough to make use of them.

Above all, a good record-keeping system must be simple to use. If it is not, chances are that it will either (1) not be used or (2) be used incorrectly. The system should also be easy to understand, reliable, accurate, consient, and designed to provide useful information on a timely basis.

Small business owners tend to cluster at either end of the bookkeeping scale. At one end of the scale they keep scraps of paper in a shoe box and write business and personal checks out of the same single bank account. At the other end they have complicated bookkeeping systems that generate reams of data and files full of reports that the owner hasn't time to digest even if there were a need for such detailed information. Of course, because of the complexity of the system, the whole thing takes much too much time and money to keep up with.

Designing the ideal bookkeeping system for your business involves a number of conditions and decisions. High on the list is your need to understand the minimum information that must be maintained for tax and other legal purposes. It is also most helpful if you have a more-than-general idea of the kind of information you would like your system to generate for you and at what frequency you wish this information presented. Once again, that dynamic duo—your attorney and your accountant—can help you establish what is mandatory and what will likely prove helpful.

RECOGNIZE YOUR LIMITATIONS

Your ability, the time you have available, your natural inclination, they all have a very real bearing on how much of the actual record-keeping chore—if any—should be your own personal responsibility.

Your abilities in the record-keeping area can range from being absolutely incapable of performing even the most elementary problems of addition and subtraction to being a certified public accountant in your own right. People in the latter category can skip this chapter entirely; those in the former probably can't read anyway. Most of us fall somewhere in between. You can and should learn at least the fundamentals of bookkeeping if you intend to operate a profitable small business.

Turning to inclination, we have an entirely different situation indeed. If you are a person who absolutely detests working with figures, it is highly unlikely that you will do justice to the necessary task at hand. Get someone else to do it. It's that simple. You should, however, understand and oversee the record-keeping process for your firm. Remember, it's *your* neck in the noose and *you* are the person responsible for making the right decisions for your business.

Probably the most difficult question of all for most small business owners is whether their time should be spent on record-keeping chores or would be more cost-efficient spent doing other things. Whether you're Superman or Wonder Woman, you still have just 24 hours in each day. The functions and tasks associated with accurate and adequate record keeping can be done by someone other than you. It very well may be that what you can do to generate income for your firm can only be done (at least presently) by you. It would then follow that your business would be better-served by your generating income and using a small portion of that income to pay someone else to keep the books.

If you really don't have time to handle your firm's record keeping personally, you'll soon be hopelessly behind in the process. When customers are waiting, phones are ringing, decisions need making, somehow, reconciling last month's bank statement or entering yesterday's sales into the appropriate journal just doesn't seem to take priority.

Your record-keeping system should permit you to know the current status of your business as well as what happened last month or last year. Inadequate records or not keeping records up to date will deny you—the boss and decision maker—access to facts that could be critical to your firm's future.

WHO'LL KEEP WHAT

We've already explored in some depth how a certified public accountant can help you keep your business on a sound basis. Among these services are setting up record-keeping procedures, interpreting your firm's records, and providing financial advice based on that interpretation. There are, however, other groups of individuals who can provide a similar service.

Heading such a list is a public accountant. This is an individual or group of individuals within a firm who offer pretty much the same services as those of a certified public accounting firm with the notable exception of the lack of certification. This may or may not be a problem. Keep in mind that the certification process does carry a rather substantial measure of assurance that the individual you'll be dealing with is competent to offer such a service. While certification is somewhat of a safeguard, don't exclude entirely the group of persons practicing public accountancy without it.

Many, if not most, of these individuals are entirely capable of setting up adequate record-keeping procedures, physically keeping your books and records, preparing and filing tax returns, generating informational reports, and performing the multitude of other functions that record keeping involves. A growing number of states are even licensing these non-CPA-type accountants to further ensure that you'll receive good services from them.

In addition, there are bookkeeping services that range from woefully inadequate to excellent. Some of these services are huge nationwide businesses. Others are a single individual moonlighting from a regular job as someone else's bookkeeper to make enough to keep the wolf from the door.

In the final analysis there are only five possible answers to the question "Who will keep the books"?

1. The CPA (or public accountant) who has set up the books may keep them. This option will probably provide the greatest accuracy. But you must weigh the cost because this professional must charge for time, operating expenses, and profits. Weigh all this against the fact that such professional advice can frequently increase your profits more than enough to cover the expense involved.

2. If you have the time and/or inclination, you can keep the whole mess yourself.

3. You may be lucky enough to locate a spouse or family member ready, willing, and able to take on this rather massive chore.

4. You can hire someone to work either full- or part-time as a staff book-keeper.

5. Last (but not least) is the freelance bookkeeping firm which—like the CPA—works for a number of different businesses.

In some places, a sixth option may be available to you: Many large, full-service banks are offering computerized bookkeeping services to their business customers. This can range from a full-charge system to handling one specific aspect of your business's financial life, such as payroll.

No matter whom you ultimately choose to be responsible for the day-to-day record-keeping responsibilities, first you've got to have a system. Information of all sorts flows into your business daily. As customers are served, data is generated about sales, cash, equipment, purchase expenses, payroll, accounts payable, and, if you grant credit to any or all of your customers, accounts receivable.

You must capture these facts and figures and turn this seemingly disjointed and unrelated batch of numbers into usable information. That's what record keeping is all about and what a good record-keeping system should do for you and your firm. Such a system usually consists of records which may be set up in ledgers, journals, or other depositories. For some small business owners, the development of small and relatively inexpensive computer systems has revolutionized record keeping.

Whether captured by quill or the latest electronic marvel dreamed up at IBM, the bookkeeping system adapted to your particular needs will contain the following basic records:

Cash Receipts: Used to record the cash which the business receives

Cash Disbursements: Used to record the firm's expenditures

Sales: Used to record and summarize daily, monthly, quarterly, or annual income

Purchases: Used to record the purchases of merchandise bought for processing or resale

Payroll: Used to record the wages of employees and their deductions, such as those for income and social security taxes

Equipment: Used to record the firm's capital assets such as equipment, office furniture, and motor vehicles

Inventory: Used to record the firm's investment in stock (such as goods for resale, raw material for processing) and is needed to arrive at a true profit on financial statements, and for income tax purposes

Accounts Receivable: Used to record the balances which customers owe to your firm

Accounts Payable: Used to record what your firm owes its creditors and suppliers

If your shop will be using a cash register, a combined sales and cash receipts record may be kept. You'll divide sales into a few categories, possibly three or four, such as wholesale, resale, and services. Or your particular business might be better served by dividing sales according to the type of merchandise being rung up. Your cash receipts will represent all cash sales and collections of accounts receivable. One bookkeeping entry is made for each day, reflecting the total cash receipts.

If your firm doesn't have a cash register, sales personnel can enter each item in the sales and cash receipts register showing the date, name, invoice number, and amount.

The day's receipts should be deposited in the bank every evening—using the night depository if necessary. Deposit the exact amount received. *Never* pay out small amounts from the day's receipts for expenses incurred in the operation of the business. Instead, use a petty cash fund. By depositing the exact amount of all receipts, your bank statement enables you to balance your cash receipts book very easily.

Just as you should deposit all receipts into your business account, all disbursements (payments) should be made by check. It should go without saying, but I'll say it again anyway: You must operate your business out of a business account and your personal expenses out of your own personal checking account. Under no circumstances ever allow your business and personal check-writing to overlap.

Whoever will be writing checks should enter in the checkbook the date, name, check number, amount, and a brief explanation of what the check covers.

As soon as bank statements are received, balance them against your checkbook. Usually a simple-to-use form is provided along with the statement from the bank to assist you in this chore. While the actual form this reconciliation sheet takes may vary from bank to bank, their substance is as follows:

Bank balance	$ _____
Add deposits not recorded by the bank	$ _____
Less outstanding checks	$ _____
Balance as per books	$ _____

One last but certainly important bit of advice regarding your bankbook: If checks are to be written by anyone other than yourself, it is strongly recommended that that person be bonded. If time permits, it is also recommended that you sign all checks. If this is too cumbersome, work with your accountant and your banker to find a solution. Many small firms designate a bonded employee as signatory on all checks up to a certain dollar amount with two signatures (of the bonded employee and the business owner) being required for checks over that designated dollar amount to be considered valid by the bank. If you absolutely cannot or will not involve yourself in this check-signing function, you may find it advisable to designate two or more bonded employees of your firm as signatories on your business checking account with the signature of several of these folks necessary to validate any outgoing check, the idea being that there's safety in numbers. There are, of course, other solutions. Again, your accountant and/or banker can help you deal with this dilemma.

I mentioned earlier the advisability of establishing a petty cash fund. Petty cash should be used for payment of small amounts not covered by invoices. A business check should be drawn for, say, $25. The check is cashed and the money placed in an appropriate cashbox or drawer. When small amounts are paid out for such items as overdue postage, freight charges, or the purchase of some light bulbs, the items are listed on a petty cash form or even on a blank sheet of paper. Some firms find it helpful to utilize a manilla envelope and place receipts for each item listed inside. When the $25 cash amount is nearly exhausted, all listed items are summarized and another check is drawn to cover the exact amount that has been expended from the fund. This second check is cashed and the fund replenished up to the original $25 amount. At all times the cash on hand in the drawer or lockbox plus the listed expenditures will equal the original amount of the petty cash fund. If it doesn't, it's time to start kicking some bottoms. Probably out the employees' entrance.

A couple of more record-keeping chores that you will want to ensure are not overlooked are (1) a list of all permanent equipment used in your business and (2) adequate insurance records. Your equipment list should keep track of all items with a useful life of 1 year or longer and having some appreciable value. Your list should include the date the item was purchased, the name of the supplier, a brief description of the item, the number of the check with which it was paid for, and the cost. If your shop owns quite a number of items, there should be separate listings for automotive equipment, tools and manufacturing equipment, and furniture and fixtures. These lists are the basis from which your accountant calculates depreciation and provides supporting data for fixed-asset accounts. Even if you don't know what in blazes I'm talking about, make the list.

Insurance records should make sense even to a record-keeping neophyte.

This list should include each policy and show the type of insurance, the coverage, name of insurer, effective dates including expiration date, and annual premiums. Have your insurance adviser and your attorney look over your list regularly—I would suggest a minimum of every 12 months—to ensure that your coverage is adequate.

If you run a fairly small, fairly uncomplicated business, you may be able to operate comfortably with simple cash basis books. Anything larger or more complex than a hot dog stand will probably require the use of accrual basis records. The choice between cash basis and accrual basis might well depend on whether your firm grants credit to its customers and on the amount of inventory required to operate.

Accrual basis is a method of recording income and expenses in which each item is reported as it's earned or incurred, without regard as to when actual payments are made or received. Charge sales are credited at once to sales and charged to accounts receivable. When the bills are finally collected, the credit is to accounts receivable.

Accruals will also be made for expense items payable in the future such as annual or semiannual interest on loans. Your accountant—or you—will make a charge to expenses to cover depreciation of fixed assets other than land. Corresponding credits are made to reserves for depreciation.

Items normally in use for 1 year or longer such as buildings, automotive equipment, tools, equipment, and furniture and fixtures are considered fixed assets. Most small businesses usually charge depreciation at the end of their fiscal (business) year, but if your firm has substantial fixed assets, you'll probably calculate depreciation monthly. Most small businesses will use straight-line depreciation based on the expected life of the items for book purposes. If, for instance, a building has an estimated life span of 20 years, that represents 5 percent depreciation each year. Automobiles that have a projected life of 4 or 5 years should be depreciated 20 or 25 percent each year. Figure 3 is a sample depreciation chart.

If you've decided to do it yourself, there are a number of copyrighted bookkeeping systems that can help you simplify the record-keeping process. Most of these systems cover the basic records necessary for both external reporting and internal information purposes and are bound in a single book complete with reasonably easy-to-follow instructions for their use. Most office supply stores have two or more of these systems available for purchase; your accountant or bookkeeping service will likely have one that they specifically prefer if they—or you—don't want to go to the expense of setting up a custom system for your firm. There are even more exotic but extremely easy to use "one-write" systems that write checks, make journal entries, do everything but turn out the lights with a single written impression.

The following is a partial listing of some of the most widely available bookkeeping systems. If your local office supply outlet does not have a

Depreciation of Buildings and Equipment (1980)

Item	Date purchased	Cost ($)	Estimated life (yr.)	Yearly depreciation (%)	Accumulated prior depreciation ($)	This year's depreciation ($)	Total accumulated depreciation ($)
Main office	Jan. 1977	$ 40,000	20	5	$ 6,000	$ 2,000	$ 8,000
Main factory	Jan. 1978	75,000	25	4	6,000	3,000	9,000
Calculator	Feb. 1978	1,200	10	10	230	120	350
Machinery	July 1978	40,000	20	5	3,000	2,000	5,000
TOTAL		$156,200			$15,230	$ 7,120	$22,350

Figure 3 Sample fixed asset depreciation chart. This sample chart suggests how you may depreciate various kinds of property owned by your business for tax purposes. Discuss establishing a depreciation schedule for your firm with your accountant.

particular system on hand, you may wish to contact the publisher at the address given with each entry.

- Blackburn's General Business Bookkeeping System. No. 19P and 33P Blackburn Systems, 366 Wacouta St., St. Paul, Minn. 55101. Provides for accounting inventory and personnel records in quick, easy entries. Lists merchandise payments, record of sales and receipts on one side of the book and operating expenses on the opposite page. Shows monthly record of sales; monthly balance sheets, showing cash on hand, amounts owed and due. Other sections include accounts payable, complete with discount columns; inventory sheets; employee Social Security and income tax records; sales record by departments; notes receivable and payable; depreciation schedule. Includes a list of suggested allowable tax deductions.

- Dome Simplified Monthly Bookkeeping Record, No. 612; Dome Simplified Weekly Bookkeeping Record, No. 600. Price $6.95. Dome Publishing Company, Ten New Way, Warwick, R.I., 02887. Available in stationery stores and chain stores. Contains the following forms sufficient for recording the results of 1 year's business: monthly record of income and expenses; annual summary sheet of income and expenditures; weekly payroll records covering fifteen employees; individual employee compensation records. Also contains general instructions, specimen filled-in monthly record of income and expenses, and list of 276 expenses which are "legal deductions" for federal income tax purposes. This record was designed by a CPA and fits every type and kind of business.

- General Business System. General Business Services, Inc., 51 Monroe Street, Rockville, Md. 20850. Locally authorized business counselors provide complete, easy-to-maintain, preprinted manual, one-write, or computerized record-keeping systems; custom-designed for sole proprietors, partnerships, and corporations, including a monthly profit and loss statement and proof of accuracy, meeting requirements of Internal Revenue Service. Service includes review and analysis of particular record-keeping requirements; furnishing a complete set of records; personal instructions on use and maintenance of records; analysis of records and financial statements with guidance throughout the year; preparation of federal and state income tax returns, both business and personal, with guarantee of accuracy by professional staff at national office; tax advisory service by tax specialists for research and answers to income tax questions; monthly tax bulletin with money-saving ideas; and supplementary services by local business counselors as required. Also offers on an optional basis accounts receivable, computerized monthly billings, collection system for delinquent accounts, and tax preparation service for employed individuals.

- Greenwood's Approved Business and Income Tax Record. The Greenwood

Company, 411 S. Sangamon St., Chicago, Ill. 60607. System No. 212. Permanently bound book, $15.00; looseleaf style, with 2½ times more sheets, $25.00. Contains the following forms: daily record of cash payments for month; monthly totals; yearly balance sheet; yearly profit and loss statements. Also includes filled-in specimen sheets. Individual and weekly payroll records are available. Write for samples.

- Ideal System: General Bookkeeping and Tax Record No. 3611. Dymo Visual Systems, Inc., P.O. Box 1568, Augusta, Ga. 30903. $11.95. Designed for any business operating primarily on a cash basis. Sufficient forms for recording the results of 1 year's business.

- Ideal System: Business Service Bookkeeping and Tax Record No. 3621. Dymo Visual Systems, Inc., P.O. Box 1568, Augusta, Ga. 30903. $11.95. Designed for every type of business primarily offering a service (as opposed to merchandise). Examples would be acting, advertising, clubs, associations, and fraternal organizations.

- Ideal System: Merchants Bookkeeping and Tax Record No. 3021. Dymo Visual Systems, Inc., P.O. Box 1568, Augusta, Ga. 30903. $11.95. Designed for any retailer or wholesaler, for anyone buying at one price and reselling at another.

- Ideal System: Weekly Bookkeeping and Tax Record No. M-2025. Dymo Visual Systems, Inc., P.O. Box 1568, Augusta, Ga. 30903. $11.95. For every business, profession, trade, farm, or ranch. Can be started anytime. Pages for sample entries plus fifty-two sheets for weekly entries.

- Ideal System: Payroll Record 1 to 25 Employees No. M-1812. $3.95. Payroll Record 1 to 50 Employees No. M-2812, $4.95. Dymo Visual Systems, Inc., P.O. Box 1568, Augusta, Ga. 30903. Both books provide one sheet for each employee. Column headings for both hourly wage and salaried employees, all taxes and other withholdings.

- Ideal System: Payroll Record No. 5812. Dymo Visual Systems, Inc., P.O. Box 1568, Augusta, Ga. 30903. $9.95. For use with any bookkeeping system. Sheets for fifty employees. Can be expanded with additional sheets.

- Ideal System: Double Entry Combined Journal No. 5831. Dymo Visual Systems, Inc., P.O. Box 1568, Augusta, Ga. 30903. $9.95. This simplified journal ledger, used in conjunction with general ledger, provides for distribution of sales, cash, purchases, disbursements, and journal entries.

- Ideal System: Double Entry General Ledger No. 5836. Dymo Visual Systems, Inc., P.O. Box 1568, Augusta, Ga. 30903. $9.95. Used in conjunction with combined journal, provides all necessary records for any business, trade, profession, farm, or ranch.

- Ideal System: Inventory Management System No. 5900. Dymo Visual Systems, Inc., P.O. Box 1568, Augusta, Ga. 30903. $9.95. Shows at a glance your inventory position by item, what to order and when, its value, prime and alternate suppliers.

- Kolor-Key. Moore Business Forms, Inc., P.O. Box 5252, Eastmont Station, Oakland, Calif. 94605. May be ordered through local Moore Business Forms representatives. System includes basic business forms (sales slip, invoice, statement, voucher check, purchase order, daily cash control, duplicate deposit slip); instructions for preparation and filing of forms; record-keeping aids. The system is adaptable to a wide range of businesses and can be easily modified as the business grows and needs for forms change.

- N.B.S. Systems, Inc., Attn: Marketing Department, P.O. Box 321, Edwardsville, Ill. 62025. Telephone: 618-692-0321. N.B.S. offers a complete line of one-write accounting systems for just about all types of businesses, large or small. They design special, custom pegboard accounting systems for small business, healing arts practitioners, contractors, and just about any special category of firm one could envision opening. In addition, N.B.S. designs special systems that interface beautifully with the mighty computer. When it comes to one-write systems, N.B.S. is one of the best. Their standard accounts receivable system with payables and accessory forms will produce daily and monthly reports, including accounts aging with analysis, cash flow forecasting, and much more valuable data that usually requires electronic data capability to generate. But it's all yours without a computer and with the single-entry convenience of a pegboard one-write system. All accounts payable, receivable, cash disbursement, and payroll combo systems come complete with easy-to-follow instruction books that pretty much take you step by step through the how-to-do-it process. N.B.S. also manufactures what they call the Porta-System, which covers disbursements and payroll. It's definitely worth looking into. This "biggie" in pegboard systems offers a three-hour continuing education course to certified public accountants in many states on their systems, a testimonial to the firm's expertise. Your accountant might want to look into attending, should you decide to go with an N.B.S. system. Check the yellow pages for N.B.S. Pegboard Systems, found under Business Forms and Systems. They're available through authorized dealers throughout the nation.

- Peg Rite Systems, Mastercraft Corporation, 831 Cobb Ave., Kalamazoo, Michigan, 49001. A classic, simple-to-use one-write pegboard system; it can be tailored to your individual record-keeping needs, so prices will vary widely.

- Practical Bookkeeping for the Small Business. Henry Regnery Company, 180 North Michigan Ave., Chicago, Ill. $5.95. Every aspect of business bookkeeping is presented and explained in detail; basic accounting reasoning and terms; the entire bookkeeping cycle, from the initial entry to closing the books; the correct uses of checking accounts and petty cash; making out payrolls, providing for deductions, and maintaining necessary payroll records; the IRS-approved cash basis and accrual basis bookkeeping methods; and how to figure state sales tax. Summary problems coordinate chapter information to facilitate complete understanding of this simple and accurate bookkeeping system.

• Safeguard Business Systems, Inc., Craig A. Ross, general market mgr., 470 Maryland Dr., Fort Washington, Pa. 19034. Offers a number of one-write systems designed to save time and assist the small business owner with record-keeping activities. Systems are installed and serviced by local representatives. Also available are computerized financial reports through the business owner's accountant. All services and products are detailed in the *Business Systems Reference Manual*, free on request.

• Wilmer Service Line, P.O. Box 1397, Dayton, Ohio, 45401. Another fine one-write pegboard system. Very comparable to the Safeguard System, with totally interchangeable forms and equipment which can be a real plus. Wilmer also manufactures a full line of regular journal supplies.

• Wilson-Jones, 6150 Touhy Ave., Chicago, Ill., 60648. This old-line firm manufactures columnar pads and is one of the world's largest suppliers of bookkeeping forms of all kinds. You'll find Wilson-Jones forms from double entry to 31 columns. The very popular G-7203, 3-column form pad runs $3.40 a pad. All Wilson-Jones columnar pads fit into special binders for ease of storage and handling. This is an extremely flexible batch of supplies and will probably be able to fill your (or your accountant's) needs at a very low price. Generally available at all stationers.

In addition to the above listed record-keeping systems which are designed for general use in any retail or service business, there are a number of book-

		Debit	Credit
Jan. 31, 1980	Interest expense	$58.33	
	Accured interest Payable		$58.33
	To record January share of interest due on First National Bank loan. Principal amount $10,000 @ 7% = $700.00 January share $58.33		

Figure 4   Sample journal entry. In accrual bookkeeping, the eleventh commandment is "for every debt there's a credit." This sample illustrates that commandment. When keeping your books, keep it in mind.

keeping systems designed for use in specific retail and service firms such as automobile dealers, barbershops, beauty salons, building contractors, appliance dealers, and bars and restaurants. Among the major purveyors of such specialized record-keeping systems are General Business Systems, Safeguard Business Systems, Inc., Ideal Systems, and Modern Merchant Simplified Bookkeeping.

If you're interested in a specific record-keeping system for your type of business and have been unable to locate one, I would suggest you contact your trade association. Several trade associations have, in fact, had such systems designed specifically for their membership.

In addition to basic records, you will need a book for journal entries. A journal entry is used to record the various business transactions which do not involve cash, such as accruals for depreciation, expenses due at some later date, and so on. Figure 4 on p. 98 is a typical journal entry.

Your firm also needs to keep a general ledger to record balances of assets, liabilities, and capital and to accumulate sales and expense items. A sample classification of accounts, all of which are recorded in the general ledger, is found in Figure 5.

At the end of each fiscal year, accounts are balanced and closed. Sales (income) and expense account balances are then transferred to the profit and loss account. The remaining asset, liability, and capital accounts will give your accountant the figures for your balance sheet.

Don't use too many accounts. You needn't make things more complex than they have to be. You should break down sales into enough categories to show a clear picture of your business. Use different expense accounts to cover frequent or substantial expenditures but avoid the microscopic distinctions that will confuse rather than clarify the issue. Use the miscellaneous expense account for small, unrelated expense items—but don't use it so often that it becomes a mushy, catchall category.

In addition to all the above, you or your bookkeeper will need to keep adequate and accurate control of accounts receivable and payroll records. For a more complete discussion of accounts receivable, refer to Chapter 8—Make the Devil Give You Your Due. Further information on payroll records can be found in Chapter 7—"Render Unto Caesar..."

GOOD RECORDS MEANS GOOD BUSINESS

By now, you're beginning to see that accounting records are involved with every activity of your business. Every time you buy, sell, order, trade, pay a bill, produce an item, provide a service, or collect a fee, some business record must be created.

You'll use these accounting records to gain information for such things as social security, wages and hours of employment, workman's compensation,

Assets (debit)

100-Cash in banks
101-Petty cash fund
102-Accounts receivable

105-Materials and supplies

107-Prepaid expenses
108-Deposits

120-Land
121-Buildings
122-Reserve for depreciation—
  buildings (credit)

123-Tools and equipment
124-Reserve for depreciation—
  tools and equipment (credit)
125-Automotive equipment
126-Reserve for depreciation—
  automotive equipment (credit)
127-Furniture and fixtures
128-Reserve for depreciation—
  furniture and fixtures (credit)

130-Organization expenses (to be amortized)

Liabilities (credit)

200-Accounts payable
201-Notes payable

205-Sales taxes-payable
206-FICA taxes-payable
207-Federal withholding taxes
208-State withholding taxes

209-Unemployment taxes

220-Long-term debt—mortgages payable
221-Long-term debt—SBA loan

225-Miscellaneous accruals

Capital accounts (credit)

300-Common capital stock
301-Preferred capital stock   for corporations

            or

300-Proprietorship account
301-Proprietor's withdrawals   for proprietorship

305-Retained earnings

Sales accounts (credit)

400-Retail sales
401-Wholesale sales
402-Sales—services

405-Miscellaneous income

Expenses (debit)

500-Salaries and wages
501-Contract labor
502-Payroll taxes
503-Utilities
504-Telephone
505-Rent

509-Insurance
510-Interest
511-Depreciation
512-Travel expense
513-Entertainment
514-Advertising

506-Office supplies	515-Dues and contributions
507-Postage	520-Miscellaneous expenses
508-Maintenance expense	

Figure 5   Sample classification of accounts. You and your accountant may wish to devise your own accounts classification system. This one is certainly adequate for most small business needs and illustrates the various categories and account numbers you'll need to establish to keep books that make sense.

income taxes, sales taxes, etc. Equally important to you is their use as a valuable tool for determining how your business is doing and how you can improve it.

When a friend asks how your business is doing, you can merely answer either good, fair, better, or worse and satisfy his or her curiosity. But when the Internal Revenue Service wants to collect taxes or when you're asking your banker to make a loan, you must be able to show them exactly how your business is doing and how you expect your business to do in the future. The only possible way you can get these answers is from good accounting records.

Since statistics show that more than 70 percent of all new small businesses will fail, keep in mind that adequate business records help increase the chance of survival and reduce the probability of failure. Likewise, for the business that has survived its first 2 or 3 fledgling years, it has been clearly demonstrated that good records increase the chances of staying in business and of earning increased profits.

Let's explore how good record keeping will decrease the chances of failure and increase your likelihood of staying in business and of earning a reasonable profit. We'll do this by listing the questions your records can and should be able to answer for you.

- How much business (cash and credit) am I doing? How much do I have tied up in receivables?

- How are my collections? What are my losses from credit sales? Who owes me money? Who is delinquent and to what extent? Should I continue to extend credit to delinquent accounts? How soon can I expect to be paid by my accounts receivable?

- How much cash do I have on hand and in the bank? Does this amount agree with what records tell me I should have, or is there a shortage? How much is my investment in merchandise? How often do I turn over my inventory? Have I allowed my inventory to become obsolete?

- How much merchandise did I take out of my store for personal family use and how did it affect my gross profit calculation? How much do I owe my suppliers and other creditors? Have I received all my outstanding credits for returned merchandise?

- How much gross profit (margin) did I earn? What were my expenses, including those not requiring cash outlay?

- What is my weekly payroll? Do I have adequate payroll records to meet the requirements of workman's compensation, wage and hour laws, social security, unemployment insurance, and withholding taxes?

- How much net profit did I earn? How much in resultant income taxes do I owe? What is my capital (of my total assets, how much would be left for me after paying all my creditors in full)? Are my sales, expenses, profits, and capital showing improvement, or did I do better last year than this? How do I stand as compared with two or three periods ago? Is my position about the same, improving, or getting worse?

- On what lines of goods or in what departments am I making a profit, breaking even, or losing money? Am I taking full advantage of cash discounts for prompt payment? How do discounts *taken* compare with discounts *lost*?

- Last but certainly not least, how do the financial facts of my business compare with those of similar businesses?

With the answers to these questions, you'll know whether something is wrong and, if so, the probable cause for this not-so-great situation. When you know sales are declining or collections are slow, when you've overinvested in inventory, or you notice that expenses are rising, you can take corrective action before you really get into trouble.

If anyone has ever managed to negotiate a business loan from a bank without having properly prepared financial statements, I've never heard about it! Your banker and other credit grantors will need to study your balance sheet and income statement in order to decide how much (or whether) credit should be extended to your shop. In most instances, these documents must be prepared by an outside accounting firm. It's not that anyone questions your veracity; let's just say that this "second opinion" of how well you're doing tends to carry a lot more weight than hearing how well your firm is doing from no one but you. In some instances, audited financial statements will be required. Again, your firm's record-keeping system will provide the basis for these statements.

Probably as important to your survival and success as the management and credit information to be gleaned from your financial statements is the requirement by federal and local government agencies for adequate records. The responsibility for such record keeping and the proof of its accuracy falls on the taxpayer/collector. That's you. Federal and local income taxes, payroll taxes, sales taxes, personal property taxes, and an ever-increasing number of laws and regulations require certain reports. They are far easier both to prepare and to substantiate if the figures are organized by a good bookkeeping system.

The records to back up these government reports must be available to the appropriate agency during the auditable period. The length of time over which you must retain these records will depend upon the statute of limitations set forth by the appropriate local and federal laws. Your attorney and/or accountant can fill you in as to the requirements of governing statutes. Most business records must, however, be maintained for a minimum of 3 to 5 years.

Keeping good business records is really like keeping score. Just imagine that you were attending a basketball game where either no score was kept or the score was posted several minutes late. You'd be confused, frustrated, and probably so disgusted that you'd end up leaving the stadium. Well, when you don't know the current score in your own business, the same thing is sure to follow. Since we already know that you're in this game to win, make sure your business records always keep you posted on the current score.

BREAKING EVEN, PLUS

Every business (and yours is no exception) has a break-even point. The break-even point is that magic number under which you will lose money and over which you will earn profits. It is the minimum gross sales you'll need, the magic "nut" you must crack.

It is a figure few small business owners know and even fewer know how to figure.

It is probably the single most important number in your business life. As a matter of fact, if you learn absolutely nothing but how to figure the break-even point for your firm, the money you spent for this book will have been well-spent.

Break-even analysis is a management control device because the break-even point clearly shows you how much you must sell under given conditions in order to just cover your costs with no profit and no loss.

Profit depends on sales volume, selling price, and costs. A break-even analysis will help you establish what a change in one or more of these factors will do to your profits. To figure your break-even point, you must separate your fixed costs (such as rent) from variable costs (such as the cost of goods sold).

If that all sounds very confusing, just memorize the following formula:

$$\text{Break-even point (in sales dollars)} = \text{total fixed costs} \div \left(1 - \frac{\text{total variable costs}}{\text{corresponding sales volume}}\right)$$

Depending on the type of business you run, the cost of operating your firm is made up of various items. In general, they're categorized as follows:

Fixed Costs

These costs remain about the same from the day you open your shop until a change is made in the actual cost of the item. Fixed costs include rent, lights, power, and depreciation. Your salary may also be included here. Fixed costs—just as the name implies—remain the same regardless of the amount of sales or production that your business generates.

Direct Costs

These are costs which go up or down as sales or production increases or decreases. The products you buy to resell to your customers or the material and labor involved in making a product yourself are direct costs. All direct costs are directly related to a particular product or service.

Indirect Costs

These costs vary from period to period but not necessarily in any direct proportion to your sales or production figures. Indirect costs are for goods and/or services which may be necessary to your business but are not directly tied to particular items you sell. You will usually have much more control over indirect costs than either fixed or direct cost items.

Just in case you're totally confused, let's give you an example of how the break-even formula works: Say you plan to open a store and you estimate your fixed expenses at about $9000 the first year. You also have estimated your variable expenses (direct + indirect = variable) to be about $700 for every $1000 of sales.

$$\text{BE point} = \frac{\$9000}{1 - \frac{700}{1000}} = \frac{\$9000}{1 - .70} = \frac{\$9000}{.30} = \$30,000$$

Just think of all the valuable information you now have! Your "magic number" is $30,000 annually. You must sell at least that much to meet your expenses. Every dollar over that figure is profit. You can break it down into monthly quotas and know, for instance, that you must sell $2500 worth of merchandise each month to stay on target. You can break that down even further and set yourself minimum weekly ($577.36) or daily ($96.23 for a 6-day week) sales goals.

Now that you know what your minimum must be, it becomes a relatively easy matter to realistically set goals which will include a modest (or even immodest!) profit.

One thing's for sure: If your break-even point is totally unrealistic, you can reexamine your business plan before you back it with your life savings or the family jewels. Maybe all you need do is adjust some of your fixed costs.

You might find a less-expensive location to lease or (perish the thought!) reduce your owner's draw (that means salary). Or you may explore a change in pricing policies. Maybe you can bump prices up a bit, keep a close rein on indirect costs, and still eventually see a light at the end of the tunnel.

And if you find out that there is absolutely no way you could realistically expect to meet your minimum sales goals and, consequently, reach and exceed your break-even point, it's certainly better to find it out before the fact. When the light at the end of the tunnel is a train coming from the other direction, you'd best stay out of the tunnel.

As I said earlier, if you don't learn another thing from this book, knowing how to calculate your break-even point puts you miles and miles ahead of most of the rest of the small business world. Not to worry; you can thank me later.

P&Ls AND OTHER MYSTERIES

All this collecting, compiling, and keeping of individual bits and pieces of your firm's activities will culminate in the compilation of business statements.

Now, business statements are simply written reports which describe the condition of your firm. Their purpose is to help you determine answers to questions such as: How profitable is my firm? What is the makeup of my business assets? How much do I owe in debts of various kinds? What costs appear to be a problem? What is my investment in the business and is it shrinking or growing? What changes have occurred since the last statement was compiled? Did I do better or worse than last month or last year?

There are basically two important business statements or reports that should be generated for your firm regularly. These are an income and expense report, or statement of earnings—commonly referred to as a P&L—and a balance sheet.

The P&L or income statement is simply a report which tells you how much money your firm made (profit) or lost (loss) over a given period of time. The report might cover a day, a week, a month, or a year or more. Most generally, your P&L will cover not less than a month or more than a year.

Following is a very simplified example of how an income statement looks:

Sales	$1000
Cost of sales	600
	$ 400
Other operating costs	200
	$ 200
Income taxes	100
Net income	$ 100

Keep in mind that the net income figure doesn't necessarily mean that there will be an increase in cash available to your firm in that amount. Some of the net income may have gone into increased equipment, inventory, etc., or toward the reduction of liabilities.

Your balance sheet is the report which shows, on any particular day, the assets you own, the liabilities you owe, and the total amount of your investment in your business.

The report is called a balance sheet because of the way it is written: The amounts on the left- and right-hand sides of the report are equal, or "in balance," as shown by this simple example:

Assets		Liabilities and Owner's Equity	
Cash	$100	Accounts payable	$100
Receivables	300	Notes payable	100
Fixed assets	200	Mortage payable	200
			$400
		Owner's equity	200
	$600		$600

The total of the liabilities and investment in your business will always equal the total of the assets. To find your investment in the business, simply subtract the liabilities from the assets.

To further confuse the issue, a balance sheet is also commonly referred to as a financial statement. That is, in fact, what it is: a statement of the financial condition of your business on a particular day.

Now it's all very well and good to freeze a moment in time and commit it to paper. But the real value in generating this kind of report is to be able to compare it with what you did last month, last year during the same month, during similar periods in previous years, and with how your firm compares with other similar business operations.

Figure 6 shows the commonly used current balance sheet form. All you have to do is fill in the blanks, and voilà!, instant balance sheet. If nothing else, it may help familiarize you with the different categories contained in a financial statement.

From these two basic reports, you or your accountant can generate any number of special reports analyzing the data on the balance sheet and the P&L statement. You might, for instance, find a statement of changes in financial position summary helpful. This will identify the sources from which cash or other current funds were obtained and how they were used. The sources of funds might include operations, loans, additional investments, etc.

CURRENT BALANCE SHEET

for

_____

(name of your firm)

As of _____

(date)

Assets

Current assets:
  Cash:
    Cash in bank $_____
    Petty cash   _____ $_____
  Accounts receivable $_____
    Less allowance for doubtful accounts   _____   _____
  Merchandise inventories   _____
    Total current assets $_____

Fixed assets:
  Land $_____
  Buildings   _____
  Delivery equipment   _____
  Furniture and fixtures   _____ $_____
    Less allowance for depreciation $_____ $_____
  Leasehold improvements, less amortization   _____
    Total fixed assets   _____

Total assets $_____

Liabilities and Capital

Current liabilities:
  Accounts payable $_____
  Notes payable, due within 1 year   _____
  Payroll taxes and withheld taxes   _____
  Sales taxes   _____
    Total current liabilities $_____

Long-term liabilities:
  Notes payable, due after 1 year   _____

Total liabilities $_____

Capital:
  Proprietor's capital, beginning of period $_____
  Net profit for the period $_____
  Less proprietor's drawings   _____
  Increase in capital   _____
    Capital, end of period $_____

Total liabilities and capital $_____

Figure 6 Balance sheet form. Fill in the blanks and you'll have a credit balance sheet for your business. You'll probably want to enlist the help of your accountant. You may even want to turn the entire chore over to him or her.

The uses of such funds might include inventory, new equipment purchases, receivables, or the reduction of liabilities, etc. Similarly, you might find a statement of retained earnings a valuable tool. This report would summarize the net income earned, any portion taken out or distributed, the balance retained for business use, and the accumulated income which has been left in the business. Another brief report that both you and your banker might find comforting is a margin of safety analysis. This simply identifies what your break-even point is and how far over or (perish the thought) under that point you happen to be currently.

There are various other supplementary schedules and statements that may also be prepared to show in greater detail some of the principal elements of your P&L and balance sheet. To further study how these statements can be the literal salvation of a small business, take a look at Figure 7, the profit and loss statement for an imaginary firm we'll call A-Z Appliance Repair Company. Then study Figure 8, the ancillary P&L statement for this same firm which shows expenses as percentages of sales.

Now, some of these numbers bounce right out and hit you on the head. For example, in Figure 7 the P&L statement shows a net profit of $3600 which probably doesn't warrant the owner getting out of bed every morning. It could have been worse; he could have lost $3600. But why the low profit?

The picture begins to clear when the firm's accountant analyzes the complete financial picture shown in Figure 8. This expanded P&L shows the results of a study where (1) sales are broken down into two categories, parts and service, and (2) expenses are allocated to each category. This information is relatively easy to accumulate when your sales records are set up to capture this information at the time of the sale.

In addition, the use of percentages to show the part of each sales dollar used by each of the various expenses is especially good for comparing current-year financial statements with those of previous years. A business owner can easily determine the trend of the business with this kind of report. It's also easy to see how valuable comparing these figures with those of other similar firms might be.

Two trouble spots jump right off the page when the expense figures of the A-Z Appliance Repair Company are broken down into percentages. One is the loss on the sale of parts. The other is an excessive payroll.

The loss on the sale of parts occurred because the owner did not price the parts properly. A careful review indicated that the owner received a 30 percent discount when parts were purchased. Therefore, the sales price—provided the owner's competition would allow it—should have been $34,286 ($24,000 ÷ 70% = $34,286), instead of $25,000. This increase in the selling price of parts would have covered the other costs and shown a net profit of $6,386

PROFIT AND LOSS STATEMENT
for
A-Z Appliance Repair Company
Jan-Dec 1980

Gross sales		$70,000
Cost of sales:		
Opening inventory	$13,000	
Purchases	25,000	
Total	38,000	
Ending inventory	14,000	
Total cost of sales		24,000
Gross profit		46,000
Operating expenses:		
Payroll (not including owner)	26,000	
Rent	3,000	
Payroll taxes	1,500	
Interest	600	
Depreciation	1,400	
Truck expense	5,500	
Telephone	2,400	
Insurance	1,000	
Miscellaneous	1,000	
Total		42,400
Net profit (before owner's salary)		$ 3,600

Figure 7 Sample profit and loss statement. Study both Figure 7 and Figure 8. Sample P&L Statement. In addition to helping you become familiar with these two reports, these charts will enable you to learn what's wrong with the A-Z Appliance Repair Company so that the same things will never be wrong with *your* company.

($10,286 − operating expenses of $3900), instead of a loss of $2900.

Now the other trouble area—payroll. More than 57 percent of the service income was being expended for payroll. A more in-depth look at this situation is definitely indicated. It's even more serious when you remember that this percentage does not include the owner's salary. This business owner must get either higher service charges or lower-paid (or fewer) service people.

There's no way we could pinpoint the reasons behind this large payroll cost from the available data. But such facts and figures would certainly ring

A-Z Appliance Repair Company
P&L Statement Showing
Expenses as Percentages of Sales
Jan-Dec 1980

	Total		Parts		Service	
	Amount	Percent	Amount	Percent	Amount	Percent
Gross sales	$70,000	100.00	$25,000	100.00	$45,000	100.00
Cost of sales:						
Opening inventory	13,000		13,000			
Purchases	25,000		25,000			
Total	38,000		38,000			
Ending inventory	14,000		14,000			
Total cost of sales	24,000	34.29	24,000	96.00		
Gross profit	46,000	65.71	1,000	4.00		
Operating expenses:						
Payroll	26,000	37.14			26,000	57.78
Rent	3,000	4.28	1,500	6.00	1,500	3.34
Payroll taxes	1,500	2.14			1,500	3.34
Interest	600	.86	300	1.20	300	.66
Depreciation	1,400	2.00			1,400	3.11
Truck expense	5,500	7.86			5,500	12.22
Telephone	2,400	3.43	1,200	4.80	1,200	2.67
Insurance	1,000	1.43	400	1.60	600	1.33
Miscellaneous	1,000	1.43	500	2.00	500	1.11
Total	42,400	60.57	3,900	15.60	38,500	85.56
Net profit (loss)	$ 3,600	5.14	$(2,900)	(11.60)	$ 6,500	14.44

(Exclusive of owner's salary)

Figure 8 Sample P&L statement. (See Figure 7)

the bell alerting us to the need for additional analysis. Somebody better come up with answers to questions such as: Is an accurate record maintained of time spent on jobs? Is the 8-hour day of each employee fully accounted for? Is travel time from one job to another job charged for and, if so, to whom? If employees are working overtime, is the additional expense reflected in the charge to the customer? Is work being done on a guaranteed price basis, or is it being billed on an hourly basis? If the firm's working on a guaranteed price basis, is the actual time spent on the job greater than what was originally estimated? If so, and if the job is resulting in a loss to the firm, was the original estimate sound? Is it time to raise prices? Is the percentage spent for payroll appropriate and in line with other similar firms' expenses?

The P&L statement for your firm may reveal a number of items that need further exploration. For example, maybe you're paying more rent than is necessary for your type of business. Or there may be a better way to schedule work so that personnel and equipment can be used more efficiently. Perhaps you can cut your telephone bill by using mail service more and long-distance phone calls less. Or the P&L statement may identify the possibility of increasing inventory turnover.

In Figure 8, the average inventory for the 12-month period covered in the report of $13,500 ($13,000 opening inventory, $14,000 ending inventory, average inventory $13,500). The cost of sales being $24,000, the firm's average inventory was used less than twice a year. Look at it another way: The ending inventory of $14,000 represents a part supply for approximately 7 months.

Upon realizing this fact, the owner of this firm was able to cut the average inventory to $10,000. While such a move would depend, of course, on the type of business and quality of service from suppliers, the owner of this firm was able to carry a smaller supply of certain parts and to rely to a greater extent on immediate delivery from wholesalers for other replacement parts.

I can only hope you're beginning to see both the value and the necessity of accurate records and timely reports. If you're bored beyond belief or hopelessly confused (or both!), I again refer you to adequate outside accounting assistance. If, on the other hand, all this stuff sounds just fascinating to you, do investigate your local continuing education opportunities through your high school, junior or community college, or university for course offerings in accounting.

Happily, there seems to be a growing awareness on the part of educators of the need for courses specifically for small business owners. If you're really a neophyte, the checklist illustrated in Figure 9 should—if followed religiously—keep you out of trouble.

SMALL BUSINESS FINANCIAL STATUS CHECKLIST
(What an Owner-Manager Should Know)

Daily   1. Cash on hand.
             2. Bank balance. (Keep business and personal funds separate.)
             3. Daily summary of sales and cash receipts.
             4. Ensure that all errors in recording collections on accounts are corrected.
             5. Maintain a record of all monies paid out, by cash or check.

Weekly   1. Accounts receivable. (Take action on slow payers.)
             2. Accounts Payable. (Take advantage of discounts.)
             3. Payroll. (Records should include name and address of employee, social security number, number of exemptions, date ending the pay period, hours worked, rate of pay, total wages, deductions, net pay, check number.)
             4. Taxes and reports to state and federal government (sales, withholding, social security, etc.).

Monthly   1. Ensure that all journal entries are classified according to like elements (these should be generally accepted and standardized for both income and expense) and posted to general ledger.
             2. Ensure that a profit and loss statement for the month is available within a reasonable time, usually 10 to 15 days following the close of the month. This shows the income of the business for the month, the expense incurred in obtaining the income, and the profit or loss resulting. From this, take action to eliminate loss (adjust markup; reduce overhead expense, pilferage, incorrect tax reporting, incorrect buying procedures; correct failures to take advantage of cash discounts).
             3. See that a balance sheet accompanies the profit and loss statement. This shows assets (what the business has), liabilities (what the business owes), and the investment of the owner.
             4. Make sure the bank statement is reconciled (that is, that the owner's books are in agreement with the bank's record of the cash balance).
             5. Ensure that the petty cash account is in balance. (The actual cash in the petty cash box plus the total of the paid out slips that have not been charged to expense total the amount set aside as petty cash.)
             6. See that all federal tax deposits, withheld income and FICA taxes (Form 501), and state taxes are made.
             7. See that accounts receivable are aged (i.e., 30, 60, 90 days, etc., past due). (Work all bad and slow accounts.)

8. Make sure that inventory control is worked to remove dead stock, and order new stock. (What moves slowly? Reduce. What moves fast? Increase.)

Figure 9 As long as you have the answers to these various categories, you'll be in good financial control of your business. Take whatever steps are appropriate to ensure that on a daily, weekly, or monthly basis (as indicated) you have these facts at your fingertips. (Courtesy of U.S. Small Business Administration.)

"Render unto Caesar . . ."

Things were a good deal simpler a couple of thousand years ago when Jesus Christ allowed as how it was appropriate for his followers to pay their taxes. Caesar set the tax rate and appointed a bunch of not-too-nice fellows called publicans to collect them. Mr. Publican skimmed some off the top for himself and passed the rest on to old Caesar, and that was that.

A citizen of the time could voluntarily comply or have his property forcibly confiscated, or face some form of physical punishment up to and including becoming some lion's dinner.

But it was simple. There was one tax, one tax collector, and that was that.

Times, as they say, have changed. Every conceivable unit of government seems to have a claim on some portion of the money that passes through your cash register. And the whole area of business taxes has become so complex that attorneys and accountants specialize not just in taxes, but in very narrow and sometimes esoteric areas of taxation. While probably the most suspect sentence in the English language is, "I'm from the IRS and I'm here to help you," taxes needn't keep you awake nights.

A little information, a bit of planning, and a businesslike approach to the subject will keep you clean, current, and in control.

DEBTOR/AGENT RESPONSIBILITIES

As the owner-manager of a small business, the first thing you must understand about taxes is that they must be paid. (I would also heartily recommend that they be paid in full and on time.) The second thing you should understand is the dual role you play in our tax-collecting system.

First, there's the role of debtor: You pay those taxes for which you personally are liable. Then, there is the role of agent: You withhold or collect taxes from others and pass them along in an appropriate manner to the taxing entity. The small business owner is literally both taxpayer and tax collector.

As a further illustration of these points, in your role as taxpayer (or debtor) each year, you owe federal income tax which must be paid out of the earnings of your business. If your business owns land and/or buildings, you will owe the applicable property tax.

In your role as tax collector (or agent), each pay period you'll deduct federal income and social security taxes from your employees' wages. In the case of social security taxes, you become both an agent and a debtor since you must match the employee contribution. You act as an agent when you collect sales and excise taxes as applicable and simply pass these monies on to the taxing entity. You don't actually owe them; you are given the "privilege" of collecting and handling them in exchange for the opportunity to own and operate your own shop.

You are, however, responsible for paying both your own taxes and those which you collect from others. By planning ahead, keeping accurate records, and setting tax monies aside as they are collected you'll discover that paying taxes is just another normal business function.

You may not ever make it a pleasure, but you can keep it from being a pain.

FEDERAL, SATE, COUNTY, AND MUNICIPAL TAXES

Dear old Uncle Sam has four categories of taxes with which you will likely find yourself involved. These are income taxes, social security taxes, unemployment taxes, and excise taxes.

The amount of income tax levied on a business depends on many factors including the form of business organization utilized (i.e., sole proprietorship, partnership, or corporation) as well as the number of exemptions, deductions, and credits for which the firm is eligible.

Generally speaking, a sole proprietor or member of a partnership will report the net income from the business on his or her individual income tax return. A partnership also files a separate information return which lists the taxable amounts that each partner reports on his or her individual return as a result of the business. The various items of income and expense from a business operated as a sole proprietorship are usually reported directly on the owner's individual tax return. The reported income is taxed by the federal government at individual rates which vary with the owner's total income, deductions, number of dependents, and all the other regular personal income tax considerations. However, the sole proprietor also files an additional schedule with the personal income tax return which identifies income and expenses from business activities.

Federal tax law requires that individual proprietors and partners pay income tax and self-employment tax liabilities on a "pay-as-you-go" basis. First, you file a Declaration of Estimated Tax (Form 1040 ES) no later than April 15 of each year. This declaration is the amount of tax the proprietor or partner expects to owe for the year. Payment of the total, however, is made quarterly and is due April 15, June 15, September 15, and January 15. If things seem to be changing drastically, adjustments to the estimate can be made at the time that a quarterly payment is submitted.

For the owner of a brand-new business, such a declaration may be required by the IRS on a date other than April 15; for example, if you had been working for wages subject to withholding and had left that job to operate your own shop. Under similar conditions, you would be required to file a declaration as follows:

For a change occurring after April 1 but before June 2, file by June 15.

If the change takes place after June 1 but before September 2, you must file by September 15.

For changes occurring after September 1, you must file by January 15 of the following year.

If your business is a corporation, the business itself pays taxes on its profit. You, in addition, are subject to an individual income tax on any salary or dividends which your corporation pays to you.

All taxable corporate income is taxed at 22 percent. In addition, taxable income over $25,000 is subject to a 26 percent surtax. So after the first $25,000, the effective corporate tax rate is 48 percent.

While the rest of the United States struggles along with April 15, corporations can pick their own "tax day." The corporation may select as its taxable year any period of 12 months. This fiscal year may—but does not have to—correspond with the calendar year. As a matter of fact, two of the most popular fiscal year periods are July 1 through June 30, and October 1 through September 30. Just remember that the income tax return of your corporation is due on the 15th of the third month following the end of its fiscal year.

Every corporation with an estimated tax of $40 or more is also required to make estimated quarterly tax payments. While income tax returns are filed annually, most firms handle payment of the appropriate tax on a quarterly basis.

Since we've all had taxes withheld from our paychecks and all annually come to grips with short forms, long forms, deductions, credits, and a test of just how far our respective moral codes go regarding the amount we'll claim as the past year's charitable contributions, the new business owner does tend to think that he or she knows something about the debtor relationship posed by income taxes and about the agent relationship inherent in withholding tax from the payroll of your newly acquired staff.

A foolish assumption at best. Both angels and amateurs should fear treading anywhere near the federal tax forest without expert assistance. The folks at the IRS tend to take this whole thing very seriously. And so should you. Advice and assistance from your accountant will not only keep you legal but very likely save you money over the long haul.

As soon as you become an employer rather than an employee, you must collect federal income and social security taxes from your employees by withholding from their paychecks the appropriate amounts of money. In turn, it is your legal responsibility to pass this money along to the feds. Here is a simplified look at how it works:

When you hire a new employee, he or she will complete and sign a Form W-4, an employee's withholding allowance certificate. This lists the exemptions and additional withholding allowance that the employee wishes to claim and gives you, the employer, the legal right to withhold these amounts and pay them—on the employee's behalf—to the federal government.

If for some reason an employee fails to provide you with such a certificate (Form W-4), you are required by law to withhold tax as if the employee were a single person with no exemptions. Every year, before December 1, you should have each of your employees fill in new W-4s if there has been any change whatsoever in the exemptions to be claimed during the upcoming year. You'll have to keep adequate records of the amounts withheld because each January you, the employer, have to furnish each of your employees with completed copies of Form W-2, the wage and tax statement, which includes the totals withheld from the employee's check all year. In addition to the copies that go to the employee, you must provide a copy to each taxing jurisdiction. A copy of this Form W-2 must be received by the Internal Revenue Service on or before February 28 each year.

The amount withheld from each paycheck will vary from employee to employee and will be based on marital status, number of children, the amount of money earned in the pay period, and other considerations. Current tax tables which show the employer how much to withhold based on each employee's Form W-4 are available from any IRS office. Your accountant can probably also provide you a copy.

Social security taxes are a slightly different situation. Here, the employer is both an agent and a debtor. As an agent, you will be responsible for deducting the appropriate tax amount from each employee's paycheck. As a debtor, you will match these deductions yourself and add them together to make one tax deposit. If you're running a business where you or your employees receive tips as part of their income, there are some special rules to be followed. Likewise, if you as the business owner will be using social security for your own retirement, some special rules apply. Assitance with any problems or questions is readily available through the Internal Revenue Service, the Social Security Administration (SSA), or your accountant.

There's really nothing terribly complicated about passing along the tax monies you have collected. It looks complex and cumbersome, but truly it simply involves withholding the money, keeping tabs on how much has been withheld from whom, reporting these amounts to the appropriate government agency using the appropriate government forms, and making deposits at certain intervals at a Federal Reserve Bank. In some very small communities, a regular old commercial bank may be authorized to accept tax deposits. It's quite likely that the bank with which you do business is, in fact, a Federal Reserve depository.

To deposit the funds which you withheld, just complete the tax return Form 941 to report withholding and social security remittances. The form and the deposited funds are usually due on April 30, July 31, October 31, and January 31. I say "usually" because there are many cases when remittances will be due before the due date of the return. The dates on which you will have to make deposits will depend on your individual business situation. Make the deposit and fill in Form 501, Federal Tax Deposits, Withheld Income, and F.I.C.A. Taxes. Simply attach a check in the amount due and take or send it to the Federal Reserve Bank (or designated commercial bank) nearest you.

Things get slightly confusing when distinguishing between when tax reports are due and when the deposits are due. The reports are always due on the last day of April, July, October, and January. The deposits are due depending on when you have withheld certain amounts of money. A general rule of thumb: The smaller your tax liability, the less often you have to make a deposit. Here's the way it works:

Less Than $200 Liability per Quarter

No deposit is required if your liability for a quarter is less than $200. Total liability for the quarter is to be remitted with the next quarterly return on or before the last day of the month following the close of the quarter.

Liability of $200 or More per Quarter but Less Than $200 Liability in Any Month

If at the end of the first month in the quarter your cumulative liability is less than $200 but by the end of the second month it is $200 or more, you must make a deposit for the cumulative amount by the fifteenth day of the third month in the quarter. Any liability for the third month of that quarter may be remitted with the return you'll be making on or before the last day of the month following the close of the quarter.

When Cumulative Liability Does Not Reach $200 until the Third Month of the Quarter

The total liability must be deposited by the last day of the month following the close of the quarter.

Liability of $200 or More but Less Than $2000

If your cumulative liability for the quarter or each of the first 2 calendar months is $200 or more but less than $2000, your deposits are due on or before the fifteenth day of the next month. For the last month in the quarter, deposits are not due until the last day of the month following the close of the quarter.

Liability of $2000 or More at the End of Any Quarter-Monthly Period

If by the 7th, 15th, 22d, or the last day of any month, your cumulative liability is $2000 or more, a deposit must be made within the next 3 banking days.

The next federal tax that your business will likely be subjected to is federal unemployment tax. If you employ one or more persons in each of 20 days a year, each day being in a different week, or if you have a payroll of at least $1500 in any calendar quarter (i.e., January, February, and March), this tax is due and payable (with a few exceptions I've noted later) by the end of the month following each of the first 3 calendar quarters (i.e., on April 30 for the quarter made up of January, February, and March). Each payment is made to an authorized commercial bank or Federal Reserve Bank and must be accompanied by Form 508, Federal Tax Deposit—Federal Unemployment Taxes. Quarterly returns are not required. Instead, report Form 940 may be filed for the whole year and is due by January 31 of the next year. If there is a balance of tax due for the year, it must be paid in January using depositary Form 508.

I mentioned that there are a few exceptions as follows: To be subject to federal unemployment tax, you must pass the test for designation as an employer. In either the current calendar year or the preceding calendar year, you must have paid wages of $1500 or more during any calendar quarter or employed one or more persons in each of 20 days in a calendar year with each day being in a different week. If you don't pass the test, you win! And you don't have to pay unemployment tax. Another variable in the quarterly payments described above is as follows: Quarterly payments are not required if the tax for that quarter plus the tax not deposited for the prior quarters in the calendar year is $100 or less. If, for example, the computed tax for the quarter ending March 31 was $90, no depositary payment would be required at that time. Then, if the tax for the quarter ending June 30 was $240, there would be a depositary payment of $330 ($90 + $240) to be made by July 31.

Please note that I have not suggested the tax rate nor the amount of wages subject to social security and unemployment taxation. Both the rate and the amount of income subject to tax have risen dramatically over the past few years. Since they are subject to such fluctuations, the only source of truly accurate information is the taxing entity (i.e., IRS, SSA) or your accountant.

The last federal tax to which you may well be subject is federal excise tax. Excise taxes are imposed on the sale or use of certain items, on certain transactions, and in certain occupations. For example, there is an occupational tax on retail dealers in adulterated butter or in beer, on retail liquor dealers, and on wholesale beer and liquor dealers. Diesel fuel and certain special motor fuels also carry a retailer's excise tax. Clear up any doubt about your excise tax liability by contacting your nearest Internal Revenue Service office or by checking with your accountant. If you're liable for excise tax, you must file a quarterly return on Form 720.

When you owe more than $100 a month in excise tax, monthly deposits of that tax must be made to a Federal Reserve Bank or other authorized depositaries in the same manner as your federal income taxes. Semimonthly deposits of excise taxes are required if your liability is for more than $2000 of all excise taxes reportable on Form 720 for any month during the previous quarter.

If your business involves gaming devices, liquor, narcotics, gambling, or firearms, you are subject to excise tax. Details of these rather specialized and sometimes complicated areas are available from your nearest IRS office. If you are dealing in any of these areas, you most certainly need the services of a competent CPA.

If you own and operate trucks in your business, you'll have to pay the federal highway use tax. Internal Revenue Service publication 349, "Federal Highway Use Tax," describes this special tax in detail. The best thing about the booklet is its price tag: It's free for the asking. Contact your friendly IRS office for a copy.

In addition to playing debtor, agent, or both to the feds, you'll find yourself in the same relationship with other units of government. Since state, county, and city taxes vary so significantly from one location to the next, there is no way to address the subject in anything but the most general terms. The three major types of taxes usually levied by one or more of these governing authorities are unemployment taxes, income taxes, and sales taxes.

Each state (plus Puerto Rico and Washington, D.C.) has unemployment taxes. Since the rules and requirements vary by state, check the authorities in your state to determine your obligations. Taxable wage base in a calendar quarter is the basis for unemployment taxes in most instances. The rate of tax charged is usually determined by your firm's unemployment experience coupled with the unemployment experience of your state (or similar businesses operating within your state). In some states, the employee is also assessed through payroll deduction.

Many states impose an income tax. When it's applicable, you will be required to deduct this tax from your employees' wages. Some state tax returns are similar to those used by the federal government. Other states use a vastly different approach. Most, however, require you—the employer—to file an informational return. Again, contact the state authorities in your area to find out exactly what requirements apply to your business. Since the reporting requirements can differ from those applicable to filling out federal income tax returns, make sure that your records will give you the necessary information to compute state income taxes.

Many states also levy a state sales tax. In handling the sales tax, you once again become an agent. You will collect the tax and pass it on to the appropriate state agency. You will be required to use whatever system the taxing jurisdiction has set up. Make sure your method of collecting, reporting, and paying state sales tax complies fully with your state's requirements.

Almost all counties, towns, and cities impose various kinds of taxes of their own. Heading the list are real estate taxes, personal property taxes, taxes on gross receipts of businesses, and unincorporated business taxes. Certain licenses to do business are also a tax even though some business owners don't think of these license fees as such. And many cities (mainly the larger ones) also have an income tax.

The last major tax category is that of property taxes. The county in which your business is located is usually the unit of government that assesses and collects property taxes. This does vary in some parts of the country, however, so seek the guidance of your attorney and/or accountant if you're in doubt. If your firm owns real estate, you will be subject to real estate taxes. If your firm leases its premises, the lease might call for you to pay real estate taxes (or the amount of any increases in real estate taxes) as part of the conditions of the lease. Real estate taxes are usually paid in several installments during the year.

Your business may also be taxed on personal property, and if you operate as a corporation, you might additionally be subject to tax on capital stock. Both of these would require the filing of a tax return. Again, it's not an area for amateurs. Seek professional help.

Taxes can be confusing. But with some professional advice and assistance, systematic deposits to a special bank account where you can hold the funds to pay your taxes until they are due—in short, a businesslike approach—will help you cope with this critical and inevitable part of your business. And it is both critical and inevitable.

REMEMBER CAPONE?

If you goof up and file a report or a return late, make an incorrect tax deposit, or deposit the funds after they are due, you're subject to some reasonably stiff penalties in the form of interest added to the amount due. If the situation gets a bit more out of hand, you can find the front door to your business padlocked and the whole kit and caboodle confiscated by the government to be auctioned to satisfy your tax debt. You can even find yourself in some very unsavory company, serving time in prison for failure to pay taxes in a complete and timely fashion.

Lest you think the IRS and the courts are a bit overzealous, look at it this way: Nonpayment of taxes—especially when you've been acting in the capacity of agent—constitutes out-and-out theft. The money you collect as an agent (whether from customers or employees) is not, never has been, and never will be *yours*. In addition, keep in mind that any business owner who utilizes tax money collected as part of operating capital is taking a totally unfair advantage that more law-abiding, taxpaying business owners do not have. So evading the payment of taxes is not only immoral, it's illegal. It's also stupid.

You can't get away with it. The best you'll do is pay a stiff penalty and/or fine. You may even lose your business entirely. And you could ultimately lose a few years of your life sitting in the slammer.

Before you pooh-pooh the notion that (1) you'd ever get caught or (2) such drastic punishment would ever be meted out in your direction, just remember Capone. Old Al terrorized Chicago and environs for quite a number of years. With all the not-nice things Mr. Capone pulled, the one that finally stuck him behind bars was income tax evasion.

Those tax guys and their cohorts in the courts take the payment of all kinds of taxes very seriously. Maybe it's because that's where their paychecks are generated. But whatever the reason, just make sure your taxes are paid in full and on time. And remember Capone.

TAX OVERVIEW

We've identified the fact that you will owe and pay and/or collect and pass along taxes to the federal government, your state government, and both the county and the municipality in which your business is located. It can seem mind-boggling. Failure to comply with any or (heaven forbid!) all your business tax responsibilities can result in heavy penalties, seizure of everything from your bank account to the contents of your shop, or a change in your address from your current residence to the nearest state or federal prison.

In short, taxes are serious business and you should act accordingly.

Your tax obligations can and should be met in a timely and businesslike manner. This keeps everyone—you included—happy.

Unlike other encounters with the law where you must be proved guilty, tax law puts the burden of proof on you. The IRS (and every other taxing entity I know of) assumes that you are a liar, a cheat, and the possessor of falsified and/or inadequate backup data, and that you owe "them" whatever it is they say you owe. Fully confusing the issue, the Internal Revenue Service doesn't mandate what books and records the small business owner must keep in order to prove (or disprove) tax-related issues. It is, however, required that adequate and permanent books and records be kept to identify the firm's income, expenses, and deductions. If inventory is a factor in determining your business income correctly or if you take travel and entertainment deductions, special supporting data are required. While the IRS doesn't dictate form, it does mandate accuracy. These records and books must be available for inspection by agents of the Internal Revenue Service and other local taxing agencies. For most businesses, the record-keeping systems discussed in Chapter 6 will provide you adequate information on which to compute your tax liability and prove your point, should it come to that.

Also keep in mind that these business records must be kept as long as their contents may become material in the administration of any tax matter. Ordinarily, the IRS statute of limitations for such records expires 3 years after the return or report is due to have been filed. If the taxpayer omits over 25 percent of gross income or files a false or fraudulent return, however, that 3-year statute of limitations flies out the window, and you could very well be called on to prove your "innocence" for a substantially longer period of time. Many of your business records should be kept for longer than this minimum 3 years.

Among records you'll want to keep for a minimum of 3 years are cash books, depreciation schedules, your general ledger, journals, financial statements, and audit reports. Records you should retain for 6 to 7 years include accounts payable and receivable, canceled checks, inventory schedules, payroll records, and sales vouchers and invoice details. You should also keep copies of income tax returns and other tax reports. Remember, you must be able to prove that your tax returns and reports have all been filed correctly.

All the news isn't grim: You can also use these records to file carry-back claims and amended returns should you and your accountant discover this would be to your benefit.

Take your role of both tax agent and debtor very seriously. But if you must make a choice, take the role of agent even more seriously. The reason is simple: In your role as agent you're playing with someone else's money, not yours. Failing to live up to either obligation ranges from stupid to criminal. Generally speaking, however, the taxing entity tends to be a little more liberal toward tax debtor than toward the tax collector or agent.

To keep clean, seek the advice of an accountant or other competent professional. You might also check with your local chamber of commerce. Many chambers make available a complete listing of all the taxing and licensing entities to which you will be subject. Your accountant and/or lawyer can also provide you with this information. The following is a list of the more common federal reports that may be required:

1. Application for Employer's Identification Number Form SS-4

2. Corporate Income Tax Form 1120 (see your accountant)

3. Partnership Tax Form 1065

4. Employer's Withholding Allowance Certificate Form W-4

5. Employer's Quarterly Federal Tax Return Form 941

6. Personal Income Tax Form 1040

7. Profit (or loss) from Business or Profession Form 1040-C

I strongly suggest that to help you meet your tax obligations you have your accountant help you fill in a chart similar to Figure 10, Work sheet for Meeting Tax Obligations. Post this in a prominent place to remind you of what and how much tax you owe, when you owe it, and to whom.

WORK SHEET FOR MEETING TAX OBLIGATIONS

Kind of tax	Due date	Amount due	Pay to	Date for writing the check
FEDERAL TAXES				
Employee income tax and social security tax	___	___	___	___
	___	___	___	___
	___	___	___	___
	___	___	___	___
Excise tax	___	___	___	___
Owner-manager's and/or corporation income tax	___	___	___	___
	___	___	___	___
	___	___	___	___

Unemployment tax   ___   ___   ___   ___
                          ___   ___   ___   ___
                          ___   ___   ___   ___
                          ___   ___   ___   ___

STATE TAXES

Unemployment taxes   ___   ___   ___   ___
                          ___   ___   ___   ___
                          ___   ___   ___   ___
                          ___   ___   ___   ___

Income taxes   ___   ___   ___   ___
Sales taxes   ___   ___   ___   ___
                          ___   ___   ___   ___
                          ___   ___   ___   ___
                          ___   ___   ___   ___

Franchise tax   ___   ___   ___   ___

Other   ___   ___   ___   ___
                          ___   ___   ___   ___
                          ___   ___   ___   ___
                          ___   ___   ___   ___

LOCAL TAXES

Sales tax   ___   ___   ___   ___
                          ___   ___   ___   ___
                          ___   ___   ___   ___
                          ___   ___   ___   ___

Real estate tax   ___   ___   ___   ___

Personal property tax   ___   ___   ___   ___

Licenses (retail, vending ma-   ___   ___   ___   ___
chine, etc.)

Other   ___   ___   ___   ___
                          ___   ___   ___   ___

Figure 10 This work sheet is designed to help the owner-manager to manage the firm's tax obligations. You may want your accountant or bookkeeper to prepare the work sheet so that you can use it as a reminder in preparing for and paying the various taxes. (Courtesy of U.S. Small Business Administration.)

Unless your background includes bookkeeping or accounting, you should use outside help in setting up your tax records. An accountant can help you determine what records to keep as well as advise you on techniques which ensure that you don't pay unnecessary tax.

For example, because of poor records one small businessman unnecessarily included $30,000 of installment sales in his income even though they would not actually be earned for 2 to 3 years. At a 22 percent tax rate, this man paid more than $6500 in "extra" taxes. He—and you, if you're at all typical—could certainly have put that money to good use.

Inventory costing is another example of the need for sound tax-related record keeping. Your records should allow you to substantiate a correct but minimum income valuation on which you're subject to taxation. The rules of the game are as follows: Pay every dime you owe but not a red cent more.

DON'T BLAME ME! WRITE YOUR
CONGRESSPERSON

There is no doubt about it. The tax system in this country stinks. And it smells worse every year.

The kindest thing I could say about our current tax structure is that it makes small business survival difficult if not downright impossible. The unkind things I could say would probably make this the first business-oriented textbook ever banned in Boston.

Profits are hard enough to come by. But the inordinate bite taken by the several taxing entities to which you are subject will leave precious little, if anything, you can call your own. Add to this the time, effort, and expense of filling in and filing the multitudinous returns and reports required of all these units of government and what we have is a mess!

Insult is truly added to injury when you discover (and you will!) that the tax dodges, shelters, and loopholes really do give big business an additional advantage over small. And those big guys don't need any more help. You and I, on the other hand, need all the help we can get.

And the place to get it is from those we have voted into office and those who hope to gain our vote in the future.

Let your local, state, and national elected officials know how you feel about the situation. Stay informed and involved in the whole political process. Join with other business owners and support trade associations in their lobbying efforts to protect the interests of small business. At the very least, these associations will strive to keep things from getting worse. In addition to becoming rightfully involved in the political process of your community and your country, seek out and take the very best available advice on tax matters. Each of the four VIPs you met in Chapter 3 can assist you in both minimizing and meeting your tax obligations. As the late Judge Learned Hand said, "Over and over again courts have said that there is nothing sinister in arranging one's affairs to keep taxes as low as possible. Everybody does so, rich or poor; and all do right, for nobody owes any public duty to pay more than the law demands."

Learn what the law demands, pay not a penny more, and do everything in your power to reduce those demands.

8

Make the Devil Give You *Your* Due

The main purpose for the existence of your business is to generate a profit. Whether you're attempting to collect money due your firm, negotiating the terms of an agreement with a national franchise representative, or determining the fair market price for your goods or services, keep that one fact clearly in mind.

In this chapter we'll explore some seemingly dissimilar topics. The glue that binds them all together is the profit motive. And the cleanest kind of profit is generated when both buyer and seller get what they deserve.

COLLECTIONS

Credit is a part of everyday living in America. Whether as individuals, as business entities, or collectively as a nation, we couldn't exist for very long without credit.

Big business learned a long time ago that credit made it possible for customers to buy what they wanted, when they wanted it, and to pay for it from future earnings. It took a while, but small business is also now very much involved in the consumer credit game.

Consumer credit can be divided into two broad categories: loan credit and purchase credit. The consumer uses loan credit to borrow from banks, finance companies, credit unions, savings and loan associations, and other lenders. Purchase credit is used to acquire merchandise or services from many different kinds of businesses.

Most medium to large firms operate their own credit departments and finance the credit thus extended, themselves. As a matter of fact, many large retailers earn as much (if not more) from the interest generated by the extension of credit as they do from the sale of merchandise or service that the credit was used to acquire.

It takes a lot of money to get into the credit-granting business, however. Since it may take from 1 month to 3 years or more for a firm to receive payment in full for merchandise sold on credit, on the average it will take three to five times as much capital to extend credit to your customers as it will to operate on a cash-only basis.

Many small firms, however, have found that by opening store charge accounts for valued customers, increased sales, consumer loyalty, and the interest or service fee generated by such accounts make it well worth the risk involved.

The major contributing factor to the great and growing involvement of small business in credit selling has been the overwhelming consumer acceptance of and reliance on credit cards. While the so-called TBA (tires, batteries, and accessories) cards issued by major oil companies and the "travel and entertainment" cards such as American Express and Diners Club have long had an impact on related small business outlets, the phenomenal proliferation of all-purpose credit cards issued by banks such as Master Charge/Master Card, American Express, and VISA has revolutionized credit purchasing over the past decade. Most large firms, in addition to carrying their own in-house credit accounts, also honor one or more of these major credit cards. And precious few small businesses can remain competitive without welcoming one or more forms of "plastic money."

Probably the major determining factor as to whether your business should accept credit cards or grant some other form of credit (or both) is what your competitors are doing along these lines. If they grant credit, so must you.

If your credit-granting decision is to go the major credit card route, there's almost no big deal involved! Simply contact your friendly banker and arrange to meet with a bank card representative. Many major banks now offer both major bank cards. If yours doesn't, negotiate for the one they do have and, should you want to offer both "majors," simply contact the bank card division of another bank in your community which does provide the services required.

The bank card representative will inform you of the whole process, sign you on as a member firm, and provide you with the necessary carbon set forms and the little machine that imprints the customer's credit card number on the form. The machine, by the way, will promptly break all your fingernails.

The issuing bank charges a percentage of the total sale on each credit card transaction and assumes all responsibility for collecting the debt and all risk inherent in the relationship. Note carefully: The percentage retained (or service fee) by the lending institution varies from bank to bank and even from one firm to another within the same bank. A little negotiating with your bank card representative is very much in order. A reduction of even a fraction of a percentage point can add up to a significant amount of money each year. And I'm sure you'd rather have those dollars in your profit column than in the bank's. If that's not how you feel, I would strongly suggest that you get a job working for someone else. You aren't very likely going to make it as an entrepreneur.

With the rather notable exception of the portion of each credit card transaction retained by the bank, the rest of the sale is very much like a cash purchase. You simply tally up the credit slips, present them to the bank, and the total (minus the service fee) is deposited into your firm's account.

The issuing financial institution's bank card representative can explain all the rules, regulations, and procedures to you and your staff. It's a quick, convenient, and almost totally risk-free method of providing the credit option to your customers.

The question as to whether your firm should make other forms of credit, such as personal charge accounts, available to your customers and potential customers is a much more serious and difficult one to answer. As stated above, most large retailers prefer to operate their own credit departments—often in addition to bank card service availability. These firms believe that there's a great deal of customer loyalty generated through personal credit service. These merchants have found that customers will shop more regularly where they have credit accounts. Many retailers tend to view credit customers as repeat business and cash customers as "one-timers." While this may not always hold true, the theory does have merit. And everyone agrees that credit shoppers tend to spend considerably more than cash customers do.

While most small businesses—should they decide to offer credit at all—find that they can manage nicely by simply honoring the major bank and/or travel and entertainment cards, some firms (maybe even yours) have found it very profitable indeed to offer their best—if not all—customers personal credit accounts.

A good case in point is a successful retailer I'll call Marilyn Yarnell. Marilyn operates an exclusive women's apparel store in a small Northeastern city. She carries designer brands, classics to high fashion, and all are uncommonly expensive. If you're one of Marilyn's "good" customers, opening a charge account is as easy as signing the bottom of the sales ticket.

Marilyn explains, "Sure, we accept Master Card, VISA, and American Express. But some of our customers would rather their husbands not know how much they paid for a particular garment. And others may not have enough room left on their bank card to charge the purchase they wish to make to it. I have very few slow-paying accounts, even fewer deadbeats, and a lot more large total sales because of our personal account option."

I would venture to add that there's a certain snob appeal inherent in utilizing this personal charge option instead of whipping out the old credit card as all the common folks do. And I can personally vouch for the wisdom in Marilyn's ways by pulling from my closet a Calvin Klein coat, a gorgeous fur-collared sweater, and several other expensive purchases that this astute "merchant princess" has happily conned me into signing for. And I have no doubt that the next time I'm in her city, I'll visit her shop and, once again, make all-too-good use of "my" personal account with her elegant little shop.

Before you attempt to enter the credit-granting arena, explore the idea thoroughly with your lawyer, your accountant, and your banker. There's a lot of legality, liability, and just plain risk inherent in managing credit transactions of this kind. You must keep the whole situation legally sound and fiscally prudent. You'll need their help to determine first whether it is necessary and/or desirable to offer some form of personal credit to your customers. If the answer is affirmative, you'll definitely need to know how much credit you can extend, and you'll need assistance in cash flow management. Last but certainly not least, you'll need legal assistance with applications, contracts, collection proceedings, and the interest or service fee (if any) to be charged.

What does all this have to do with collections? Simple. Until you grant credit, there's nothing to collect. When you deal in cash, you've made all the collection to which you are entitled at the time of sale. The acceptance of major credit cards simply involves a slight reduction in the total dollars each sale represents and a small delay in transferring those monies to your firm's checking account. But you don't have to worry about collections. When your firm of and by itself extends credit, however, collecting those accounts receivable amounts is very much your concern.

Ask your attorney to explain the Consumer Credit Protection Act of 1968 to you. In addition to its truth-in-lending features, the act applies to credit, advertising, wage garnishments, and extortion on credit transactions. Many states have also passed the Uniform Consumer Credit Code. Find out if and/ or how these and possibly other local and state regulations impact your firm.

You'll also want to join and make use of your local credit bureau. This is usually a locally owned and operated small business which collects pertinent data on persons living in your retail trade area. Businesses such as yours which need information on the relative creditworthiness of a specific individual join the credit bureau for a set fee and then pay a small service fee for each credit reference check they request from the bureau. Your local credit bureau most likely belongs to a nationwide association of credit bureaus linked by sophisticated computer equipment so that credit information on people from other parts of the country can be obtained by contacting your local bureau.

Similar credit information is collected and disseminated on business firms by such organizations as Dunn & Bradstreet. Shortly after you go into business, you will probably be contacted by one or more of these firms to request information on your business and its financial condition.

It will, of course, be necessary for you to contract for the services of Dunn & Bradstreet or some other business credit service if your firm will be doing business with other businesses. There are also several excellent credit control and billing systems you may wish to investigate. The American Billing Corporation, whose national headquarters is located at 4014 North Seventh Street, Phoenix, Arizona 85014, has developed a simple four-step third-party system for controlling accounts receivable that is both effective and easy to maintain. This ABC system is a real time-saver which can increase cash flow, help maintain businesslike relationships with credit clientele, increase billing and credit operation efficiency, and is completely controlled by you at the point of use (your shop) with no communications gaps or time delays. Another very large plus is the very low price.

Another excellent system has been developed by the American Accounting Credit Control Systems, Inc., 1055 East Tropicana Avenue, Las Vegas, Nevada 89109. Again, the advantages are many and the cost is low. Either of these firms will be most happy to provide you with complete information about its systems and services. You might also want to check with your accountant for other suggested services or systems for you to consider.

Whichever way you go, credit and collections will both likely change drastically over the next 10 or so years. Recent developments in electronic data processing are rushing us all headlong into a truly cashless society. The Federal Reserve System is up to its ears in the development of electronic funds transfer system (EFTS) transactions which should be perfected some time in the 1980s. If you're at all interested in the new developments (and you should be), next time you take your banker to lunch, ask for an explanation over your club sandwich.

A FAIR PRICE, A FAIR PROFIT

Coming up with an equitable price for your goods or services is no easy matter. I will assume that you intend to operate a retail or service business and confine my remarks to that area.

If you intend to enter the manufacturing arena, I can only point out the four elements you must consider in setting prices: (1) direct costs, (2) manufacturing overhead, (3) nonmanufacturing overhead, and, last but not least, (4) profit. You will need to explore direct costing, price-volume relationships, the value of the raw material you'll utilize in your manufacturing process, to name just a few. Your efforts to maximize profits might include price-setting based on a contribution per labor-hour, contribution per pound, contribution per machine-hour, or a return-on-investment approach.

Obviously, it's a rather complex and critically important process. I can only suggest that, should you be headed in this direction, you get some professional assistance. The likeliest place to find it is within the hallowed halls of your certified public accounting firm.

While equally critical, coming up with the right selling price in retail or service firms is a much smaller headache. Always remember that the "best" price for a product or service is not necessarily the price that will sell the most units. It may not be the price that will bring in the greatest number of total sales dollars. It is, rather, the price that will maximize the profits of your company.

The "best" selling price is both cost-oriented and market-oriented. It must be high enough to cover your costs and help you make a profit. It must also be low enough to attract customers and build sales volume.

In retailing, certain markups (the difference between the wholesale price and the retail price) have already been established and are considered acceptable by the marketplace. This markup can range from a fraction of 1 percent in the case of some food and grocery items to 400-plus percent for fine jewelry and other luxury items.

Recognizing full well the dangers inherent in making assumptions, I will assume that along with your hopes and dreams you will open your retail shop armed with good, solid, practical firsthand retail experience. If this be the case, look to your experience to assist you in determining the right selling price. Also look to your trade association. The price you set on each piece of merchandise will be determined by everything from the manufacturer's suggested retail price to your projected total sales volume annually. No matter what kind of shop yours will be, the bottom line is all. And for survival's sake, that bottom line figure must meet or exceed your firm's break-even point. It surely wouldn't hurt for you to go back to Chapter 6 and review the section called Breaking Even, Plus. Accurately estimating your overhead, realistically projecting your gross sales volume, and determining your break-even point should all be a part of setting a fair price and making a fair profit.

The process is somewhat different when you are selling a service. Here, basically all you have to sell is time. And don't you forget it. Because while a manufacturer can increase output by the addition of new equipment or more streamlined processes, and the retailer can hope to generate larger sales by aggressive marketing or by adding a new product line, the businessperson is yet to be born who can add more hours to the day. Your only options are to increase the charge per hour generated by you and/or your staff, to increase the number of staff generating income, or both.

There is obviously a limit as to what the market will bear vis-à-vis the cost per hour or charge per service unit (i.e., a service call and/or repair of a specific nature: the performance of a specific task), and you must be especially sensitive to what your competition is doing. By the same token, if you are charging too little for your services, the addition of more staff will simply hasten your demise.

As we discussed earlier, the cost of operating your proposed business must be considered in setting prices. There is no conceivable way to make a profit until you've covered basic costs. Let's briefly review these costs:

Fixed Costs

These are the costs which are about the same from the day you start in business until a change is made in the fixed-cost items. Rent, light, power, and depreciation are types of fixed costs. Your salary may also be included here. Fixed costs are the same regardless of the amount of your sales or production.

Direct Costs

These are the costs which go up or down with increases or decreases in your sales and production. The product you buy to resell to your customer or the material and labor of making or delivering the product or service yourself are direct costs.

Direct costs may be material costs if they originate with a purchase you make, or they may be labor costs if they come from your payroll. All direct costs can be related to a particular product or service.

Indirect Costs

These costs may vary from period to period but not necessarily in proportion to your sales or production. They relate to those goods and services which are necessary to your business but are not related to particular items you sell.

From this oversimplified explanation of cost factors you can determine that the cost of your product or service at the point in time that it is ready to be sold includes the direct cost of the material and labor going into it plus some portion of the fixed and indirect costs. The total amount of fixed and indirect costs that each product or service must carry depends on the number or volume of items produced and sold.

At the end of any given period, the volume is known and the actual cost can be determined. However, you cannot await the end of a period to determine your costs and the related selling prices. It is therefore necessary to estimate the volume before you can estimate the cost.

Be both honest and realistic. The person who stands to be hurt the most by overestimating sales or underestimating costs is you. Your estimate of volume should represent a truly realistic balance between your ability to produce goods or services and your ability to sell them. In most cases, the amount of fixed and indirect costs to be added to the direct cost of an item can best be stated as a percentage of the direct cost.

For example, if your estimated monthly volume is 500 units at an average direct cost of $20 each, estimated monthly fixed costs are $1000, and estimated indirect costs are $500, the overhead rate and unit costs would be as shown in Figure 11.

Therefore, your selling price must be set based on a $23 cost. In addition to the costs we've already explored, you will probably have selling costs and other general administrative costs. The selling costs would include sales salaries, commissions, advertising, and similar items related to your sales effort. General administrative costs would include office salaries, supplies, interest, taxes, and similar items. If you've not included them in either direct or indirect costs, now is the time. Now's also the time to include a little something for you: It's called profit.

Assuming we've covered all sales and general and administrative costs in coming up with our $23 sales unit, all we need do is add on a fair profit and, voilà!, we have a fair price. Notice I said fair profit. This could be anything from a fraction of a percent to two, three, a hundred times or more the unit cost itself. What constitutes a fair profit will differ from person to person and situation to situation. Ideally, you'll look at everything, including the profit margin considered to be the norm for your industry or profession, the amount of risk inherent in the deal, the market conditions of the moment, and the extent of your personal greed.

Just don't get too greedy. Sound businesses are built on repeat performance. You can gouge some of the people once. But precious few of them twice.

In some types of businesses, it is advisable, if not downright necessary,

	Fixed cost	$ 1,000
	Indirect cost	500
Your overhead =	Total	$ 1,500
Direct cost = 500 × $20		$10,000
Overhead + direct =		$11,500

Your overhead rate is:

$$\frac{1,500}{10,000} = 15\%$$

Unit cost = $20 + 15% = $23
500 units × $23 = $11,500

Figure 11 Formula for fixing price based on estimated volume. Price = direct cost + indirect + profit

to break out inventory and/or functions into cost centers. A careful examination of what merchandise or services are generating sales, what pattern—seasonal or otherwise—may be inherent in such sales, and the relative profitability of these various sales-generating areas can and probably will lead to changes for the better. You may find, for instance, that a particular line of merchandise is utilizing 17 percent of your available floor space but is generating only 3 percent of your total gross sales and 1 percent of your total pre-tax profit. Obviously, something is wrong. You may decide to reduce the amount of inventory you maintain or to discontinue the product or service altogether, with no real adverse effect. As a matter of fact, you may find that when you fill the now-available floor space with faster-moving and more-profitable merchandise, your profit picture suddenly looks much brighter. The same kind of examination of your hours of operation can both lighten your load and increase your profit.

Not long ago, I worked with a young couple I'll call Jim and Jeanine Murphy. Jim and Jeanine had opened a convenience food store, and, thinking to go the competition one better, they opened for business 7 days a week, 24 hours a day. The business was just breaking even, and it was obviously only a matter of time before the Murphys' health and/or marriage broke down.

A careful examination of their more-than-adequate business records and some honest questions and answers led us rather quickly to the discovery that staying open the 8 hours between 11:00 P.M. and 6:00 A.M. accounted for 27 percent of the Murphys' overhead and roughly 6 percent of their gross sales.

They took my advice, changed their hours of operation from 6:00 A.M. until 11:00 P.M., and almost overnight (if you'll pardon my pun) drastically increased the profitability of their store.

They lost very little of the sales that had been made during these late night–early hour periods of operation, and while some of the fixed overhead continued whether they were open or not, the net result was very beneficial to their balance sheet.

Reducing the strain on their respective bodies and collective marriage also proved to be a good move.

Which leads us back to my original point: Setting both prices and policy must be done to maximize profits.

In some businesses, outside professional assistance in pricing and related matters is not only recommended, it's downright essential. A good case in point is the everyone-wants-one restaurant.

Unless you are a veritable fountain of knowledge regarding the restaurant industry, seek out and engage the services of a competent restaurant consultant. A consultant can help to determine what selections should be included in your menu, what size portions should be offered and at what price, what equipment is essential and what merely nice to have around, what steps should be taken to reduce employee pilferage and other forms of shrinkage (and there are a million ways to be "had" in the restaurant business!), how to lay out a floor plan and work stations for maximum efficiency, and a dozen other areas, all directly related to a profitable food and beverage operation.

If you don't know of a good consultant in the field, contact your local restaurant association for suggestions. You might also check with your local U.S. Small Business Administration office. Most SBA offices (especially at the regional level) have consultants on call contracts. You may even be eligible for such services at no charge to you—whether you are an existing or potential SBA borrower or not.

This kind of government-funded consultant service is available in many, if not most, areas. Ask and ye just may receive.

BUYING AND SELLING EXISTING BUSINESSES (WOULD YOU BUY A USED CAR FROM THIS MAN?)

Purchasing an existing business can be anything from a stroke of financial genius to a total disaster. Selling your business runs the same gamut. It is also almost always traumatic.

That's to be expected. After all, you've nurtured this going and growing concern from infancy to the point where now, we hope, someone will purchase the fruits of your labor. Ideally, you'll recoup your investment plus a nice, tidy profit based on the firm's future income-generating potential and the so-called goodwill that your past business efforts have produced.

Since at this stage of the game it is far more likely that you're in the market to buy an existing business rather than to sell one, let's take a look at some dos and don'ts, shoulds and shouldn'ts, and a couple of never evers. Learning what to look for as a buyer will also stand you in good stead when and if you find yourself in a position of seller.

The first question I ask clients to ask themselves regarding the business they wish to purchase is "why?" Why do you want to purchase an already established firm? Why this firm in particular? Why does the owner wish to sell the business? If you could establish a brand-new business complete with comparable inventory and similar location for less money, there should be one heck of a lot of "goodwill" covered by the price differential between the purchase price and what a new business start-up costs. If the firm that you're considering purchasing has a good reputation, be advised that it won't nec- essarily last long. If, on the other hand, the firm has a very bad name in the community, hanging an "under new management" sign in the front window will not change the store's negative image to a positive one. Paying too much for a store's good reputation is closely related to financial suicide. Paying anything for a store's bad reputation *is* financial suicide.

Do be cynical. If you're reasonably convinced that the deal looks good, insist on a fresh audit of the books and a complete inventory of all the stock and equipment that is to be included in the purchase price. And speaking of stock and equipment, always assume that much of it is obsolete at best. In all likelihood, this will prove to be the case. You'll be lucky to sell some, if not most, of the stock at pennies on the dollar. Likewise, the owner well may have taken every cent of depreciation potentially allowable on furniture, fixtures, and equipment. You may have the dubious pleasure of purchasing a bunch of junk that looks great on paper but is, in reality, as extinct as the last dinosaur.

If physical location is playing a large part in your thinking, make very sure that the owner doesn't know something you don't—like plans for major road construction that will make the business inaccessible to customers for 8 of the next 12 months, a freeway imminently about to displace the firm entirely, or a major chain planning a new store a block up the street. While I, like you, assume most people in this world to be decent and honest, you, like I, should assume that anyone attempting to sell you a business is part crook, part con artist, and hasn't been to church in years.

Finding out the real reason behind a decision to sell a business may be impossible. And there are business owners who, due to age, illness, or other family crises, really are willing to sacrifice a bit of profit to see their beloved firms left in good and capable hands. But for safety's sake, don't assume "your" owner is one of them.

Before signing anything, or deciding anything more final than a desire to explore the possibilities further, call on the services of your attorney, your accountant, and your banker. Any—or all three—may have some special knowledge of new competition, construction, or other real reasons behind the seller's desire to sell. Your accountant should examine (if not perform) the business's audited financial statement and other records and verify the audited inventory. Your accountant can also use this information to determine the true worth of the business. The two of you can then come to grips with a fair bid. While not absolutely mandatory, it might well prove helpful to consult a commercial real estate broker at about this point. He or she should be able to provide you with asking and purchase prices for similar firms in the area. A word of caution: When dealing with a commercial real estate broker (or any real estate broker), keep in mind that he or she does not necessarily have your best interest at heart. What a broker might tout as the deal of the decade will result in a commission for the broker and could lead you straight into bankruptcy court.

At about this time, your attorney begins to play an active part in the transaction. Utilize your legal counsel to review all appropriate documents pertinent to the purchase, including leases, lease-purchase agreements, notes, and all legal documents such as partnership agreements, articles of incorporation, and the like. Your lawyer should also prepare and present your offer to the business owner and, should the deal be brought to fruition, should draw up the necessary purchase agreements and other documents of sale.

Throughout the process seek input and concurrence from your banker. Not only will you need his or her OK when it comes time to finance the deal, but also of all your outside consultants, your banker is in the best position to know of or be able to obtain pertinent inside information regarding the business you wish to purchase, the person or persons you're buying it from, and the like.

Never ever buy a business sight unseen. With precious few exceptions, never ever buy a business about which you know nothing. And never ever skip any of the foregoing steps when making and acting on a decision to purchase someone else's "baby."

It's better to let the "chance of a lifetime" get away from you than to have to live through, with, and down the mistake of a lifetime.

A couple of other important points to cover: Take the necessary legal steps to ensure that the current business owner will be prohibited from directly competing with you and "your" new firm for a reasonable number of miles, a reasonable number of years, or both. If it appears potentially important, try to legally ensure that key personnel, customers, and suppliers will likewise remain with the business. It is possible (and often profitable) to retain the owner as a part of the management team for a period of time to assist in the orderly transition from the old guard to the new. Approach the purchase of an existing business with the same healthy cynicism that you'd take to Honest John's car lot. Don't just kick the tires and drive the old clunker around the block. Assume you're about to buy someone else's headache, have the old heap checked out thoroughly by qualified mechanics, and get the best guarantee possible in writing.

Last but not least, if you find that you can start a similar new firm with comparable location, equipment, inventory, and personnel for considerably less money, give that option the careful consideration it deserves.

FRANCHISE SCHEMES AND THINGS

Question: When are you starting a new business at the same time you are purchasing an existing business? Answer: When you become a franchisee.

While I will not denigrate the veritable revolution that franchising represents in American small business today, please be aware that there are at least as many (maybe more!) horror stories as happy endings in the franchising storybook.

Franchising is essentially a system of distribution. Depending on the contract, an individually owned business is operated as though it were part of a large chain and uses "corporate" trademarks, design, equipment, symbols, and standardized products or services. It can cover a single product or involve an entire turnkey business operation.

We will confine our exploration of franchising to the "package deal" definition of the term.

While it is possible to purchase a franchise from a franchisee (all the rules of buying an existing business apply plus, in most instances, the need to gain the approval of the franchisor—or parent company—before culminating the deal), most potential franchisees deal directly with the franchisor; put up varying amounts of cash; wait varying amounts of time while a site is selected and construction or renovation is completed; and the "store of their dreams," complete with stock, personnel, and grand opening banners, is ready for business. During the wait, the franchisee (that's you) has had varying amounts of input into the process and received varying amounts of training in how to generate varying amounts of profit from the new franchise.

Needless to say, the results also vary from the small and not-so-small fortunes made by franchise owners of McDonald's hamburgers and Kentucky Fried Chicken outlets to the financial disaster experienced by both franchisor and franchisee in the now-defunct Minnie Pearl chicken operation. Many attempts at local, regional, and national franchisor activities fail, taking lots of life savings along with them. Many more franchisors tend to quietly ignore the individual franchisee who doesn't make it, or what may even be the majority of franchisees who have risked their financial future for the "privilege" of working inordinately long hours for a barely living wage.

A good franchise is expensive and usually very difficult to come by. A bad franchise may start out cheap, end up expensive, and will almost always be a snap to purchase.

There are some very good things a good franchise operation offers the aspiring entrepreneur. The right franchise can minimize the risk of failure since you won't be starting a "new" business, but rather a "branch" of an already accepted and established product or service complete with corporate trademark and loyal customers.

In addition to the "instant" product identification and customer loyalty that a good franchise can represent, one of the major pluses to the brand-new business owner is the training, management, and technical assistance provided by the franchisor. This assistance can include everything from a school of several weeks at company headquarters to hiring and training the personnel necessary to adequately staff your establishment. Some franchisors even offer financial assistance, granting the necessary lines of credit to qualified franchisees to establish or expand their outlets.

Now for the bad stuff. Operating a franchise can be very confining—while you own your own business, you will have and answer to numerous supervisors from franchise headquarters. Your franchise agreement will likely mandate certain standards of quality, conduct, and rules and regulations under which you must operate or be subject to the loss of your franchise. To many entrepreneurs, these constraints rankle emotionally. Many others have found them both restrictive and costly in a bottom-line sense.

Some franchises come into existence because a manufacturer or distributor needs a regular outlet for a specific product or service. A large flour mill operation, for example, started a pizza franchise as a means of "growing its own" market for white flour products. The franchise operation proved extremely successful. However, the franchisees and franchisor eventually ended up in court when the franchisees discovered that the extremely high-priced "special recipe" pizza mix they were mandated to use was nothing more than the franchisor's own flour with a few other ingredients—all priced several times over their true market worth. The franchise contract under which the franchisees operated forbade the purchase or use of any pizza ingredient from any source save the franchisor. It took a long and costly court fight to break that contract clause.

Such sole-source clauses are extremely common in franchise contracts. Proceed with great caution and lots of good legal advice if the franchise you're interested in comes complete with such clauses.

A number of franchise holders of a moderately successful women's boutique chain, for instance, had great difficulty getting their orders filled on a timely basis. Since their franchise contract precluded them buying clothing on the open market, the slow service was more than frustrating—it was financially detrimental, to say the least. There was no intentional wrongdoing on the part of this franchisor; it was simply a matter of too-fast expansion for the production department back in New York City to cope with. That sort of explanation is very small consolation, indeed, when it's *your* store that needs merchandise right now!

If you approach franchising knowing full well what it is and what it isn't, its advantages and disadvantages, you'll infinitely enhance your prospects for a pleasant and profitable experience.

The number 1 advantage of franchising is that it enables you, the investor, to capitalize on experience you might otherwise have to get the hard way—through trial and error. Your parent company will use its experience in business location, management, publicity, advertising, product research and development, etc., so that you'll start and operate your outlet with optimum efficiency, minimum frustration, and maximum profitability. Especially if you're buying into a truly successful franchise, it would probably take years of promotion and investment to build comparable identity and goodwill.

Your first contact with a franchisor could come as a result of spotting a classified advertisement, magazine ad, or a discreetly placed sign in another franchisee's already operating outlet. Some parent companies mandate extensive personal interviews, psychological evaluation and testing, and specific background requirements, in addition to the always-present capital investment requirements. Many a potential franchisee has been both shocked and angered to discover that it takes more than money to be granted a franchise. As a matter of fact, the easier it is to purchase a franchise, the more leery you should be! Many of the "fast buck" or "front-money" people who will sell a franchise to anyone with the initial investment are really selling nothing but equipment and a catchy name. Once you own the equipment, they couldn't care less whether you succeed or fail.

Be certain that you're dealing with a reputable company. Absolutely check with your local Better Business Bureau, the National Better Business Bureau, your local chamber of commerce, and your banker before proceeding with negotiations. You should get a complete credit report on the company offering the franchise. It's also a good idea to obtain a similar credit report on the individuals involved as principals in the franchise operation. Your banker can help with the credit checks.

One other good technique for validating the company and its track record is to obtain a list of existing franchisees. Write letters and make phone calls and (if at all possible) personal visits to as many of the franchise locations as you can. Count and observe customers, what they buy, how much the average ticket totals, and so on. Ask the franchisees not only about their individual businesses, but also about their views of the franchisor and its service—or lack thereof—to the franchisees.

In dealing with the parent company, find out when the firm was established. Request a specimen contract that your attorney can study and approve. If they won't provide such a document, better run fast in the opposite direction.

Find out how many franchises are currently operating and, even more important, how many have been sold that are no longer operating—and why they're not. Check the company policy regarding the resolution of differences with franchises. How does the company provide continuing assistance for its franchisees? Will you have regular visits from parent company personnel? Will someone come when you cry help or are you pretty much on your own?

The key to franchising success is the license or franchise contract. They can range from a simple one-page letter of agreement to highly complex legal documents in which every conceivable detail of your business operation is covered. Some contracts, in addition to specifying the exact products and services which a franchisee may sell under the company's name, also dictate the hours and days of business, the types of uniforms (if any) to be worn by franchisees and their employees, and from whom you may obtain all the materials and supplies necessary for business operation.

A franchise contract should never be signed without legal counsel. Your attorney may be able to negotiate a change or a compromise in the contract language that will be to your distinct advantage. Among the areas your attorney should check are:

Is there a franchise fee? If so, what is the basis for it?

What is the total cash investment required? What are the terms for financing the balance? Does the cash investment include payment for fixtures and equipment? How do prices charged for such furniture and equipment compare with current competitive prices in the open marketplace?

Are there continuing royalties? If so, how much? How are they determined? By whom are they determined?

Will you be required to participate in company-sponsored publicity and promotion? If so, to what extent? Will you have any say in how such an advertising fund is utilized?

Under what conditions may your franchise be canceled?

If the parent company's service or product is protected by patent or liability insurance, is this same protection extended to you, the franchisee?

Under what terms may you sell your franchise?

Will you be mandated to sell any new products introduced by the parent company after you have opened your business?

What form of continuing assistance is the parent company obligated to give you after you are operating your business? Is such training mandatory on your part?

How can you terminate your franchise agreement if you're unhappy with the situation?

Even the very best of franchise opportunities is not a ticket to ride. There just is no such thing as a free lunch. The right franchise, properly managed and staffed, can be an excellent place to invest your time, effort, and money. The wrong franchise has been, is, and will be a great way to lose it all for the sucker naive enough to be taken in. And in between the two are hundreds and hundreds of small franchise outlets at which the owner (or owners) works much too hard, much too long, for much too little.

Whether you are interested in becoming a franchisee or think that your thriving business could, itself, be successfully franchised, seek and take the best available legal advice. Franchising—whether you're the buyer or the seller—is based on a contractual relationship. And the professional best-equipped to oversee what goes into or out of a contract (depending on your point of view) is a lawyer.

BUSINESS HAS GOT TO BE BUSINESS
(SELLING TO AND WORKING WITH FRIENDS
AND FAMILY)

Management problems in a family-owned business can be somewhat different from the problems faced in a nonfamily business. Emotions tend to interfere with business decisions when close relatives work together. Some family-owned companies find the control of daily operations a real problem. In others, the high turnover rate of nonfamily staff members presents a problem. Still other firms find some relatives unwilling to plow profits back into the business while the rest view change of any sort as an affront to family tradition.

Every family has a turkey or two who just can't seem to hang on to a job or always have money problems. A family-owned business is usually under special pressure to hire this black sheep brother-in-law or nerd of a niece. The equitable division of both workload and profit can present some highly emotional problems. In truth, the problems of operating a small firm owned and/or staffed by family members or close friends are the same as any other batch of small business problems. Only more so.

I would strongly recommend full discussion and commitment to paper of all rights, responsibilities, privileges, and payoffs of each family member involved in the business operation. If the business will be operated as a corporation, naming individuals who are not relatives to the board of directors can often inject both balance and reason into the firm.

Come to a firm agreement regarding the firm's policy toward other family members not involved directly in the business operation. The same should be done for close friends.

The decision may well be that business has got to be business, no matter whether the customer is your mother-in-law or your spouse's best army buddy. Some family-owned firms solve the problem by offering a uniform discount on goods and services to all family members or close friends.

It's not an easy subject with which to come to grips. And there is no right or wrong way to deal with it.

Three books that may offer a little insight and assistance are:

Edwin J. Bradley (Ed.), *Close Corporations*, Learner Law Book Company, Inc., Washington, D.C., 1967 (available in paperback).

Theadore Ness and E. L. Vogel, *Taxation of the Closely Held Corporation*, Ronald Press Company, New York, 1972.

F. H. O'Neal, *Expulsion or Oppression of Business Associates*, Duke University Press, Durham, N.C. 27708, 1961.

My final words on the matter are "Good luck!"

9

Money Matters

"It takes money to make money."

Gee! I wish I'd said that!

Most budding businesspersons have a little money. Some even have a lot of money. But almost none have enough money.

Owing directly, I suppose, to their lack of management ability, too many small business owners compound the undercapitalization problem they face by expending too much of their precious cash on leasehold improvements, inventory, equipment, and the other necessities of business life that lead to opening day.

Very often, astute business owners can negotiate some—if not all—the necessary leasehold improvements into their monthly lease payments, or a combination of increased lease payments and a "balloon" payment can be arranged at some date in the future when cash reserves of the business should be in an improved condition. Proper inventory management could result in more liberal trade credit agreements and, perhaps, inventory delivery at timed intervals which would keep the shop's stock at the proper levels but would not force the owner (that's you!) to pay for inventory that does nothing but sit on the back shelves for weeks or even months.

In the case of fixtures and equipment, almost without exception new entrepreneurs have the mistaken notion that they must purchase rather than rent everything they need immediately. At least at the start, your rule should be "never buy when you can lease; seldom lease without a purchase option; and think *used* before you think new."

While I'm sure a few crusty old arch conservatives still exist who'll caution you against ever borrowing money, and, on the other side of the spectrum, there are some wildly successful dynamos of business who'll expound that you should never use your own money—always borrow—I take a moderate, middle-of-the-road approach to the subject. Borrow when there's a need, never borrow too much, and never borrow too little.

One of the most valuable skills a business owner can have is knowing *how* to borrow money. It *is* a skill; consequently, it can be learned.

Probably the most important thing to determine is what kind of money you are seeking. You have three basic options: short-term money, term money, and equity capital.

The purpose for which the funds are to be used and the source of repayment are both important factors in deciding the kind of money needed. It's not always a clear-cut situation. You may be using some of various kinds of money at the same time and for the same purposes. Short-term bank loans are probably the most common form of business financing. You can use short-term bank loans for purposes such as financing accounts receivables, for, say, 30 to 60 days. Or they can be used for building a seasonal inventory over a period of 5 to 6 months. Usually, lenders expect short-term loans to be repaid as soon as their purposes have been served. For example, an accounts receivable loan is paid as soon as the outstanding accounts have been paid by your customers, and inventory loans are serviced shortly after the merchandise has been sold.

Banks can grant such money either on your general credit reputation with an unsecured loan or on a secured-loan basis—against collateral.

An unsecured loan relies entirely on your credit reputation. The secured loan involves a pledge of some or all your assets. If you don't pay the loan in a satisfactory manner, the bank can seize the collateral which it will then liquidate to pay off the loan.

Term borrowing provides money you plan to pay back over a fairly long period of time. It is sometimes broken into two forms: (1) intermediate—loans longer than 1 year but less than 5 years—and (2) long-term—loans for more than 5 years.

To help you match the kind of money you seek to the needs of your company, think of term borrowing as a kind of money which you will probably pay back in periodic installments from earnings.

The difference between term borrowing and equity capital tends to confuse some people. There is a big difference. You don't have to repay equity (or investment) capital. It is money you obtain by selling a part interest in your firm. In so doing, you take investors into your business who are willing to risk their money by buying into it. They are interested in potential income rather than a fairly immediate return on their investment. Equity capital is not borrowed money. But it is sometimes the ideal—or at least preferable—source of funds and should never be overlooked.

How much is enough? The amount of money you need to borrow depends on the purpose for which you need the funds. It is relatively easy to figure the amount of money required for business start-up, construction, conversion, or expansion. Suppliers, equipment manufacturers, architects, and builders will be more than happy to supply you with cost estimates. It is much more difficult to estimate the amount of working capital you'll need since that varies widely and depends upon the type of business you're in and how cost-efficiently you can operate your firm.

While rule of thumb ratios can provide a starting point, a detailed projection of sources and uses of funds over some future period of time (usually 12 months) is a better approach. These projections are developed through the combination of a predicted budget and cash forecast. The budget is obviously your best estimate of your firm's performance during the coming period. The cash forecast is your estimated cash receipts and disbursements during the same budget period.

To plan your working capital requirements, you must know the cash flow which your firm will generate.

In addition to assisting you in establishing goals and quotas for your staff and yourself, your cash flow projections can assist you in borrowing what you need, when you need it, in a planned, orderly fashion.

Bankers (those folks from whom you borrow) are usually rather conservative human beings. As such, they do not react well to individuals or businesses that seem to survive in chaos and crises. We've already established the fact that the worst time to borrow money is when you really need it. Your cash flow projection can minimize crisis borrowing, enhance your image with your banker, and maybe even keep your ulcer under control. It is a written, month-by-month estimate of how much cash you'll have—and need—over the next year or two.

It's easy to imagine how much more favorable the response will be when you approach your banker in February to secure a line of credit to be used to cover a projected (planned and expected) cash shortfall in June and July and (barring an act of God) to be repaid in equal installments come October, November, and December.

The opposite of this nice, tidy, orderly picture is the all-too-common scenario in which our neophyte entrepreneur approaches the loan officer in a state of panic on a hot, late-August afternoon and announces: "My account's overdrawn, I can't meet next week's payroll, and several of my suppliers are threatening to cut off my credit unless I pay immediately! Things are bound to get better around Christmas. You've just got to give me this loan!"

The simple cash flow form provided in Figure 12 (see p. 184) may be used as a guide to help you project and plan for your operating capital needs. If this is your first shot at a cash flow projection, you might want to enlist the aid of your accountant. If the process absolutely boggles your mind, assign the responsibility for filling out, monitoring, and updating your firm's cash flow to someone adequate to the task.

Before a bank or any other lending institution will lend you money, the lending officer must feel satisfied with the answers to the following five questions:

1. What sort of person are you, the prospective borrower? The personal character of the borrower comes first. Second in importance is your ability to manage your business.

2. What do you plan to do with the money? The answer to this question will determine the type of loan, short or long term. Loan proceeds to be used for the purchase of seasonal inventory will require quicker repayment than money which will be used to purchase fixed assets.

3. When and how do you plan to repay the loan? Your banker's judgment as to your business ability and the type of loan will both be deciding factors in the answer to this question.

4. Is the "cushion" in the loan large enough? In other words, do the business projections and the requested loan amount make suitable allowances for unexpected developments? The loan officer will decide this question on the basis of your financial statement, an analysis of the projected cash flow of the firm, and/or on the collateral pledged to secure the loan.

5. What is the general business outlook? What is the outlook for your particular firm?

Banks want to make loans to businesses which are solvent, profitable, and growing. The two basic financial statements used to determine those conditions are the balance sheet and the profit and loss statement. The balance sheet is the yardstick for solvency; the profit and loss statement measures profits. Analyzing a continuous series of these two statements over a period of time is the principal means for measuring the financial stability and growth potential of an existing business.

When you are seeking to borrow money for a brand-new firm with no proven track record, your personal experience and character, enhanced by a first-rate loan proposal package, are all the loan officer has to go on. So it behooves you to make them look as good as possible.

It helps to know exactly what a banker looks for in deciding whether to accept or reject the loan application. In interviewing you, the loan applicant, and reviewing your firm's records, the loan officer is especially interested in the answers to the following questions:

General Information

If yours is an existing business, are the books and records up to date and in good condition? What is the condition of accounts payable? Notes payable? What are the salaries of the owner, manager, and other company officers? Are they in line with prevailing rates being paid by similar firms in the market?

Are all taxes being paid currently? Is there an order backlog? What is the number of employees? What is the firm's insurance coverage?

Accounts Receivable

Has any portion of the accounts receivable already been pledged to another creditor? What is the accounts receivable turnover? Of the total accounts receivable, which are in the 30-, 60-, 90-day or 120-day-and-over column? Has a large enough reserve been set aside to cover uncollectible accounts? How much do the largest accounts owe? What percentage of total accounts receivable do these large clients represent?

Inventories

Is merchandise in good shape, or will it have to be marked down to be sold? How much raw material is on hand? How much work is in progress? How much of the inventory is finished goods? Is there obsolete inventory on hand? Has an excessive amount of inventory been consigned to customers? Is inventory turnover in line with industry averages? Is too much money being tied up for too long in inventory?

Fixed Assets

What is the age, type, and condition of the firm's equipment? What are the depreciation policies? What are the details of mortgages, leases, or conditional sales contracts? What are the firm's future acquisition plans, if any?

Sometimes, your signature is the only security the bank needs when making a loan. At other times, the bank requires additional assurances that the loan will be repaid. The kind and amount of security (collateral) depend on the bank, the amount of the loan, and the borrower's individual situation.

If the borrower's financial statements alone cannot justify lending the amount requested, the types of security lenders usually find acceptable are endorsers, comakers, guarantors, assignment of leases, trust receipts and floor planning, chattel mortgages, real estate, accounts receivables, savings accounts, life insurance policies, and stocks and bonds.

In addition to expecting prompt debt service (paying principal and interest on time and in full), lenders will sometimes set limitations and restrictions under which you must operate your business during the period of time the loan is outstanding. The limitations and requirements which you will usually run into when you borrow money concern (1) repayment terms, (2) pledging or use of security, and (3) periodic reporting.

Restrictions that may be set down in the loan agreement will be found in the section known as covenance. Negative covenants are things which the borrower may not do without prior approval from the lender. Such approval, incidentally, must usually be obtained in writing. Some examples of moves requiring approval are further additions to the borrower's total debt, pledges to others of the borrower's assets, and issuance of dividends in excess of the terms of the loan agreement. On the other hand, positive covenances spell out things which the borrower must do. Examples are maintaining the minimum net working capital amount, carrying adequate insurance, repaying the loan according to the terms of the agreement, and supplying the lender with financial statements and reports at stated and agreed-upon intervals. Sometimes the lender will mandate that these financial statements and reports be prepared by a certified public accountant.

Some business owners resent the limitations and restrictions a lender attaches to the loan transaction. I admire an independent spirit and remind you that the option always exists to tell the lender to keep his or her money. I would also remind you that reasonable limitations and restrictions are a protection not only for the lender, but also for you, the borrower: They set forth rules a good manager would seek to follow whether or not they were imposed.

Also be advised that loan agreements may be amended from time to time and exceptions can be made. If, for instance, you find during the life of the loan that it is very much in the best interests of your business to increase your debt by adding a certain piece of equipment or by increasing the size of inventory in order to take advantage of market conditions conducive to profits, your banker would have to be bonkers to turn down such a request. It goes without saying that the request should be made properly and come complete with substantiating documentation. But the banker and you share the same interests during the life of the loan: namely, that the business succeed and prosper.

Certainly, you'll want to negotiate the terms under which the loan will be made before you sign. No matter how badly you may need the money, it's good business to get the loan papers in advance of closing and have them reviewed by your attorney and/or accountant. Remember, once the terms and conditions under which the loan has been granted have been finalized by your signature, you are bound by them. Negotiate them carefully, have the legal documents reviewed by your trusted advisers, and don't sign what you (a) don't agree to or (b) don't understand.

Most financing for small business comes from banks and other private lending institutions. A good number of these small business loans are made possible through the U.S. Small Business Administration's (SBA) guarantee program. Under this program, the loan is made by the lending institution and the federal government, through the SBA, guarantees 90 percent of the total amount of the loan. This cuts the bank's exposure to 10 percent of the transaction total and has definitely made possible business financing where none would have been available without the guarantee program. It requires the filling out of several additional forms and adds a couple of weeks to the time it takes to complete the transaction, but it is sometimes the only way a business loan can be obtained.

In addition, the SBA guarantee program tends to make the lowest possible interest rates available to the small business owner and makes possible long-term financing. The SBA sets the maximum interest rate allowable on a guaranteed loan, and it's often a point or two lower than you'd pay on a non-SBA guarantee note.

As a rough rule of thumb, I would not recommend seeking the SBA's participation in a loan of less than $5000 or in a situation where your firm could comfortably effect a payoff within 3 years or less. The SBA guarantee program is ideal for larger amounts of money spread over a longer period of time.

While there are no minimum loan amount requirements set by SBA, there are maximum limits currently set at $350,000. This upper limit can be pushed as high as $500,000 if you happen to be a member of a legally recognized minority group and are seeking to purchase a Federal Communication Commission (FCC)-licensed property (i.e., a radio or television station). The SBA didn't lend money on FCC-licensed radio and television stations or newspapers and other mass communication businesses until very recently when a growing awareness of the need to assist more minorities in obtaining media ownership led to new rules and priorities.

The guidelines for the SBA Loan Guarantee Program suggest that a business be turned down by two commercial banks before the SBA guarantee can be sought and obtained. While it's certainly no big trick to get two banks to say no, I have assisted clients in obtaining hundreds of SBA guaranteed loans without ever going through the nonsense of obtaining two bank turndowns. Do check it out if you're interested: There's considerable variance in interpreting the regulations, and your SBA regional office may stick closer to the rule book than some of the others.

The SBA annually receives a very small amount of money (relatively speaking) to be utilized in special direct loan programs. Included are equal opportunity loans which are earmarked for minorities and women who can prove social and/or economic deprivation and who have absolutely no chance for obtaining funding through open-market sources. Also included are loans to physically handicapped entrepreneurs. Chances for obtaining one of these direct loans, even if you meet the criteria, are really slim to nonexistent. The demand for dollars far exceeds their supply. But it's worth looking into (if for no other reason than that the interest rates tend to be one-half or less than the prevailing rates being charged by commercial banks).

The need and/or desirability of SBA involvement in your business loan is a decision only you can reach. I would venture to say, when it's time to seek long-term big bucks, you'll both want and need the SBA Guarantee Program.

With or without the government's participation, the documents and data you should compile and present to your banker when requestng a loan can—and will—make the difference between yes and no. I warn you: It takes quite a lot of work to do it right. But here's how it's done.

THE PERFECT LOAN SITUATION

The perfect loan situation involves the coming together of a variety of conditions. If you're starting a new business, you must show the financial institution with whom you are working that you have adequate personal experience in a business similar to the one you want to start. At least some of this experience should have been in a management or supervisory capacity. You can get creative and substitute related experience if you lack actual direct experience in the type of business you are opening. It is also possible to have a management team (two or three persons) to substitute for one well-qualified owner. The team could be made up of (1) an owner who has good management experience but little knowledge of selling, (2) someone with a strong sales background who has little or no management experience, and (3) a supervisor knowledgeable in producing the product or service but with little or no selling or management experience. All members of the team need not have ownership or a financial interest in the new firm. If they do not, it will strengthen your loan position if you have an employment contract and/or if part of the team members' compensation is related to the profitability of the firm.

You should be able to prove to the financial institution that you're a good money manager by showing a good personal net worth, a savings account commensurate with your income, and a good credit rating. You will also be able to reflect stability through such things as the time you've lived in the local area, the length of time at your present residence, the length of time on your present job, and the number of years you have been married (if applicable).

A loan officer will want to feel that you have planned adequately for this business venture. You can prove this by demonstrating the length of time you've been planning to go into business and any steps you've taken to prepare yourself for opening day. These can include full- or part-time employment, volunteer activities, and any special education you've obtained to prepare yourself for successful business operation.

You'll be able to show initiative by showing the loan officer that you've done more than could normally be expected of you. If, for example, you're an engineer and you want to open a shoe store, you may be able to prove that you've had a part-time job in a shoe store for the past 5 years and have consequently learned all phases of the shoe business. It is also critically important to show family involvement. Even if your spouse is not going to be directly involved in day-to-day business operations, having his or her full support can be extremely important to the success of the firm.

Last but certainly not least, you must have *in cash* from 10 to 30 percent of the total amount estimated as necessary to start the business. In a few rare instances, financial institutions will lend more than 90 percent if there is an exceptionally good reason why you've not been able to come up with the standard cash injection. If, for example, you have a very large family and a relatively low income. A 20 percent cash injection is a lot more "ideal."

Loan requirements for existing businesses are very similar; add to the above list financial statements that show that the business has been profitable or (at a minimum) has shown a loss but has been indicating marked improvement in sales and profits in recent months. The financial statements must show why the money must be borrowed and for what purposes. The analysis of these statements must show how the loan will improve the profitability of the company. In general, with an existing business your financial statements are the main basis for determining whether your loan request will be approved or rejected.

Now we come to the important stuff: how to put together a first-rate loan *proposal*. And the difference between a loan proposal and a loan application is very often the difference between a "yes" and "no."

Any imbecile can apply for a loan. But it takes some smarts, effort, and hard work to put together a first-rate loan proposal. Your loan proposal should be designed to answer any potential questions before they're asked, explain away any weaknesses that might exist in your individual business situation, show that you have what it takes to operate your business profitably and to pay back the loan you're seeking, and make it easy for the loan officer to say yes instead of no.

It is a collection of meaningful documents put together in an orderly and comprehensive manner. It includes the following:

Personal Data

Include your personal résumé and personal financial statement. The résumé should stress direct and related professional experience. If you are operating as a partnership or corporation, include the résumés of all partners and stockholders with more than a 20 percent interest in the corporation. If you are augmenting your own personal experience with a management team approach, include the résumés of all key staff members.

Tax Returns

Include your personal income tax returns for the past 3 years. If you are already in business, include informational or corporate tax returns. This will provide the loan officer with valuable information on your past, present, and projected incomes. It will show, for instance, that you are not planning to pay yourself an inflated salary, using the proceeds of the loan to accomplish this payment.

Legal Documents

Include copies of your lease agreement (or intent-to-lease information), partnership agreements, articles of incorporation, lease-purchase agreements, notes, and any and all legal documents that impact your current and future business operation.

Loan Application Forms

Include completed, accurate application forms required by the lending institution with whom you're dealing. If you are seeking an SBA guaranteed loan, also include the requisite forms, again accurately completed and signed.

Collateral

Provide a complete list of the collateral you're pledging to secure the loan. As applicable, the listing of collateral should include the current value of each item and serial numbers and/or descriptions. If you will be using any of the loan proceeds to purchase inventory and equipment which will become collateral when acquired, include them too.

Business Financial Statements

For an existing firm, include financial statements as current as possible, certainly no older than 60 days. For a new firm, provide pro forma statements. Keep your projections conservative. It's a big plus also to include a break-even analysis and margin-of-safety analysis.

Profit Forecast

Include a 2-year cash flow analysis and profit forecast. You can sometimes get by with 1-year projections, but 2-year figures are by far the more ideal way to go.

Use of Loan Funds

Here, spell out very carefully exactly how you will use the proceeds from the loan, if granted. Include backup documentation such as quotes, estimates, bids, price lists, etc. If working capital is part of the total amount requested, don't ask for more than 3 months' worth. This is especially crucial with an SBA guarantee. N.B.: The SBA won't (and bankers don't like to) lend new firms money to purchase land and/or buildings. The SBA *will* lend for this purpose to existing firms with a proven track record.

Business Plan

On two to four neatly typewritten pages, commit the following information to paper:

1. Structure of business: Let the banker know whether you're a sole proprietor, involved in a partnership, or doing business as a corporation. You'll want to include an organizational chart if the size of your staff warrants this.

2. Your contribution to the business: Include a brief synopsis of what you bring (or brought) to the firm. Include both monetary and personal contributions. Keep in mind, the banker wants to feel that you have a bigger stake in this business than does the bank.

3. Source of customers: Explain the need and/or demand for your product or service. Also include information on how you intend to draw customers to your firm; how you intend to advertise and promote your shop.

4. Competition: List competitors, include their location, geographic proximity to your firm, their major strengths and weaknesses, how those strengths and weaknesses compare with yours, major differences between your operation and theirs, and how you intend to capitalize on or minimize those differences.

5. Facilities: Describe your physical location, including the type of building; adequacy of parking; position vis-à-vis major thoroughfares and traffic patterns; pertinent lease details such as renewal clauses, number of square feet, and potential for expansion if pertinent and applicable. It's a good idea to include a floor plan and architect's sketches, if available.

6. Need for product or service: Spell out the reasons your firm should come into existence (or grow a little bigger).

7. Other pertinent facts: Add anything you think will strengthen your case not already covered by all the above. This might include a quote from a major publication indicating upward trend in your industry or any special personal information about yourself such as awards or honors.

This "mini-feasibility study" should assume that the loan officer knows absolutely nothing about your specific kind of business.

Loan Proposal Highlights

Use this section to point out any strong points and to explain away the few not-so-strong ones.

Miscellaneous

This section of your proposal might include copies of newspaper or magazine articles providing background data on your specific business or on the geographic location in which you will operate. You might want to include letters of intent from existing or potential customers as applicable, letters of recommendation or commendation, copies of advertising material; in short, anything that will help the loan officer better understand your business.

It's obviously a lot of work to put together a good loan proposal. The finished product may be 2 to 3 inches thick! But it immediately indicates to the person with veto or approval power over your request that you've got your act together; that you're a serious, informed, knowledgeable businessperson who knows where you're going and how you're going to get there.

You may want to get help putting your loan proposal together. Possible sources of such help include your attorney, your accountant, a management consultant (some of them know what they're doing), or a nonprofit business development organization. You'll find information on such organizations in Chapter 15 (Parting Shots, Where to Look for Help).

In any event, when you've got it all assembled, make three copies of the entire proposal if you are seeking SBA participation in the loan; two copies if it's just you and the bank. Present the loan officer or branch manager with one or two copies, depending on whether the SBA is to be involved. Keep the other copy for your own future use.

I have personally used this loan proposal format to successfully obtain millions of dollars in small business loans.

It truly is the ideal way to request a business loan. You'll not only enhance significantly the chances of your loan request being approved, you'll also know one heck of a lot more about what you're doing, why you're doing it, how you're doing it, where you're going, and how you're going to get there. With all that knowledge and all that money you ought to have it made.

THE NOT-SO-PERFECT LOAN
SITUATION

What do you do when all is not well? When, say, your credit record's a little less than sterling, there's something in your past you'd rather forget, or you waited too long to seek a loan and now your business is in considerable trouble?

There are dozens and dozens of facts and situations that can make you or your firm a not-so-perfect loan candidate. Whatever the problem, whatever the situation, whatever can you do?

Obviously, if you have time to rectify the situation, fix it first and then apply for the loan. Your next best strategy (and it's an absolute must!) is to tell the truth. The cardinal rule when applying for a business loan is "no surprises."

Whatever the situation, whatever the facts, you're a lot better off having your loan officer hear it from you, not the credit bureau, or the FBI (which runs a background check in the case of an SBA or other government-backed loan). I have obtained SBA guaranteed business loans at some very conservative banks for business owners with not just one but two bankruptcies in their background! Similarly, loans have been negotiated for business owners who served time in prison, some of them for some pretty heavy-duty offenses!

I remember one case in particular where a loan was granted to a woman who had served several years in a state penitentiary for the second-degree murder of her spouse. The loan officer's response, once he'd regained his composure, was simply, "Well, she obviously didn't much like her husband. Maybe she had good reason. I'm sure she'll like her customers a lot better. It would be bad for business to kill them off!"

The remark was perhaps not in the greatest taste, but it is a good illustration of how almost anything can be explained away if done properly.

If you blew it, you blew it. Explain what happened, why, and how the money you're requesting will help you turn things around, the specific steps you are taking to preclude this particular bit of history from repeating itself. You can turn almost any negative into a positive with some thought and effort. If, for instance, you got stuck with a couple of rather large bad debts, your loan proposal should stress what happened, why, and, most important, what specific steps you have taken to ensure that this will never happen again. This might include a new "COD-only" policy or new, tighter credit and collection controls.

This is where the loan proposal can save both you and your business. Your proposal provides you the opportunity to identify whatever problems exist and to outline your solution to each of them. You honestly point out the negative, but don't stop there: Every mistake can be a lesson learned; every foolish move can leave you wiser. Continue every negative to a positive conclusion.

Lest you think I'm Pollyanna, let me ask you two questions:

1. Did you learn anything from your mistake or are you as dumb as before?

2. Do you want this loan or not?

If the answer is (1) "yes," and (2) "yes," do as I say.

THE SBA AND OTHER ACRONYMS

I'd like you to meet my favorite federal agency, the United States Small Business Administration (fondly referred to as the SBA). It's not perfection, but it's the best we've got going.

Since it was established by Congress in 1953, the SBA has provided a wide range of services to potential, promising, thriving, and failing firms, throughout these fifty states. In many cases, SBA assistance made it possible for folks to start businesses, save businesses, or expand businesses. In not a few instances, the bureaucrats at SBA did too little and/or too late. Those firms aren't with us anymore. But, then, nobody's perfect.

While I confess to being a reasonably devoted SBA fan, there are two areas at SBA with which I have major concerns. The first is a lack of staff capability to provide one-on-one management and technical assistance, including the ability to assist a business owner in the development of a loan proposal. About all you'll get at most SBA field offices are the blank forms and a cheery "good luck!"

Some offices just provide the forms.

My second major concern are the variances in service from one federal region to another, one field office to another. I guess it's to be expected since there are ten regions and ninety-plus SBA field offices. But I still find it a little hard to understand why one SBA office can process a loan application and give you a "yes" or "no" in a maximum 10-day time frame, while an SBA office halfway across the country takes four times as long. Oh, well.

The SBA Guarantee Loan Program is probably the agency's most important and widely used program. By law, the agency may not make a loan if your business can obtain funds from a bank or other private source. Theoretically, you're supposed to seek funding and be turned down by a couple of private lending institutions before SBA steps in to save the day and guarantee the loan. In actuality, no one's all that sticky about it. After all, all you have to do is ask a banker the wrong way, and I assure you, he or she will be most happy to provide you with a letter of rejection.

The SBA's Equal Opportunity Loans Program (EOL) is one of its most misunderstood programs. There's precious little money for them to lend through this program—which operates directly from SBA with no lending institutions. As I said early on, there is precious little EOL money available they are made at interest rates considerably below those of the market, and they are available exclusively to minorities and those few nonminorities which can prove extreme social and/or economic disadvantage. An EOL loan absolutely requires written proof of loan denial by several commercial lending instutitions. As I said early on, there is precious little EOL money available and the competition is fierce. If you think you might be eligible and interested, get the details from your nearest SBA field office, and pray.

In addition to regular business loans and equal opportunity loans, SBA provides a number of special financial assistance programs. These include local-development company loans, state-development company loans, pool loans (not as in swimming pool but as in corporations formed and capitalized by groups of small business companies to purchase materials, equipment, etc.), revolving line of credit guarantees, displaced-business loans, handicapped assistance loans (for the physically handicapped—extending to both private and nonprofit operations), disaster recovery loans (for both small and large businesses, and private homes), and base-closing economic injury loans (yes, as in military base).

The exotic list continues with strategic arms economic injury loans, emergency energy-shortage loans, and regulatory economic injury loans.

SBA guaranteed surety bonds have made the difference between success and failure to many small and emerging contractors who have found bonding otherwise unavailable. The SBA can guarantee up to 90 percent of losses incurred under bid, payment, or performance bonds on contracts valued up to $1 million.

It's a fairly well-kept secret, but SBA also licenses, regulates, and, in some cases, finances small business investment companies (SBICs). These SBICs can provide both venture capital and long-term financing. Some also provide management and technical assistance to the small businesses they serve. There is also the 301(d) small business investment companies which do the same thing for members of ethnic or racial minority groups. Venture (or risk) capital is about the hardest money in the world to find when you need it. It's the difference between what you have, what you can borrow, and what you need. The SBIC and 301(d) SBIC programs are making a truly significant contribution to the small business community across the nation.

In the area of procurement assistance, the SBA is responsible for monitoring the federal "set aside" program to ensure that small and minority-owned firms have an opportunity to seek and obtain government contracts. In addition, the SBA has developed subcontracting opportunities for small firms.

If you're at all interested in doing business with government, get your SBA field office to place your firm on their procurement source list. It's a fairly simple process, and could add a significant new revenue source to your firm.

The SBA is also capable of providing certificates of competency which attest to a small firm's ability to perform a specific federal contract. The SBA also runs contract-opportunity workshops and helps coordinate property sales and energy-related mineral lease contracts to ensure small business access to these sometimes, possibly, or potentially lucrative opportunities.

I've already said that I've got a problem with the lack of management assistance available through SBA. But they do try. Some of the staff are even competent to provide such counseling. In addition, there are the SCORE/ACE and Professional Association Volunteer programs; the Service Corps of Retired Executives/Active Corps of Executives provides a very real service.

You'll sometimes get "assigned" to a real turkey, but since it's free, the price is certainly right. Most of these volunteer consultants are both competent and dedicated.

In addition there are SBA Small Business Institutes scattered throughout the nation where upper-class and graduate-level students, under supervision of a faculty member and an SBA management assistance officer, provide no-cost help to small business owners.

My special favorite is the SBA Call Contract program, which provides professional management and technical assistance to small business owners from professional consulting firms under contract with SBA. Assistance ranges from accounting to engineering; consultants can be specialists in restaurants, or writing television commercials. Keep in mind that these are professionals in their field, the SBA pays the tab, and you don't even have to be an SBA borrower to be eligible. This is another well-kept secret. But now *you* know and that's all that matters.

The SBA also puts on a variety of courses, conferences, workshops, and clinics on the various subjects relating to the successful operation of a small business. Some of them are even kind of interesting. All are either free or offered at minimal fees.

Another area where SBA really does some good work is in the field of publications. The agency issues hundreds of management, technical, and marketing publications on every conceivable aspect of small business operations. Most are free of charge; others can be obtained for a small fee from the Superintendent of Documents at the U.S. Government Printing Office in Washington, D.C. The "freebies" are available at any SBA office. You can also pick up an order-by-mail blank for both the free and fee publications.

Probably the next best friend that small business has in government is the United States Department of Commerce. Commerce provides some pretty good publications, seminars, and workshops on importing and exporting. Given the balance of trade deficits we face, they are much more interested in helping you export products to other countries, but they do cover both situations when pressed.

Your local Department of Commerce office also can provide some pretty fair one-on-one technical assistance and advice on doing business overseas. When you call, ask for a trade specialist.

Tucked away in a little corner of the Commerce Department is the Minority Business Development Agency (MBDA). The MBDA is the conduit for funding a variety of business development organizations (BDOs) that provide much-needed management, technical assistance, and educational services to the minority small business community. Unfortunately, these organizations are specifically mandated to serve only firms owned and operated by members of racial or ethnic minority groups. Also unfortunate is the very limited budget MBDA has to work with.

One of the best MBDA-funded agencies, in my opinion, is the National

Economic Development Association (NEDA). Headquartered in Washington, D.C., NEDA operates offices in some eighteen cities—from Los Angeles to New York, from Chicago to San Juan, Puerto Rico. Its clientele is predominantly Hispanic. So if you live in an area where there are significant concentrations of these folks and you think you might be eligible for NEDA's services, call for an appointment. As a matter of fact, it wouldn't be a bad idea to seek them out in any event. They usually know where additional community resources are buried and will be most willing to direct you to them.

There are a number of other organizations similar to NEDA but more local in scope, such as CEDCO (The Chicago Economic Development Corporation). This agency has several offices in the greater Chicago area and serves predominately the black business community. Out in California there's a BDO called Asian, Inc. Obviously, this one serves Asian-American business owners. There are numerous others; rather than recite every conceivable letter of the alphabet, I suggest that you contact your nearest SBA and/or Department of Commerce office. Ask them where to find the nearest business development organization.

A word of warning: Everyone connected with the government speaks acronyms instead of English. They erroneously assume everyone else in the world (including you) knows what they're talking about. If they're wrong and you don't, stop them in midsentence and ask for clarification.

WHERE ELSE DO YOU GO FOR MONEY?

We've discussed the role played by banks and other lending institutions and the Small Business Administration in securing finances with which to start up or expand your shop. But where else do you go?

Back a few paragraphs I mentioned the SBICs—probably a new term to you. Your nearest SBA office can advise you of your nearest SBIC. The SBIC can be a source of venture capital (also called risk capital). This is usually the difference between what you have and what a lender will lend you. In other words, if the bank says they'll go for 80 percent of the funds you need with an SBA guarantee, you still have to come up with the 20 percent. If you only have 10 percent, an SBIC could be the source of the missing 10 percent.

In the realm of borrowed capital, you can always seek a loan from friends or family. You won't always get it, but you can always seek it.

Another relatively common source is your insurance policy.

Explore what your credit union might have to offer. There's the possibility of refinancing your home or taking a second mortgage on the old homestead.

A source of funds almost everyone overlooks is the sale of something(s) of value which you may own such as artwork, collections, stocks and bonds, jewelry, property, etc. Any or all of these things could also be pledged as collateral to make your loan request more acceptable to the lender.

You can sell an interest in your firm (remember, equity capital doesn't have to be repaid!); part of the pie is better than no pie at all. You can seek trade credit from the vendors and suppliers with whom you'll do business.

If your existence would provide a needed product or service or fulfill an EEO/AA requirement for some large company in the area, it's possible that it will either finance you or arrange for financing. Mind you, I didn't say it was likely; I said it was possible.

As an absolute last resort, there are individuals and firms who will invest in promising products or businesses. Most of them want an arm, a leg, and 90 percent ownership. It all boils down to how badly you want and/or need the money you're seeking.

Commercial banks are still the most likely source of small business financing. Keep in mind, one "no" doesn't mean that that's the final word on the subject from the banks of the world. Taking your proposal from one branch to another can make all the difference. I had a client not long ago who heard "no" twelve times. Thirteen was her lucky number. The thirteenth banker to whom she submitted her loan proposal said "yes"!

That's perseverance. And that's what it takes.

10

What the Heck Does Marketing Mean?

The word "marketing" is one of many in the English language that tend more to confuse than to clarify. It's a sort of umbrella term that covers numerous tasks, activities, and disciplines.

If, for example, a young college student claims to be a "marketing major," you're talking with someone whose academic training might lead anywhere from selling used cars to ending up chairman of the board of United Airlines.

In its most general definition, marketing is the directing of the flow of goods and services from producers to consumers or users. In retail, marketing includes buying, pricing, display, promotion, advertising, public relations, customer services, and research.

There are five basic functions you should consider when developing the marketing plan for your shop:

1. Pricing
2. Product determination
3. Distribution
4. Promotion
5. Marketing research

Pricing involves an intricate collection of events ranging from determining your firm's profit goals for the year to what percentage of markup (difference between wholesale and retail price) you will add to each of the goods or services you offer.

Product determination consists of establishing the assortment of goods to

165

be sold (or produced), as well as their qualities and physical characteristics.

Distribution, obviously, encompasses everything that's involved in getting goods and materials from where they are to where you want them and, ultimately, to where your customer wants them.

Promotion covers both personal selling and advertising. It includes deciding on what image your store will project and communicating that image to your customers and potential customers.

Marketing research is concerned with the gathering, processing, and analyzing of market information. It is an aid in the evaluation of actions already taken, as well as a guide to future planning and budgeting.

Marketing, then, is all activities, events, and circumstances that produce sales and profits for a business. It encompasses product, price, distribution, and promotion and is tied together by research which will help you set necessary goals and develop plans and strategies on how you will attain those goals.

Most small business owners neglect marketing planning even though they plan some of the other areas of their firm's operation. Formalized marketing planning is an important tool for both short-term and long-range sales and profit.

A written marketing plan provides a detailed, comprehensive blueprint that sets forth, well in advance, exactly how sales increases and gross profit goals are to be achieved. Further, it will help you coordinate all your firm's resources into a cohesive, comprehensive team effort aimed at achieving your stated goal.

To ensure continued profitability and expansion, your marketing efforts and plans have to go beyond sales projections, quotas, and cost budgeting. Your plan must elaborate the inventory you will carry, when this inventory will be ordered and delivered, and how you will support the efforts of your sales staff with compensation, advertising, sales promotion, public relations, merchandising, and display. Without this written "game plan" it is easy for one area or activity to go astray and foul up the whole works.

Begin by determining what your company can expect to do next year. Put on paper the answers to such questions as: How much of a total sales increase should the company shoot for? What dollar volume can you expect to sell next year? How will that dollar volume break down by product, service, or area? What will your gross profit on this dollar volume total? What will be the gross profit by product or service?

Determining your profit objective is a critical marketing step. Your gross expected profit determines the absolute amount you can spend to achieve that sales objective. If your goal, for example, is a 10 percent sales increase which would bring you to a gross profit of $75,000, you cannot (as a general rule) afford to spend $76,000 to attain it. You must know your anticipated gross profits before you can determine how much you can spend to get that sales increase.

Profitable marketing is based on two sets of facts. One set of facts includes information about the *market* in which you do business. You need to know the vital statistics, trends, and current data about your market for your type of business. Keep in mind, you are looking for both your long-range and your short-term probabilities. If possible, go back several years in your data collection to uncover trends on which you can base potential sales figures. County and "market area" data of the U.S. Census are available for almost every element that has a major bearing on your particular business prospects. Determine which of these market factors affect you and get the figures that have a bearing on those factors. This could be information on family income, the number of new single-family dwellings constructed in the area, the number of people employed outside the home in your area, the number of women of a certain age group, or any of dozens of other information categories—depending on the type of business in which you are involved.

You can interpret all these facts and figures and predetermine your opportunity for a sales increase and whether you'll have to go with or against the stream.

The other set of facts is about *your* marketing: about what you and your people do in selling your products or services. Look at everything: Your purpose is to seek out and eliminate weaknesses which will hamper your effort to reach your stated sales goal. Check your inventory mix, pricing, and ordering and delivery schedules, sales approach and quotas, displays, and advertising.

When you have both sets of facts, you are ready to lay out each of the segments of your individual marketing plan. Develop each part (i.e., advertising, inventory ordering and delivery, sales promotion and compensation) of your written marketing plan under definite timetables: monthly, quarterly, 1 year, 5 years. Develop a written plan for each part and use it for reference. Establish guidelines to steer you on a set course. Absolutely refuse to allow employees to vary from these guidelines unless you are aware of such variance, concur, and make a corresponding change in your plan. Regularly review and assess how you're doing and adjust your marketing plan accordingly.

In developing these written plans for the next 12 months, be sure to include any activities that bear on your goals for the next 3 to 5 years. For example, if you hope to introduce a new product line the year after next, you may need to prepare an advertising campaign in the last months of next year.

As you address each segment, you'll probably have four or five separate plans—one for advertising, others for sales promotion, public relations, sales management, and inventory control.

Your overall marketing plan should spell out in detail exactly what is to be done in each of these areas. For example, your advertising plan will spell out what is to be done each month and for each product, division, or service. If you're going to have a sale in November, you must plan to order the merchandise in, say, April; take delivery in October; order media exposure and write copy, and so on, in September; plan staffing patterns in early October; and attend to all the other details that add up to a successful sale. Get the picture? It, as well as each of the other separate plans, should state clearly who is responsible for the various activities to be accomplished each month for each product, and so on.

Be sure to maintain flexibility. You must always be alert to possibilities that might offer you a competitive edge or require correcting of a flaw in the initial plan. In addition, don't change your entire marketing program annually. Give your plan a fair chance. Be sure it has proper emphasis and support and, above all, enough money to do the job. Put everything on a cost versus results basis: Stay away from doing "cheap" projects that turn out "expensive" because of poor results.

The efficiency of your marketing plan will be enhanced with controls and follow-up. They are necessary to ensure that you and your employees stay within the framework of your marketing plan. The budgets which you establish must be maintained, the sales quotas reached or exceeded. And you should check frequently to ensure that your sales objectives are achieved at the profit levels you had planned. If you reveal weaknesses, use them to set benchmarks for improving the next marketing plan you develop.

You may want to establish record-keeping and reporting procedures that will, for example, give you information on the comparative performance and comparative cost of each of your salespeople. You might also find information helpful on what percent of your total customers are generating what percent of your total gross sales. Many small firms have discovered that, say, 20 percent of their customers were generating up to 70 percent and more of their gross sales. Armed with this information, the business owner could change advertising strategies, effect considerable savings, and maintain or increase sales at current or reduced cost levels.

Other data similarly generated might suggest a change in merchandise mix, the total elimination of an unprofitable service, or an adjustment in hours of operation.

If all this sounds like a great deal of work, it is. But the end very definitely justifies the means.

Your marketing research and the resultant written marketing plan that you and your employees will follow will help you identify (1) who your customers are, (2) where your customers are, (3) what specific goods and services you'll offer to them, (4) how and when you will reach them with information about these goods and services, (5) what your customer will find when he or she visits your shop, (6) exactly how Mr. or Ms. Customer will be treated, (7) how much all this will cost that customer, and (8) how much money this activity will generate for you and your employees.

In answering the following checklist developed for the SBA by Colorado State University Marketing Professors George Kress and R. Ted Will, you will be reminded of what you may still need to do to round out all marketing aspects of your business.

CUSTOMER ANALYSIS

Who Are Your Target Customers and What are They Seeking from You?

	Yes	No
Have you estimated the total market you share with competition?	☐	☐
Should you try to appeal to this entire market rather than a segment(s)?	☐	☐
If you concentrate on a segment, is it large enough to be profitable?	☐	☐
Have you looked into possible changes taking place among your target customers which could significantly affect your business?	☐	☐
Can you foresee changes in the makeup of your store's neighborhood?	☐	☐
Are incomes in the community apt to be stable?	☐	☐
Is the community's population subject to fluctuation or seasonal?	☐	☐
Do you stress a special area of appeal, such as lower prices, better quality, wider selection, more convenient location, or more convenient hours?	☐	☐
Do you ask your customers for suggestions on ways to improve your operation?	☐	☐
Do you use "want slips"?	☐	☐
Do you belong to your trade association?	☐	☐
Do you subscribe to important trade publications?	☐	☐
Have you considered using a consumer jury or consumer questionnaire to aid you in determining customer needs?	☐	☐
Do you visit market shows and conventions to help anticipate customer wants?	☐	☐
Do most of your customers buy on weekends?	☐	☐
Do sales increase in the evening?	☐	☐
Does the majority of your customers prefer buying on credit?	☐	☐

BUYING

Have You a Merchandise Budget (Planned Purchases) for Each Season?	Yes	No
Does it take into consideration planned sales for the season?	☐	☐
Does it achieve a planned stock turnover?	☐	☐
Have you broken it down by departments and/or merchandise classifications?	☐	☐
Have you a formal plan for deciding what to buy and from whom?	☐	☐
Have you a system for reviewing new items coming into the market?	☐	☐
Have you considered using a basic stock list and/or a model stock plan in your buying?	☐	☐
Are you using some sort of unit control system?	☐	☐
Do you keep track of the success of your buying decisions in previous years to aid you in next year's buying?	☐	☐
Do you attempt to consolidate your purchases with two or three principal suppliers?	☐	☐
Have you a useful supplier evaluation system for determining their performance?	☐	☐
Have you established a planned gross margin for your firm's operations and are you buying so as to achieve it?	☐	☐

PRICING

Have You Established a Set of Pricing Policies?	Yes	No
Have you determined whether to price below, at, or above the market?	☐	☐
Do you set specific markups for each product?	☐	☐
Do you set markups for product categories?	☐	☐
Do you use a one-price policy rather than bargain with customers?	☐	☐
Do you offer discounts for quantity purchases or to special groups?	☐	☐
Do you set prices so as to cover full costs on every sale?	☐	☐
Have you developed policy regarding when you will take markdowns and how large they will be?	☐	☐
Do the prices you have established earn planned gross margin?	☐	☐

Do you clearly understand the market forces affecting your pricing methods?	☐	☐
Do you know which products are slow movers and which are fast?	☐	☐
Do you take this into consideration when pricing?	☐	☐
Do you know which products are price sensitive to your customers, that is, when a slight increase in price will lead to a big dropoff in demand?	☐	☐
Do you know which of your products draw people when put on sale?	☐	☐
Do you know the maximum price customers will pay for certain products?	☐	☐
If the prices on some products are dropped too low, do buyers hesitate?	☐	☐
Is there a specific time of year when your competitors have sales?	☐	☐
Do your customers expect sales at certain times?	☐	☐
Have you determined whether a series of sales is better than one annual clearance sale?	☐	☐
Do you know what role you want price to play in your overall retailing strategy?	☐	☐
Are you influenced by competitors' price changes?	☐	☐

Are There Restrictions Regarding Prices You Can Charge?

	Yes	No
Do any of your suppliers "fair trade" their product by setting a minimum standard at which it can be sold?	☐	☐
Does your state have fair trade practice acts which require you to mark up your merchandise by a minimum percentage?	☐	☐
Are there any state regulations on how long "close-out" sales can be advertised?	☐	☐
Are you sure you know all the regulations affecting your business, such as two-for-one sales and the like?	☐	☐
Do you issue "rainchecks" to customers when sale items are sold out so they can purchase later at sale price?	☐	☐

PROMOTION

Are You Familiar with the Strengths and Weaknesses of Various Promotional Methods?

	Yes	No
Have you considered how each type might be used for your firm?	☐	☐

Do you know which of your items can be successfully advertised? ☐ ☐

Do you know which can best be sold through personal selling? ☐ ☐

Do you know which can best be sold by demonstrations? ☐ ☐

Do you know when it is profitable to use institutional advertising? ☐ ☐

Do you know when product advertising is better? ☐ ☐

Do you know which of the media (radio, television, newspapers, Yellow Pages, handbills) can most effectively reach your target group? ☐ ☐

Do you know what can and cannot be said in your ads (Truth in Advertising requirements)? ☐ ☐

Can you make use of direct mail? ☐ ☐

Is a good mailing list available? ☐ ☐

Are your promotional efforts fairly regular? ☐ ☐

Do you concentrate them on certain seasons? ☐ ☐

Are certain periods of the week better than others? ☐ ☐

Is There Available Financial or Technical Assistance Which You Can Use to Enhance Your Promotional Efforts?

	Yes	No
Can you get help from local newspapers, radio, or television?	☐	☐
Are cooperative advertising funds available from suppliers?	☐	☐
Do you tie your local efforts to your suppliers' national programs?	☐	☐
Do you join with other merchants in area-wide programs?	☐	☐
Have you looked for guidelines or ratios to estimate what comparable firms are spending on promotion?	☐	☐
Do you study the advertising of other successful retail firms, as well as of your competitors?	☐	☐
Have you some way of measuring the success of the various promotional programs you are using?	☐	☐

Are Your Products Displayed to Maximize Their Appeal Within the Store?

	Yes	No
Do you know which of your items have unusual eye appeal and can be effective in displays?	☐	☐
Have you figured out the best locations in the store for displays?	☐	☐
Are you making use of window displays to attract customers?	☐	☐
If you use multitiered display stands or gondolas, do you know which shelves are the best sellers?	☐	☐

Have you a schedule for changing various displays? ☐ ☐

Do you display attention-getting items where they will call attention to other products as well? ☐ ☐

Do you know which items are bought on "impulse" and therefore should be placed in high traffic areas? ☐ ☐

Where price is important, do you make sure the price cards are easy to read? ☐ ☐

Do your suppliers offer financing of accounts receivable, floor planning, and so forth? ☐ ☐

Do You Know What Type of Credit Program (if any) You Should Offer?

	Yes	No
Does the nature of your operation require some type of credit for your customers?	☐	☐
Have you discussed credit operations with your local credit bureau?	☐	☐
Would a credit program be a good sales tool?	☐	☐
Is a credit program of your own desirable?	☐	☐
Have you looked into other programs of credit cards?	☐	☐
If you set up your own credit program, do you know what standards you should use in determining which customers can receive credit, for what time periods, and in what amounts?	☐	☐
Do you know all of the costs involved?	☐	☐
Will the interest you charge pay for these costs?	☐	☐
Do you know about the Fair Credit Reporting Act?	☐	☐
Are you familiar with the Truth-in-Lending legislation?	☐	☐
Have you determined a safe percentage of your business to have on credit that won't jeopardize paying your own bills?	☐	☐
Have you discussed your credit program with your accountant and attorney?	☐	☐

Do You Offer Some Special Customer Services?

	Yes	No
If you offer delivery service, do you own your vehicles?	☐	☐
Have you considered leasing them instead?	☐	☐
Have you thought about using commercial delivery service?	☐	☐
Do you charge for delivery?	☐	☐
If not, do you know how to work the delivery expenses into the selling price of your products?	☐	☐
Have you a policy for handling merchandise returned by customers?	☐	☐

Have you considered certain obligations to your community, in terms of charitable contributions, donations for school functions, ads in school yearbooks, etc.? ☐ ☐

Do you participate in activities of your local chamber of commerce, merchants' association, better business bureau, or other civic organizations? ☐ ☐

MANAGEMENT

Have You Developed a Set of Plans for the Year's Operations?

	Yes	No
Do your plans provide methods to deal with competition?	☐	☐
Do they contain creative approaches to solving problems?	☐	☐
Are they realistic?	☐	☐
Are they stated in such a way that you know when they have been achieved?	☐	☐
Have you a formal plan for setting aside money to meet any quarterly tax payments?	☐	☐

Are You Organized Effectively?

	Yes	No
Are job descriptions and authority for responsibilities clearly stated?	☐	☐
Does your organizational structure minimize duplication of effort and maximize the use of each employee's skills?	☐	☐
Do employees understand how they will be rated for promotion and salary increases?	☐	☐
Does your wage schedule meet the local rate for similar work and retain competent employees?	☐	☐
Would you or some of your employees profit by taking business education courses offered at local schools?	☐	☐
Will training help your employees achieve better results?	☐	☐
Do your experienced employees help train new and part-time employees?	☐	☐
Have you provided for good working conditions?	☐	☐
Do you use positive personal leadership techniques such as being impartial, giving words of encouragement and congratulations, and listening to complaints?	☐	☐
Are you familiar with the Fair Labor Standards Act as it applies to minimum wages, overtime payments, and child labor?	☐	☐
Do you avoid all forms of discrimination in your employment practices?	☐	☐

Do you have a formal program for motivating employees? ☐ ☐

Have you taken steps to minimize shoplifting and internal theft? ☐ ☐

Have You an Effective System for Communicating with Employees?

	Yes	No
Are they informed on those plans and results that affect their work?	☐	☐
Do you hold regular meetings that include all personnel?	☐	☐
Do your employees have their own bulletin board for both material you need to post and items they wish to post?	☐	☐
Have the "rules and regulations" been explained to each employee?	☐	☐
Does each employee have a written copy?	☐	☐
Is each employee familiar with other positions and departments?	☐	☐
Do you have an "open-door" policy in your office?	☐	☐

FINANCIAL ANALYSIS AND CONTROL

Have You Established a Useful Accounting System?

	Yes	No
Do you know the minimum amount of records you need for good control?	☐	☐
Do you know all the records you should keep to aid you in meeting your tax obligations on time?	☐	☐

Do Your *Sales* Records Give You the Key Information You Need to Make Sound Decisions?

	Yes	No
Can you separate cash sales from charge sales?	☐	☐
Can sales be broken down by department?	☐	☐
Can they be broken down by merchandise classification?	☐	☐
Do they provide a way to assess each salesperson's performance?	☐	☐

Do Your *Inventory* Records Give You the Key Information You Need to Make Sound Decisions?

	Yes	No
Do they show how much you have invested in merchandise without the necessity of a physical inventory?	☐	☐
Do you know the difference between inventory valuation at cost and at market?	☐	☐
Can you tell which one shows a loss in the period earned?	☐	☐

Can you tell which one conserves cash? ☐ ☐

Do you understand the pros and cons of the cost method of inventory accounting versus the retail method? ☐ ☐

Have you found an accounting method that shows the amount of inventory shortages in a year? ☐ ☐

Do Your *Expense* Records Give You the Key Information You Need to make Sound Decisions?   Yes   No

Do you know which expense items you have the greatest control over? ☐ ☐

Are the records sufficiently detailed to identify where the money goes? ☐ ☐

Can you detect those expenses not necessary to the successful operation of your business? ☐ ☐

Do You Effectively Use the Information on Your Profit and Loss Statement and Balance Sheet?   Yes   No

Do you analyze monthly financial statements? ☐ ☐

Can you interpret your financial statements in terms of how you did last year and whether you met this year's goals? ☐ ☐

Do your financial statements compare favorably with other similar businesses in terms of sales, cost of sales, and expenses? ☐ ☐

Are you undercapitalized? ☐ ☐

Have you borrowed more than you can easily pay back out of profits? ☐ ☐

Can you see ways to improve your profit position by improving your gross margin? ☐ ☐

Do you use the information contained in your financial statements to prepare a cash budget? ☐ ☐

INSURANCE

Have You Adequate Insurance Coverage?   Yes   No

Do you have up-to-date fire coverage on both your building equipment and inventory? ☐ ☐

Does your liability insurance cover bodily injuries as well as such problems as libel and slander suits? ☐ ☐

Are you familiar with your obligations to employees under both common law and workmen's compensation? ☐ ☐

Do you spread your insurance coverage among a number of agents and take the risk of overlapping coverage or gaps which may raise questions as to which firm is responsible? ☐ ☐

Has your insurance agent shown you how you can cut premiums in areas like fleet automobile coverage, proper classifications of employees under workmen's compensation, cutting back on seasonal inventory insurance? ☐ ☐

Have you looked into other insurance coverage, such as business interruption insurance or criminal insurance? ☐ ☐

Do you have some fringe benefit insurance for your employees (group life, group health, or retirement insurance)? ☐ ☐

It's your business, and your potential profit or loss. And that's what marketing means.

11

Advertising North, South, East, and West of Madison Avenue

According to Mr. Webster, advertising is a noun which describes the action of calling something (such as a commodity for sale or a service offered or desired) to the attention of the public, especially by means of printed or broadcast paid announcements. Webster continues the definition by informing us that advertising is the business or profession of designing and preparing advertisements for publications or broadcast.

Most small business owners could come up with definitions of their own. Some would view it as a necessary evil, others a total waste of money. Some would define it as a pain in the neck (or some other portion of the human anatomy), while a few would state unequivocally that advertising is a rip-off that doesn't work and that everyone concerned and connected with advertising as a business (or profession) is a thief, a charlatan, or both. Occasionally, you'll find a smiling business owner who will attribute the success of his or her venture almost exclusively to advertising.

There is probably some truth—ranging from a little to a lot—in each of these opinions. Most small business owners are confused by, baffled over, leery of, and just plain scared of advertising.

Their problem is compounded by a number of factors including a lack of knowledge, no clear-cut understanding of what they want or need their advertising effort to accomplish, and a lack of professional assistance.

Here again, the "big guys" have a decided edge. Large companies can spend millions of dollars on their advertising effort annually and draw advice and counsel from the most knowledgeable and creative advertising professionals in the field to ensure that their advertising dollar is spent efficiently and effectively, and that the company's message is presented in a manner both creative and memorable. Add to this the fact that when you have millions to spend, it's very difficult to make a mistake. When you have lots of money to spend and lots of people to help you spend it, the chances are exceptionally good that someone will do something right.

The small business owner, on the other hand, often faces the cold, cruel, competitive business world with an advertising budget only slightly larger than the average family food budget. Money for mistakes is simply not available, and because of the nature of the advertising business, professional help may not be either.

Advertising agencies are, themselves, small businesses. With the exception of the twenty or so largest advertising agencies in the world, the rest are mere financial "babies" when compared with the clients they serve. Since an advertising agency normally works on a commission basis, the small amount of money budgeted for advertising by most small businesses makes it fiscally infeasible for an agency to handle such an account.

Most advertising agencies operate on a commission of 15 percent of what is paid to the media. For example, if an advertising agency places a $1000 television schedule for a client, the bill to the client (that's you) is $1000. But the advertising agency only pays the television station $850. The balance of $150 is the agency's commission. Charges for artwork, photography, typography, and certain other "out-of-pocket" expenses are passed on to you—the advertiser. In some instances (such as photography) the amount is also commissionable between the advertising agency and the supplier (in this case, the photographer).

When you consider that the advertising agency must cover direct and indirect costs and generate a modest profit—just as you do—it becomes totally understandable why most advertising agencies are just not available to most small business owners. Fifteen percent of a small advertising budget is minuscule. The majority of advertising agencies have established policies regarding the minimum annual expenditure they can afford to handle on behalf of a client. This varies with the size of the market and the size of the agency. Some newer, smaller, and/or hungrier advertising agencies will take on almost any account. Some agencies—including some of the major advertising firms—have gone to a set fee or fee/commission combination as a way to be compensated for handling accounts. Some smaller advertisers have found this new set-fee compensation system a way to gain access to professional advertising assistance.

As a rough rule of thumb: If your advertising budget is $12,000 *annually*, you're probably on your own. If it's $12,000 *monthly*, there are probably a dozen agencies who will be happy to beg for your business.

With or without professional help, you need to know a few basic facts about advertising. You can learn to competently and creatively do it yourself. And if you're working with an agency, you'll be a much better client and consequently end up with a better and more productive advertising campaign by being adequately equipped to communicate with your advertising agency.

ADVERTISING

First, an absolute: View advertising as an investment—not an expense. In order for this approach to pay off, you must know exactly what you expect the advertising you place to do for your shop. It is helpful to divide advertising into two basic categories: immediate response advertising and image (or attitude) advertising.

Immediate response advertising is designed and placed to persuade a potential customer to buy a particular product or use a particular service within a relatively short period of time—today, tomorrow, this weekend, or next week. An example of such decision-triggering advertising is one that promotes normally priced merchandise that has immediate appeal, such as selling snow shovels immediately after a big snowstorm. Other examples are ads which use price appeals such as clearance sales, special purchases, and seasonal events such as Easter sales, back-to-school merchandise, and white sales. For such advertising to be deemed effective, projected sales goals should be achieved or exceeded because people responded in a timely manner to your exhortation that they "buy now."

The second general category of advertising—that of image or attitude advertising—simply keeps your firm's name before the public, enhances your store's image, and ideally will result in a customer utilizing your services or buying your products when the customer is buying what you are selling. There is almost never a price mentioned in this kind of advertising message, and the general tone is that of "when you're ready, we'll be glad to serve you." Advertising professionals sometimes refer to this as a "soft sell."

Some very profitable businesses have been built on this almost subliminal advertising approach. It can be disastrous, however, to run this kind of message when you are really expecting people to rush right in and purchase a specific item. By the same token, if you want to build a quality image and all you ever run are advertising messages screaming "sale," "this week only!," or "big savings this weekend," don't be surprised or disappointed when the image your customers and potential customers have of your store is as a store of less than first quality. Many small business owners blame the media, when the message is really the culprit.

Next, take a look at your location. Where your firm is located has a great deal to do with how much of an advertising budget is enough. First, your location will in great measure determine the appropriate media from which you can profitably select. If you operate a small neighborhood drugstore located in a suburban area, it is likely going to be both prohibitively costly and grossly inefficient for you to purchase time or space in media such as the major metropolitan daily newspaper or the radio and television stations which cover a vastly larger area than your primary trade zone. Looking to your suburban weekly newspaper, a shopper's publication that covers your specific geographic area only, or other media which permit you to target your message to just those folks living in reasonably close geographic proximity to your firm will both save and make you money. There will be immense savings in not paying for the vast circulation represented by the major media reaching far more people than you could reasonably expect to frequent your drugstore. And you'll make money by ensuring that those potential customers most likely to be interested in hearing your message will, in fact, be reached by it.

The second major factor to be considered in location as it relates to advertising budgets is that of "destination versus high traffic." As we discussed in Chapter 4, "It's a Great Location, but Don't Sign Anything Yet!," if you locate in a high-traffic area such as a major shopping center, your advertising budget can be significantly smaller than if you locate away from such a ready pool of consumers and, therefore, require that your customer must travel specifically to your place of business. As stated in Chapter 4, it will take a significantly larger advertising budget to inform your potential customer of your whereabouts and convince this cynical consumer that you're really worth the trip. It's almost axiomatic: What you save in rent you'll pay out in advertising and vice versa.

Now for the heavy stuff. How many bucks are enough bucks to place in your advertising budget?

Only you can answer that question. I can suggest that you get averages on what similar businesses are allocating and expending nationwide from your trade association. Your public library likely has a copy of the Robert Morris & Assoc. National Averages-Annual Statement Study which outlines average percentages allocated nationwide by all manner, shapes, and sizes of firms in everything from advertising to executive compensation. You can purchase this publication for $22.20 from Robert Morris & Assoc., P.O. Box 8500 S-1140, Philadelphia, Penn. Payment must accompany your order. If all else fails and you simply cannot find *anything* to use as a guideline, my standard "guesstimate" is always that 3 to 5 percent of gross sales should be budgeted for advertising.

Keep in mind that this is a last-resort figure only, as some industries average less than one-half of 1 percent while others budget 50 percent or more of their anticipated gross sales annually for advertising.

But 3 to 5 percent of gross sales gives you something to start with. And if you're just starting a new firm or location, plan on expending a sum equal to your approximate annual advertising budget within 4 to 6 weeks of your grand opening. To clarify this a bit further, if your anticipated gross annual sales are $100,000 and you are budgeting 5 percent for advertising, your advertising budget for your first year will be $5000. Since yours is a brand-new firm, you will budget an additional $5000 to be spent during, say, the week prior to your physical opening and 4 weeks thereafter. You would subsequently spend the $5000 budgeted for your first year over the following 11 months. Your first year's advertising budget would, in effect, be $10,000. Thereafter, you would pull back your advertising expenditures to the "normal" 5 percent of anticipated gross sales.

There is a very valid reason for doing it this way. It gives you a means to ensure that your potential customers know who you are, where you are, what you do, when you do it, and why they should frequent your new place of business. It will permit you to establish an image with the customer. If done correctly, it will assist you in gaining your appropriate share of the market (or better!). It will help you overcome the considerable edge your competitors currently hold over you since they are better-known and better-established in the community. As my final "selling point" I simply state that the "big kids" do it exactly this way. Major retailers across the country budget 100 percent of their annual budget within 4 to 6 weeks surrounding the opening of a new outlet and expend a like amount in the next 11 months. It works rather nicely for them; it will work rather nicely for you.

Also keep in mind that advertising expenditures of a one-time nature such as grand opening advertising can be included legitimately in your request for a small business loan. By the same token, your monthly advertising expenditures can—and should—be included in your overhead and can also be included in your loan request under operating capital (for 3 months).

I cannot overemphasize the importance of budgeting your advertising dollar. It is critical not only to allocate an annual advertising budget and control this budget adequately but also to plan and budget your monthly advertising expenditures.

If, for example, you have $5000, it is absolutely absurd to simply divide that figure by 12 and spend $416.66 monthly, no matter what. You must come to grips with the concept of "seasonality."

In a nutshell, seasonality is the ebb and flow of sales natural to any business endeavor. Any category of business has its peaks and valleys. Some businesses do 90 percent of their gross annual sales volume in 3 months of the year. Others have a slightly "flatter" sales curve. But none to my knowledge are absolutely flat, with an equal sales volume each and every month all year long.

	JAN	FEB	MAR	APR	MAY	JUN	ANNUAL TOTAL
% of Sales	4	5	5	4	10	8	12 mos. (100%) ($100,000) ($5000)
Monthly Ad. Budget	$200	$250	$250	$200	$500	$400	
	JUL	AUG	SEP	OCT	NOV	DEC	
% of Sales	6	7	7	10	15	20	
Monthly Ad. Budget	$300	$300	$350	$500	$750	$1000	

Figure 12 Allocating advertising dollars by anticipated monthly sales goals. This simple chart indicates how you can allocate advertising expenditures based on percent of gross annual sales projected for a full calendar year.

A sense of seasonality accepts this fluctuation and goes along with the sales tide by allocating an appropriate percentage of the total advertising budget monthly in direct relationship to anticipated sales volume.

Now that sounds really confusing, but it's a very simple process. Again, look to your trade association. The nice folks there will be able to provide you with national averages on sales trends for past years. Your local chamber of commerce and your friendly banker are also good sources of information regarding general sales trends in your specific geographic area.

By simply charting when sales are most likely to occur on a month-by-month basis, you can allocate your advertising budget in a manner that really makes some sense. In Figure 12, I have projected (for a hypothetical business) the percentage of total gross sales anticipated for the year to be achieved in each of the 12 months. This would mean that while gross annual sales would reach $100,000 at the end of the calendar year, during some months sales would be only $4000, while in other months sales would be $20,000. It seems less than absurd to spend an equal number of advertising dollars and expect to achieve such vastly different sales results!

Since we've already determined that we will spend 5 percent of anticipated gross sales (or $5000) on advertising for the year, the monthly advertising budget is a direct reflection of the percentage of annual sales to be achieved in a specific month. Take a quick look at Figure 12. I think you'll get the idea rather quickly.

Remember, advertising is a completely controllable expense. If it's doing what it should for you, you can increase your sales volume by increasing your advertising expenditures.

Remember, too, the function of your advertising budget is to control advertising expenditures. This is most easily done through a monthly tabulation, as shown in Figure 13. With this simple record, the danger signals start flashing when your advertising budget is overextended.

Whether your advertising budget is $5000, $500,000, or $5 million per year, this simple system of allocating advertising dollars based on monthly sales patterns is extremely sound. Remember to back up the expenditures for advertising by 2 to 4 weeks to achieve the desired end. This simply means that in Figure 12 where December's advertising budget of $1000 represents 20 percent of the annual advertising budget and is expected to generate 20 percent of the annual anticipated gross sales for the firm, it is necessary to start expending this money in early to mid-November. If you simply back the calendar up by 2 to 4 weeks, many of your immediate decisions regarding when to start an advertising campaign will be made automatically. The whole process is really remarkably simple and, best of all, it works!

The last budgeting approach or theory I'd like you to become familiar with is that of pulsing and flighting. Just keep in mind that in advertising, generally, more of one is better than less of many. If you have a very small budget with which to work (such as our imaginary shop owner in Figure 12), a multimedia campaign is out of the question. Our business owner must pick one advertising vehicle and purchase that vehicle as wisely as possible. The theory extends to picking one of one: That is to say, if radio is the

Account	Month		Year to Date	
	Budget	Actual	Budget	Actual

Media
    Newspapers
    Radio
    TV
    Literature
    Other				

Promotions
    Exhibits
    Displays
    Contests				

Advertising Expense
    Salaries
    Supplies
    Stationery
    Travel
    Postage
    Subscriptions
    Entertainment
    Dues				

Total				

Figure 13   Advertising budget form. Advertising is a completely controllable expense. The function of the budget is to control advertising expenditures. This can be done through a monthly tabulation, as shown in the chart. With this record, the danger signals flash when the budget is overextended. The accounts listed in the chart are not comprehensive; they serve only as examples. For instance, some companies include publicity in the advertising budget, others treat it separately.

medium of choice, *one* radio station is probably as "deep" as our business owner should attempt to go. Buying ten spots on one radio station will be far more effective than buying one spot each on ten radio stations—get the picture?

The concept of pulsing and flighting is simply an additional refinement of this concept. Those self-same ten spots on our single radio station will sound like many more if run on 2 days of the week rather than scheduling them over 5 days. By the same token, flighting the spots—scheduling 2 weeks out of 4—or on 1 week, off 3 weeks—and so forth, will make a much greater impact on the listener. These approaches to scheduling advertising can give the impression of a much larger advertising budget and make a much more lasting—and therefore profitable—impact on a potential consumer. Many major firms use these techniques very effectively to fool consumers into believing that they hear or see the advertising message much more often than they really do.

Before you can select the appropriate advertising medium (or vehicle, i.e., radio, television, newspaper, etc.), you have to know exactly whom you are trying to reach. It is also essential that you understand your own business. Take a good look at both yourself and your customers. You need the answers to such questions as:

What business am I in?

What quality of merchandise do I sell?

How do I compare with competition?

What customer services do I offer?

What kind of image do I want to project?

Who are my customers?

What are their tastes?

What are their likes and dislikes?

What are their income levels?

Why do they buy from me?

By this miniprofile of yourself and your customers, you'll be better able to direct your advertising message to those most likely to buy and, thus, you will make more effective use of your advertising dollar. For example, if you own a clothing store and you're planning a sale of jeans and t-shirts, an advertising schedule on a local contemporary or top-40 radio station would be a much better choice than a similar schedule on a classical music station. If it's during the school year, it also makes good sense to specify that you want your announcements scheduled before and after school hours or on Saturday mornings if your anticipated customers are teenagers.

To carry this just a bit further, aim for a composite picture of your "ideal" customer. Notice that I said customer, singular; not customers, plural. While you certainly want more than one customer, the ideal way to reach the "gang" is to target your message and its placement toward one ideal customer.

The Pepsi-Cola Company has accomplished this in so effective a manner, they could literally write the book on targeting advertising. Depending on the Pepsi product to be sold, the media buyer places advertising to reach a specific and very narrow "ideal" target audience. For Pepsi-Cola, for example, all media placement is bought with 12- to 17-year-olds in mind. Granted, children much younger than 12 and adults significantly older than 17 drink Pepsi-Cola, but the Pepsi-Cola Company felt—and now knows—that those both younger and older than their target audience will get the message and buy Pepsi anyway.

For Diet Pepsi, they aim for women in their thirties. Again, granted that many males watch their waistlines and we've got pudgy females under 30 and over 40, Pepsi buys just for their ideal customer for this particular product. The rest follow along as they should.

It works for the big kids, and it will work for you. Absolutely insist on media that will reach your primary or ideal target audience and, wherever possible, negotiate rates based on a cost per 1000 basic to reach these ideal customers.

When you know what you want to advertise and whom you want to reach with your message, you must next select the advertising medium that will reach them most effectively. Let's take a quick look at the major media available: how each works, who it reaches best, and a few nuts-and-bolts facts that may prove helpful.

Radio

Owing to the advent and enormous growth of television viewing, radio stations throughout the country have reexamined and repositioned themselves over the past 25 years. In many ways, radio has emerged stronger than ever and become an extremely viable advertising medium once again.

To answer the TV challenge, most mid- to large-market radio stations identify a specific segment of the listening audience to which they plan to appeal. The stations then format their programming to attract that specific target audience. In an average-size market you will, therefore, find one or more radio stations with programming geared to a teenage population, another programming country-western music only, still another offering all news or news-talk programming, one reaching for the classical music enthusiast, while still another may program in a foreign language when the minority population warrants such attention. Basic formats include top-40, middle-of-the-road (MOR), classical, news-talk, contemporary, religious, foreign language or ethnic, "beautiful" music, nostalgia or "golden oldies," and special novelty programming such as disco or punk rock—this latter group of programming options tends to change rather rapidly to take advantage of whatever is new and "trendy" in the music business.

Some stations also place especially heavy emphasis on news or sports programming, which tends to appeal to the male listener.

There are two radio bands with which you must contend: AM and FM. In many markets, FM radio now boasts larger listening audiences than does AM. While this sounds confusing, it really makes purchasing radio time for your business much simpler. Some choices are extremely clear-cut: For example, if you sell western apparel, veterinary supplies, saddles, or other related types of merchandise, it is obvious that the country-western station would be a likely candidate for your advertising dollars. By the same token, if you're selling orthopedic shoes to the over-60 crowd, you'll automatically eliminate the top-40 and contemporary stations from your list.

Keep in mind that radio is sold in time increments, usually 10, 20, 30, or 60 seconds in duration. The cost varies, dependent upon the length of spot, the time of day in which it will run, and the station on which it will be heard. The price is always based on the number of listeners who will likely hear the commercial. Generally speaking, the most expensive "day parts" (a radio term describing time segments) on radio are early morning (6:00 to 9:00 A.M.) and afternoon drive time (4:30 to 6:30 P.M.). Some FM stations attract their largest listening audiences in mid-afternoon and early evening. The most costly times to advertise on these stations are, therefore, during these day parts.

When buying radio, keep in mind that they all claim to be number 1. And they probably are. Number 1 in something or some category. But it may not be a category of interest to you. The number 1 station for men 45 to 72 years of age is hardly of use to you if you run a women's maternity shop. By the same token, the number 1 teen radio station has little to offer the average Cadillac dealership.

The more spots you purchase on a given radio station, the less each spot will cost you. Most stations also offer discounts for long-term contracts covering a set number of spots to be run during a given time period. It is, therefore, much less costly per spot if you have signed a contract for, say, 500 radio commercials to run within a 1-year period. These special packages, or "deals," can be explained by your radio station account executive. This "time" salesperson will provide you with a station rate card, explain its use, and also provide you with valuable information on the audience the station will reach for you.

This demographic information is generated by audience surveys conducted several times each year by outside firms. The largest of these rating firms currently is Arbitron, referred to as ARB by the stations.

Always ask for audience information for the specific target group in which you are interested and figure the cost per 1000 for your radio schedule based on this information. You will sometimes find it much more cost-efficient to purchase time on two or three radio stations simultaneously than to run a schedule on the so-called top-rated station in your market. Since you are only interested in reaching your primary target market, the vast numbers of people outside this narrow target group reached by the "number 1" station may represent an increased cost with a decreased efficiency rating.

Your radio station account executive can—and should—do all this figuring for you as part of his or her service. When in doubt, simply divide the number of people reached by the spot (remember, target audience only!) into the cost of the spot. If a radio spot costs $20 and reaches 4000 people in your marketing target, the cost per 1000 is $5.

Using this cost per 1000 approach, you can scientifically compare schedules on various radio stations to get the best deal for yourself.

Radio also represents a medium of immediacy: You can get on it very quickly and get results from it very rapidly. Production costs are low, and it reaches people even in their automobiles where response time to your message can be measured in minutes. It is the ideal way to reach teens and, at certain times of the day, men and women of specific interests and age groups. Relatively speaking, the cost of a radio commercial is low and can often be negotiated even lower by using the cost per 1000 approach.

To purchase radio time, simply call one or more of your local radio stations and ask to speak to a sales representative.

A final caveat: Don't buy time on your favorite station unless it also happens to be the station appealing to your target audience. Remember, your commercials are not on the air to reach you—they are on the air to reach your potential customers. You may be addicted to classical music, and your target audience may be listening to contemporary or middle-of-the-road programming.

Television

TV is the giant of advertising media. Unlike radio, television does not generate great viewer loyalty to a specific channel—with the exception of local news programming. Rather, viewers tend to change channels every 30 to 60 minutes as they respond to their favorite programs, not their favorite television stations.

With television you, therefore, purchase "adjacencies"—spots within or next to specific programs.

Like radio, television is surveyed regularly to generate demographic data and information on the total number of viewers at any given time. Arbitron and Nielson Station Index are the top rating firms currently: View any other figures *very* cynically! Again, like radio, your television account executive can provide you with this information. Likewise, cost per 1000 should be the bottom line when purchasing television.

Television has some real pluses, including the fact that it utilizes a multisensory message delivery system. TV involves motion, color, sight, and sound all simultaneously delivering and reinforcing your commercial message. Because most people in this country receive news and information—and believe what they see and hear—through television news and other special programming, television commercial messages tend to increase credibility in a service or product—rightly or wrongly.

It also has several drawbacks: It is expensive (but less so when purchased on a cost per 1000 basis); it involves some time delays due to scheduling and production requirements; production can often be quite costly; and since it is technically a bit more difficult to work with, many small business people are scared off by its complexity.

This needn't be the case since almost all television stations can provide copy, graphics, and production services—for a fee.

For information and assistance, simply call one or more of your local television sales departments and request that an account executive call on you.

As with radio, keep in mind your specific target audience and don't be swayed by so-called cheap spot availabilities. If the time slot being touted reaches the wrong audience for you, it's anything but cheap.

Television time periods include "housewife," which runs from sign-on until approximately 4:00 P.M.; "early fringe," which runs from approximately 4:00 P.M. until 6:30 P.M.; "prime time," which extends from 6:30 P.M. through 10:30 P.M.; and "late fringe," which includes 10:30 P.M. until sign-off. Prime time is obviously the most expensive per spot but can sometimes be the most cost-efficient, again based on your cost per 1000 calculations.

By the same token, the less-expensive "housewife" time period may be just exactly what you're looking for.

Television production costs vary enormously: from under $100 to tens of thousands of dollars for a single 30-second spot commercial. This is, of course, in addition to the cost of the television time itself.

While it's out of the reach of the smallest of small businesses, television should be carefully explored and evaluated as an advertising medium for many small firms. And the power of television can certainly be credited with helping some small businesses become big businesses in a relatively short period of time.

Yellow Pages Advertising

For small businesses, Yellow Page advertising is usually a must—and sometimes an "only."

Many small firms get the majority of their new customers from the Yellow

Pages. High on the list would be beauty salons, barbershops, plumbers, heating and air-conditioning contractors, appliance repair firms, and pest control services. While this list is in no way all-inclusive, most people needing these services first look to the Yellow Pages for the location of the business nearest them.

As I said, in some cases Yellow Pages advertising is the only (or major) advertising vehicle utilized by small firms. As a matter of fact, many a new small business has failed simply because the owner did not coincide the opening of the firm with the Yellow Pages' deadlines. Since the Yellow Pages are published once each year, it can be a very long dry spell between your grand opening and the time the majority of your potential customers will know who you are, where you are, and how to reach you.

Yellow Pages deadlines (the time past which no further ads or listings are accepted) occur in early September. Two to three months later, the new telephone directories are distributed. Keep this in mind when planning to open a new business or a new location of an existing business.

For complete information on costs and advertising deadlines, contact your Yellow Pages sales representative. You'll find the number listed—obviously—in the Yellow Pages.

Newspapers

Depending on size, almost every community in America is served by one or more daily and/or weekly newspapers. They can be a fruitful advertising medium.

Keep in mind that newspaper readers tend to be older (teenagers can't or don't read!), better-educated, and more affluent. Certain categories of businesses feel (rightly or wrongly) that they cannot survive without newspaper advertising. Included in this list are automobile dealerships, real estate agencies, supermarkets, and major retail outlets.

Newspapers (and other print media) sell advertising space by either the agate line or the column inch. In a few instances (such as some classified advertising), space is sold on a cost per word basis.

Here are a couple of easy-to-remember rules to simplify the space–cost relationship: There are 14 agate lines to a column inch. If space is being figured by the agate line and you want to purchase a 2-column by 4-inch ad, simply multiply 14 by 2 (agate lines by columns) and multiply that total by 4 (number of inches in the ad). To clarify: If the cost per agate line were $1, you would multiply $1 × 14 (cost per column inch) × 2 (2-column ad) = $28 × 4 (number of inches in ad) = $96.00. The cost of your 2-column by 4-inch ad would be $96.00. The second rule of thumb: If you're purchasing space priced by the column inch, simply multiply that price by the number of columns and *that* total by the number of inches in order to arrive at the cost for the ad.

Most newspapers offer special contract rates which reduce the cost per column inch significantly when you agree to purchase a set number of column inches over a specific time period, for example, 1000 inches in 52 weeks.

Newspaper space is also divided between display advertising and classified advertising. The deadlines differ, with display advertising requiring a longer lead time prior to publication.

You can increase the effectiveness of your ad by specifying the specific section of the newspaper in which it is to be placed, for example, the sports section for a male-oriented ad or the "women's pages" for a product or service aimed at women. Most papers won't guarantee placement, but they do their best to comply.

Strive to make your newspaper ads easily recognizable by using consistency in your store logo and the ad layout, including typeface and border. This way, readers will recognize your ads before they even read them.

Use a simple layout. Ads should be easy to read, and the layout should carry the reader's eye through the message easily, and in proper sequence, from illustration to headline to explanatory copy to price to store name. Avoid using too many typefaces and overly decorative borders and reverse plates. All these devices are distracting and will reduce the number of readers who will receive your entire message.

The first question a reader asks of an ad is, "What's in it for me?" Use a prominent-benefit headline which selects the main benefits which your merchandise or service offers. This message can often be effectively amplified in a supportive subheadline and body copy.

Whenever possible, let white space work for you. White space is that important layout element in newspaper advertising that has absolutely no words or pictures in it. White space focuses the reader's attention on your ad and will make your headline and illustration stand out. When a busy or crowded ad is necessary, such as for a sale, departmentalize your items so that readers can find their way through them easily.

Dollar figures have good attention value. Don't be afraid to quote your price, even if it's high. Readers will often overestimate omitted prices. If the advertised price is high, explain why the item represents a good value: superior manufacturing or materials, extra luxury features, etc. If the price is low, support it with factual statements which create belief, such as information on your closeout sale, special purchase, or clearance. Point out the actual savings to the reader and spell out your credit and layaway plans, if available.

Include related items: You can often make two sales instead of one by offering, for example, matching gloves and handbags in an ad for women's shoes. If an item is a known brand, say so in your advertising. Manufacturers spend large sums of money to sell their merchandise. You can and should capitalize on their advertising, while enhancing the reputation of your store, by featuring brand names.

Urge your readers to buy now. Ask for the sale. You can stimulate prompt action by using phrases such as "limited supply" or "this week only." If mail-order coupons are included in your ad, provide spaces large enough for customers to fill them in easily.

As a general rule, the larger the ad, the greater the response. Carefully weigh and consider this when deciding whether to run three tiny ads or one large ad.

You don't have to be an artist to effectively utilize newspaper space. Almost all newspapers have graphic artists and copy people on their staff and will be most happy to prepare layouts for your approval. In addition, many of your product lines provide newspaper layouts and other forms of advertising such as radio and television spots, brochures, etc., that simply need local adaptation.

When exploring newspapers as a possible advertising vehicle, don't overlook the neighborhood "shoppers" or small suburban weekly newspapers. They are often much more affordable and much more likely to reach your primary target audience than the more costly big-city daily that will reach thousands and thousands of people who will absolutely never visit your shop because of the geographic distance between you and them.

Magazines

Magazine advertising used to be a vehicle only for the major national advertiser. Since the magazine industry got smart and designed special local-edition sales plans, this is no longer the case.

The major national magazines all offer city or regional-edition prices which bring them into the realm of the affordable for many small firms.

You can, for instance, purchase an ad in *Time* magazine or *Better Homes and Gardens* and have the ad appear only in those issues of the magazine which are sold or delivered in your geographic area. This has significantly reduced costs for an ad and greatly increased its efficiency since only those people in your geographic target area will see the ad. This local-edition approach has provided smaller firms and local businesses with the opportunity to utilize this medium.

Certain firms can now reach a target with great potential to them, or can enhance their corporate image by becoming associated with the reputation of a major magazine. While this is not a vehicle for all—or even many—small firms, some small businesses will want to explore this option more fully.

You can research costs and obtain contact information by visiting your public library and asking to see a copy of the Standard Rate and Data Service magazine directory.

Standard Rate and Data Service (SRDS) publishes great information on all advertising media, including newspapers, radio and television, direct mail, and special obscure publications you didn't know even existed. The entire SRDS series is available at most major public libraries. Major advertising agencies subscribe to the series as a matter of course.

You would, of course, have to turn to Standard Rate and Data Service directories for information on regional or national media if you were interested in purchasing space or time on anything other than a local basis.

Magazines have much longer copy deadlines than other media, with most publications requiring copy and layout material 2 to 4 months before publication date.

Brochures and Fliers

In addition to newspapers and magazines, you can get your message in print by utilizing brochures, catalogs, and fliers. Fliers are especially important to many small firms since they are inexpensive to produce and can be delivered—either by mail or personal distribution—in the specific geographic area from which the firms draw the majority of their customers.

Any good printing firm will be able to assist you in designing and producing such printed pieces.

Direct Mail

Direct mail can be extremely expensive. It can also be extremely effective—which results in great cost-efficiencies. While I will discuss direct mail in some detail later in this chapter, the direct mail I refer to here is simply the sending of a specific piece of advertising (i.e., a brochure or announcement) to a specific list of people—either existing customers or those chosen because of their geographic proximity or a specific interest area. You might, for instance, want to send an announcement of your grand opening of a new sports equipment store to all of the members of your area's jogging club, soccer and bowling leagues, and tennis clubs. These lists are readily available from direct-mail list brokers. Check the Yellow Pages under advertising for direct-mail outlets. They'll be happy to help you.

In addition, many markets now have private mail services which will deliver your printed material to areas or special groups.

As I said, it can get expensive. But you're not paying for readers, viewers, or listeners who have absolutely no interest in what it is you're selling. So it can be an efficient way to go.

Signs and Displays

The image you choose to portray, the amount of money you have to spend on such items, and local ordinances will all play a part in how you utilize these advertising vehicles. Especially with signs, carefully check with city hall to ensure compliance with all local sign ordinances.

Outdoor

Outdoor, or billboard, advertising can be divided into three rough categories; junior or "pony" panels—those small, everywhere-you-look "little" boards—twenty-four-sheet standard billboards, and painted "spectaculars," the oversized billboards that sometimes encompass moving parts and/or "extensions," sections of the artwork that extend beyond the boundaries of the sign itself.

Boards come in two overall types: illuminated (those with light sources which increase their effectiveness during nighttime hours) and unilluminated. In addition, special light-reflecting paint can be utilized (a product usually referred to as "scotch lighting," after one of the major suppliers of the product) to use vehicle headlights to increase readership on a nonilluminated board after dark.

Boards can be purchased for varying periods of time, usually ranging from 1 month to 1 year or more. In addition, most outdoor advertising companies will contract with you for the use of their boards based on a system the outdoor industry terms a "showing." A 25, 50, 75, or 100 showing is the most common unit of sale in the industry. A number 75 showing, for example, would include a varying (from market to market) number of billboards which would produce a traffic count daily equal to 75 percent of the total population of the geographic area. A 100 showing should result, obviously, in a total traffic count equal to 100 percent of the population.

This doesn't, however, mean that every single person in the market would see your sign every day. It would mean that the aggregate number of people viewing at least one of the billboards carrying your message would total the approximate number of people residing in your geographic area. Many people might see your boards five times; others wouldn't see them at all.

Outdoor is expensive. Production for outdoor is expensive. It is my professional opinion that billboards should not normally be used as a single medium but rather as part of a multimedia campaign.

You should also remember that a billboard has but a few seconds before the vehicle or pedestrian whizzes by. You must, therefore, strive to reduce your message to seven or eight words or less. The more bold the graphics, the fewer the words, the more effective the billboard as a general rule. Billboards are, however, essential for giving directions to your customers and potential customers regarding your location and how to find it. Especially if you are physically located off the beaten path, outdoor advertising can effectively be utilized to direct people to you. As a medium, outdoor offers an extremely low cost per 1000 bottom line. How many folks rush right over and purchase an advertised item they've seen on a billboard is *very* questionable.

In some communities, local sign ordinances prohibit new outdoor advertising construction. In these markets, the pros and cons of billboard advertising are moot. Since you can't purchase it, who cares how it works, when it works, or why it works?

You might also want to keep in mind that in some communities, some customers react very negatively to outdoor advertising. If your firm is trying to positively influence a target audience likely to contain significant numbers of environmentalists or others opposed to outdoor signs, you had better find another way to spread your word.

Vertical-Interest Publications

Many small firms totally neglect this highly specialized method of reaching target audiences. *Horizontal* publications, such as *Time*, *Life*, *Newsweek*, *Harper's*, and other such broad-interest publications, are those which reach broad masses of people. *Vertical*-interest publications, on the other hand, target a smaller but very specific group of people. Examples of such publications include *Active Retirement*, *Teacher's News*, *Apartment Living*, *RX Golf and Travel*, *Association Management News*, and a host of other special-interest publications.

There is a vertical-interest publication for almost any special group of people you could imagine. This includes *Spelunker's Journal*, for those idiots who like to climb into caves, *Motorcross Magazine*, for another group of idiots who like to bounce around the countryside on high-powered two-wheel motor vehicles, and on and on. There are special publications for individuals interested in arts and crafts of all sizes, shapes, and kinds; publications for almost every single occupation and profession known to man and woman; something for almost every age group, hobby, vocation, avocation, and vice.

Obviously, if you're selling something of special interest to architects, it makes pretty good sense to advertise in the vertical-interest publication reaching architects. Likewise, if you're selling backpacks and other such goodies, it follows that a magazine or newspaper edited for and reaching those among us who would rather walk than ride would make pretty good advertising sense and dollars.

Vertical-interest publications are everywhere. And more spring up every month. Shop through a good newsstand, visit the periodical section of your public library, or refer to the Standard Rate and Data Service directory on special publications. The cost can be surprisingly low and the results surprisingly high.

Goodwill Advertising

I do not view this as a media category. Although it's truly made up of all manner and sorts of media and vehicles, I am here to tell you that goodwill advertising is *not* advertising. It is a contribution, sometimes a tax-deductible contribution, but in precious few instances will it result in any sort of consumer response.

What I mean exactly by goodwill advertising is advertising placed in programs, stitched to the back of Little League uniforms, painted on the side of race cars, and any of the other multitude of ways groups and individuals can help separate you from your advertising dollar.

There are a few exceptions: If you cater very specifically to an after-theater audience, it might make some semblance of sense to advertise in a theater program. By the same token, if you sell Little League uniforms, you may expect some small payoff for sponsoring a Little League team.

Most usually, this kind of expenditure should come under the contributions column of your annual budget—not the advertising column. Your advertising dollar is limited, and it has a long way to go. You *must* expend it in the areas that will return maximum results.

Co-Op Dollars

Again, this is certainly not an advertising medium, but if you get nothing else from this chapter, in fact from this whole book, the following information on co-op dollars may save you thousands.

Almost every manufacturer of almost every product makes available co-operative advertising dollars to retail outlets nationwide. Whether you sell Levis, lawn mowers, mattresses, high chairs, or nail polish, chances are that there are co-op dollars available to pay for part of your advertising expenditure.

The way the process normally works is as follows: A small percentage (usually 1 to 5 percent) of your annual purchases is rebated in the form of co-op advertising. This would result in the manufacturer sharing in the cost of certain advertising for his product—sold through your outlet—so long as you complied with certain rules and regulations set forth by the manufacturer. This could include the use of a specific medium such as newspaper or radio only, the use of copy either provided by or approved by the manufacturer, a prohibition regarding the mention of other products in the commercial or ad, or the fact that the name of the product has to be mentioned a specific number of times in the ad or commercial. Sometimes, there are almost no restrictions whatsoever; the cooperative budget is simply paid to you by the manufacturer upon presentation of appropriate verification that the com-mercials or ads actually ran.

For a long time, the smaller firm had precious little chance at an equitable co-op arrangement. Recent changes in legislation now mandate that a man-ufacturer offering co-op advertising programs make them available to all wholesale customers—large or small. The law did not, however, mandate that every single wholesale customer be advised of the existence of co-op advertising plans, simply that if they were available, the little guys had to get the same deal as the big guys. Therefore, it is incumbent upon *you* to ask your manufacturer's rep what co-op deals are in effect and what the restrictions are governing their utilization.

Co-op plans sometimes pay up to 50 percent and more of the total media cost. Some top-notch electronic and print production is also available from manufacturers. All you need do is localize the ad or spot with your store name, address, and/or telephone number.

Obviously, stretching your advertising dollar by as much as 50 percent is something to thoroughly explore and carefully consider.

Almost all media are adept at handling co-op advertising schedules and will provide you with the usually necessary notarized affidavits of performance and multiple copies of invoices. Ask your manufacturer's rep for details, understand the program thoroughly and comply with it completely, and advise your media respresentatives of exactly what you need from them in the billing department. The co-op dollars you use can cut back the expenditure you make and consequently increase your profit, make it possible to increase your advertising budget at the manufacturer's expense, or a combination of the two. It can certainly add up to increased advertising efficiencies and increased profits for you.

If you're big enough to need, want, and/or afford an advertising agency, what should you look for: first, an agency with some financial stability; second, an agency with a creative capability you feel good about: one whose past work meets your approval. You can find out the first by checking with some of the local media representatives. You can find out the second by taking a look at some of the ads and commercials produced by the recommended agencies.

Probably most important, however, find an agency with whom you feel comfortable. If you cannot communicate with your agency account executive, no matter how good the firm or how creative the people, the results will be less than satisfactory for you. Advertising is the business of communicating. You must be able to communicate with your advertising agency, or they can hardly be expected to communicate your message to your potential customers.

Don't be overly impressed by an agency's awards; many award-winning commercials and campaigns cost too much and/or produced little or no sales results. In some instances, the account was lost because of the plaque-winning production!

Keep in mind, however, that you can do it yourself with some readily available assistance. Almost all the media have copywriters, artists, technicians, directors and producers, and talent either on staff or available to them— and you. The same is true of printers and other suppliers. In more-major markets, you can contract for specific chores such as copywriting, production, media placement, and other activities normally handled by an advertising agency.

If you have absolutely no talent or inclination along these lines, it would definitely behoove you to employ an advertising agency—even if it means the addition of a fee over and above media and production costs in order to do so.

Some last thoughts: Remember that a good ad will hasten the demise of a bad product. Advertising cannot turn the old sow's ear into a silk purse. Also remember to sell what people want to buy. It is highly unlikely that a moving and storage company would manage to increase its sales by even one move if it slashed its regular fee in half during Christmas week. People just don't want to move during Christmas week. They will not utilize the services of a moving company unless they are going to move. Until they want—or have—to move, you're not going to get their business.

By the same token, it is highly unlikely that you'll sell many sleds in July or bikinis in January.

It is a good general rule to stay away from humor in your advertising copy. It's extremely difficult to write and almost always either offends too many people or entertains them rather than informs them. Keep your copy simple. Plan your ad around only one idea or product. Just give the folks the facts about your merchandise and services. Always identify your store fully and clearly. Make sure they know who you are by the time they've gone on to the next message.

Aim for consistency and similarity by utilizing the same typeface, logo, border, general layout, and—insofar as practical—the same background music and/or narrator. You want to build immediate identity and recall; you don't do that by changing the way your ad or commercial looks every single time. By the same token, if an ad or commercial works well, repeat it. Repeat it again. And again. Stop running it when it stops pulling for you.

Advertising (with the exception of mail order) can only inform, encourage, educate, titillate and precondition. You and your sales staff have to do the actual selling. An ad can get folks in the front door: whether or not they leave you a bit of their money is *your* job.

PUBLIC RELATIONS

We all know there's no such thing as a free lunch. But public relations (PR) offers a relatively inexpensive means for small business owners to get their firms noticed and remembered. If sought intelligently and creatively, publicity—while not absolutely free—may gain you recognition and help save or augment your advertising dollars.

A sound public relations program, often thought of as something only giant corporations involve themselves in, can give added strength and recognition to a small business by the people who use and need its product or service.

Public relations involves projecting a desired image. First, you must know the image you want your firm to project. It should be something unique, something that makes you different from your competition. It goes without saying, the image you decide to present has got to be true. A false front won't hold up long.

Remember, the image you choose for publicity must be tied to the overall promotion program of your business. There must be complete consistency between the image you project in your advertising, the personal selling of your staff, and the image you project through your public relations effort.

Next, select your specific public or publics, the people to whom you want to communicate your image. If, for example, you sell typewriters, it may not be profitable to project your image to people who do not type; but should you offer typing lessons, nontypists would be your main public.

Your public relations efforts might well include the cultivation of opinion leaders: those people who shape and influence the opinions and attitudes of others. This could include the mayor, city council, business leaders, legislative representatives, civic club leaders and members, area media representatives (newspaper editors and publishers, television and radio station owners and managers), school board members, teachers, and student leaders. While these folks may never have a need for your product or service, they influence members of your key publics. They might also wield legislative influence over how your business (or industry) will be operated and regulated in the future.

A sample list of media through which you can communicate information about your firm and its image could include trade publications; television; newspapers; radio; brochures; special events such as grand openings; tours; contests, etc.; slide presentations; speeches; personal letters; and meetings.

Your local newspaper offers many opportunities for projecting an image other than through the purchase of advertising space. Get to know the editor, news editor, or a reporter. Try to determine what the editor regards as newsworthy. The best way to provide information to such an individual is through a news release or fact sheet. The standard practice is to ask yourself who, what, where, when, why, and how. The answers to these questions are the news story. Mention the most important items first, such as what is happening, where, when, and to whom.

You might interest a reporter in doing a special feature on your business, one aspect of your business, or an outside interest or activity in which you are involved. Just seeing your firm's name mentioned in a positive story about some aspect of your activity will generate some residual goodwill for your business.

The same holds true for television and radio. You can finagle your way into a talk show guest appearance, or interest a reporter in doing a special feature on some aspect of your firm, if you can make it interesting enough to sell the idea.

Speeches and demonstrations are a valuable method for becoming recognized as an expert in your field.

Prepare a short 15- to 20-minute presentation or demonstration explaining the topic in terms nonexperts can understand. You may wish to include slides or photographs to accompany your presentation. Contact your area's civic and business clubs, high schools, women's groups, Boy and Girl Scout troops, and so on to see if they would be interested in hearing the presentation.

If you operate a garden supply store or nursery, you may find great interest in a plant care demonstration. Likewise, a florist could well develop a short talk on what flowers have meant down through the ages or how to arrange flowers attractively. A client of mine recently ended up with a 5-minute vignette on the top-rated news station locally by explaining his very unique map store to the television reporter. They happily chatted about everything from maps of old mining claims to maps charting outer space. My client merrily guided the camera through his attractive shop and pointed out globes, decorative wall maps, and special topographic charts of all kinds. Needless to say, his business increased dramatically after this almost-priceless public relations exposure.

Community involvement is another method of becoming known as the person to contact for a particular service or product. Carefully select those clubs, organizations, projects, or causes that will gain you proper exposure.

Magazines and newsletters that deal with your specific area of business or trade (commonly referred to as trade publications) can be a worthwhile means of gaining recognition. They will normally accept information on new employees, growth announcements, feature stories on companies, success stories on firms or products, new product or service announcements, and the like. Once your story has appeared in a trade publication, take it a step further and provide copies to local mass media such as newspapers and television.

Special events can be constructed to provide valuable public relations benefits. Open houses, plant or office tours, anniversary celebrations, demonstrations, displays, special commemorative days, holidays, dedications, contests and competitions, and so on, if planned thoroughly, can be useful means of gaining exposure for you and your business. Many of these events, in and of themselves, are newsworthy.

Many growing firms have found it advantageous to contract with a public relations firm to handle this aspect of their marketing effort. The fees are usually quite modest—especially when compared with the benefits that can accrue from a first-rate public relations campaign.

PROMOTION

Special promotions can—and should—be a part of your ongoing advertising and public relations efforts.

In addition to special sales promotions and contests for your customers, keep in mind the extreme value of in-house promotions for your staff—especially your sales personnel.

Offering special incentives for special efforts and increased results on their part can be both a morale booster and a profit builder.

Some small firms have become quite creative in their approaches to incentive promotions for their sales personnel. They can't, for example, offer a trip to Hawaii, all expenses paid for two. They can, however, offer the top salesperson of the month dinner for two at a nice local restaurant, or a Friday afternoon off with pay.

Some firms have found it most profitable to offer special discounts to senior citizens, students, or other special groups within their target population. And planning special sales promotions around local and national holidays and special events is a well-known sales builder.

In-store promotions should be supported by displays, decorations, signs, employee badges, special printing on shopping bags, banners, anything you can think of to support the notion that something unique is occurring.

DIRECT MAIL

There is a special category of business—and a special category of advertising vehicle—that deserves some special attention.

And that is direct mail.

Direct mail is both an advertising vehicle and a way of doing business. I mentioned early in this chapter that some firms spend 50 percent and more of their gross sales in advertising. This is the category of a firm that does exactly that. Because with direct-mail selling, the advertising is the majority of the overhead. With many direct-mail firms, there is little or no fixed overhead.

Some direct-mail firms do not have retail outlets; they operate exclusively through the mails, and, consequently, the cost for generating a catalog and distributing same constitutes almost the entire cost of doing business. This cost, however, can be considerable!

But so can the profits.

Take the firm of L. L. Bean, Inc. Leon Leonwood Bean started the firm in 1912 with $400 in borrowed capital and a funny-looking rubber-bottomed hunting boot he designed himself and sold around the country by mail. When the fine old fellow died in 1967 at the age of 94, his firm had annual sales of $3 million and 120 employees.

Today, L. L. Bean, Inc., is a giant in the speciality mail-order business and will send out 8 million catalogs each season next year—for a total of some 32 million pieces mailed out. A highly computerized, sophisticated marketer of its Bean boots, down parkas and sleeping bags, chamois cloth shirts, plaid lumber jackets, long underwear, and all manner of outdoor garb and sporting paraphernalia, the company expects 1980 sales of $120 million, up 28 percent from 1979.

We're all familiar, I trust, with the fact that Sears Roebuck, Montgomery Ward, and J. C. Penny—those giants of the retail industry—started as mail-order firms and still generate significant chunks of their corporate profits from this order-by-mail marketing effort.

Other mail-order giants include the book and record clubs. But there are some lesser-known and growing members of the mail-order industry including the Abbey Press—run by a bunch of monks who are effectively marketing religious articles through the mails—the Metropolitan Museum of Art, which sells everything from greeting cards to museum reproductions through the mail, and a long list of retailers who also utilize direct-mail marketing including Sakowitz, I. Magnin, and Nieman-Marcus.

You can literally purchase anything from raw oysters to gold-plated automobiles through the mail.

Many small firms enter the arena tentatively by placing a mail-order coupon or response ad in a customer publication accepting such advertisements, such as *Woman's Day*, *Better Homes and Gardens*, or *Sunset Magazine*—just three which have special sections devoted to order-by-mail advertisers.

Others market a single product or complete product line through the development of catalogs and the distribution of these catalogs through the mail using special mailing lists obtainable—for a price—from a number of large companies.

Take my word for it, *your* name, address, probably your telephone number, and other vital statistics concerning you, your family, and your income are available on computerized lists all over the country.

Many firms also generate their own lists by gathering and maintaining information on what product or services you have purchased from them in the past. This "house list" is probably the most valuable list of people you could possibly mail to. If customers used you before, the chances are they'll use you again. Many mail-order shops end up generating additional profit by selling their "house list" to brokers or other mail-order merchants.

Because I have purchased several items of some value by mail in the recent past, I am currently being inundated with catalogs from every conceivable direct-mail firm in the nation—and a few outside our national boundaries as well!

It's a highly specialized business and one for which you should either already have experience or seek adequate professional counsel. Counsel is, however, rather readily available. Locally, check your Yellow Pages under advertising direct mail. For information on national mailing list houses, have your librarian locate the Directory of Mailing List Houses, B. Klein Publications, Inc., 11 Third Street, Rye, N.Y. 10580, 1972. This directory includes the names of 2000 list specialists.

Most of these firms can provide not only mailing lists but also artwork; printing; automatic folding, inserting, sealing, stamping, and metering of mail; and all the other services attendent to the production and distribution of direct-mail pieces.

For information on specific mailing lists, you can contact one or more of the following brokers:

Accredited Mailing Lists, Inc., 15 East 40th St., New York, N.Y. 10016*

Accredited Mailing Lists, Inc., 5272 River Rd., Washington, D.C. 20016

Allison Mailing Lists Corporation, 329 Park Ave. South, New York, N.Y. 10010*

George Bryant & Staff, P.O. Box 190, 71 Grand Ave., Englewood, N.J. 07631*

The Coolidge Company, Inc., 11 West 42d St., New York, N.Y. 10036*

Dependable Mailing Lists, Inc., 425 Park Ave. South, New York, N.Y. 10036*

Dependable Mailing Lists, Inc., 1025 Vermont Ave., N.W., Washington, D.C. 20005*

Dependable Mailing Lists, Inc., 16661 Ventura Blvd., Encino, Calif. 91316*

Direct Marketing, Inc., 150 Purchase St., Rye, N.Y. 10580

Alan Drey Company, Inc., 333 North Michigan Ave., Chicago, Ill. 60601*

Alan Drey, Inc., 420 Lexington Ave., New York, N.Y. 10017*

Walter Drey, Inc., 130 East 18th St., New York, N.Y. 10003

Eastern Admission Services, 4881 Northgate Dr., Manlius, N.Y. 13104

Bob Engle Advertising, Inc., 5906 North Milwaukee, Chicago, Ill. 60646

Gale-Ramsey, Inc., 23 East 26th St., New York, N.Y. 10010

George-Mann Associates, Inc., Six Old Cranbury Road, Cranbury, N.J. 08512

Guild Company, P.O. Box 160 Engle St., Englewood, N.J. 07631*

Leonard G. Holland Associates, Inc., 549 Allen Rd., Woodmere, N.Y. 11598*

KMS-List Broker, 1000 West 25th St., Kansas City, Mo. 64108

Walter Karl, Inc., P.O. Drawer J, 20 Maple Ave., Armonk, N.Y. 10504*

Lewis Kleid, Inc., Division Dart Industries, Inc., 230 Park Ave., New York, N.Y. 10017*

E. J. Krane, 20 Nassau St., Princeton, N.J. 08540*

Willa Maddern, Inc., 215 Park Ave. South, New York, N.Y. 10003*

Mosley Mail Order List Service, Inc., 38 Newbury St., Boston, Mass. 02116*

Names in the Mail, 215 Stemmons Tower West, Dallas, Tex. 75207

Names In the News, 31 East 28th St., New York, N.Y. 10016*

Names In the News, 105 Montgomery St., San Francisco, Calif. 94104*

Names Unlimited, Inc., 352 Park Ave. South, New York, N.Y. 10010*

Prescott Lists, 17 East 26th St., New York, N.Y. 10010

Religious Lists, 20 South Main St., New York, N.Y. 10956*

Russell Rose Associates, 27 Locust Ave., White Plains, N.Y. 10605

William Stroh, Inc., 568–570 54th St., West New York, N.J. 07093

Florence Wolf, Inc., 919 North Michigan Ave., Chicago, Ill. 60611*

This list was supplied by the Direct Mail Advertising Association, 230 Park Avenue, New York, N.Y. 10017. The Association also publishes a booklet entitled *How To Work With The List Broker*, which sells for $2 a copy.

In most instances, rather than purchasing a list, you actually rent the use of the list and purchase the labels covering all the names and addresses it includes. In other words, you don't own the list. You simply contract for its one-time use. And the lists are extremely categorical. You'll find lists of everything from individuals who have contributed more than $20 to a conservative political cause to those who have purchased a mail-order item of more than $100 in value within the past 6 months.

Lists are also broken out by zip code, income, profession, political persuasion, and any of dozens of other characteristics.

If you're selling an automobile accessary, you can find lists of people who have automobiles of a certain model, make, and year.

If you're selling expensive jewelry or artwork, the names of every household with incomes of $50,000 or more is just a computer button away.

As life becomes more hectic, stores more crowded, gasoline more expensive, and time at more of a premium, it is very likely that purchasing by mail will become an even more popular option to consumers. Mail-order merchandising can be a lucrative option—or addition—to your retail outlet. Direct-mail selling is, however, one area where I would strongly encourage you to get professional assistance. It's a tough, competitive arena, and the neophyte needs all the help available.

*Many of these firms also are members of the Mailing List Brokers Professional Associations, 541 Lexington Ave., New York, N.Y. 10022. This association can be helpful in finding brokers geared to particular needs of users.

12

If You Don't Plan for It, It'll Happen Anyway

BUSINESS PLANS

Before beginning a journey to a new destination, anyone with even a modicum of good sense will pull out a map and carefully chart the best course. The wise traveler will note when to turn right, when left, and when to continue straight ahead. Special landmarks that will prove helpful in keeping you on the right track will be noted, along with any problem areas you can predetermine such as a road under construction, a bridge washed out, or a less-than-favorable weather report that might impede your progress.

The traveler who does this simple yet sensible kind of trip planning almost always gets where he or she is going right on (or even a little ahead of) schedule with few—if any—problems. This kind of person very likely also carries battery cables, emergency flares, a spare tire (always properly inflated), a roll of electrical tape to temporarily patch a defective water hose, and just about anything else necessary to treat an unexpected emergency as a minor inconvenience, rather than a major catastrophe.

On the other hand, I'm sure you know at least one individual who never bothers to check the best way of getting from one place to another. This is the sort of traveler who bumbles along getting totally lost, refusing to stop to ask for directions until he or she has driven 50 miles out of the way, and who always arrives late—if at all. It goes without saying that this type always has a spare that's flat, a jack that won't work, a lug wrench that's in the garage—or all three conditions—concurrent with every flat tire. I've known one or two of these nonplanners who have somehow managed to get where they were going most of the time. But one day their overworked guardian angel will take a vacation or their good luck will turn to bad, and they'll end up stranded, too.

What has this to do with business planning? Absolutely everything. You have obviously never guided your particular business through this particular time because this particular time has never before existed. Breakthroughs in technology, market conditions, interest rates, the availability of product and resources, changes in your competition, the overall political and economic situation, a multitude of constantly changing factors will influence your business positively or negatively. You can act in a planned and orderly manner to take maximum benefit of positive influences and to minimize negative influences, or you can react each time an inevitable crisis occurs, scrambling to gear up so as to take advantage of the peaks before they once again become valleys and desperately striving to survive the bad times that inevitably come.

A business plan offers you at least four major benefits. The first, and most important, is that a plan gives you a route to follow. A business plan assists you in making the future what you want it to be for your firm. It will help guide you through the bad times and to the good.

The next major benefit is that a business plan makes it much easier for your banker to be of assistance to you. By reading (or hearing) the details of your plan, your banker will have real insight into your situation and be much more likely to lend you money.

The third major benefit that a business plan affords you is that of communications. Your plan will become the tool you need to orient sales personnel, suppliers, and others with a need to know about your operations and goals.

Last, but not least, a business plan will help you develop as a manager. It will assist you in thinking about and planning for competitive conditions, promotional opportunities that present advantages to your business. It is a tool which, when used properly, can help increase your ability to make sound business decisions.

First and foremost, you must determine what business you are in. Once you have answered that crucial question, your business plan will consist mainly of asking yourself questions and providing yourself written answers to them.

When you have decided what business you are in, you're ready to consider another important part of your business plan—marketing. Successful marketing begins with you, the owner-manager of your firm. Your marketing plan moves on to determine your sales potential, decide how and when you will go about attracting customers, and the manner in which you and your sales personnel will sell to customers.

Lest you pooh-pooh the importance of a written business plan, let's examine just one small area that should be included in your marketing section: how you will go about attracting customers. Once you have determined your location, you must now figure out how you will attract customers to your store. How will you pull business away from your competition? Obviously, you can't possibly pull it away from your competitor unless you know every possible and conceivable detail about how the competition is operating. You must find your competitive advantage and take full advantage of it. Along these same lines, you must decide what image your store will project.

Another important aspect of attracting customers is your pricing policies. In what price ranges are your lines of merchandise to be sold? Will you handle only highest quality, go for medium-priced goods, position yourself as a low-priced outlet? What merchandise range will you stock? Will you sell only for cash? What services will you offer to justify your prices if they are higher than those charged by your competition? Will you offer credit? If so, remember credit costs have to come from somewhere. Recognize and plan for them. If you use a credit card system, what will it cost you? Will you have to add to your prices to absorb this cost?

And then there are customer service policies that must be dealt with. The services you provide your customers may be free to them, but they're not free to you. For example, if you provide parking, you must pay for the parking lot somehow. How? If you provide free gift wrapping, what will it cost and how will it be handled? How many services must you provide just to meet competition? Are there other services which would attract customers but which competitors are not now offering? If so, what are your estimates of the costs of each of these services?

Now you must proceed to plan your advertising. You've identified your store's strong points, major differences from your competitors, and the important facts about your store and its merchandise that your advertising must cover. You now come to grips with how much to spend, when to spend it, and where it will be spent. Finally, you must firmly define how you can measure the effectiveness of your efforts to attract customers.

I hope you can now see that each aspect of your marketing plan is anything but simplistic. It requires an investment of time, a great deal of thought, and the making of some tough decisions. But the final product, your business plan, will help guide you in the weeks and months to come, and it will assist you in gaining the cooperation and support of others—staff, lenders, suppliers, etc.—so that you're all pulling in the same direction and at the same time.

Your business plan will include a written plan for buying merchandise including the name of the item, the name and address of suppliers, discounts offered, the delivery time, freight costs, and fill-in policies. Your plan will include provisions for any fixtures and equipment that might be necessary for stock control and shipping and receiving.

Any behind-the-scenes work will be considered and systematized.

Getting the work done in an appropriate and timely fashion is relatively easy if you're the only employee of your company. All you have to do is never get sick and work like a dog. When you start adding employees, you also add the need to organize and systematize. This, then, becomes another important part of your written business plan. At a minimum, it will include a simple organizational chart, job descriptions for each employee, and whatever policies and procedures are necessary to ensure that everything that must get done does exactly that.

At about this point in your business plan, it's time to think about dollars. How many will it take and how many will you make?

Last, but certainly not least, you need to commit to paper your plans for control and feedback of your entire business plan. It obviously won't do you much good to commit all this data to paper and then never look at it again. And if you only plan to review your business plan once each year, it will be of minimum, if any, value to you. Your plan should be reviewed often, at regular intervals, and revised and adjusted to meet current conditions. At a minimum, plan to review your business plan once each month.

Obviously, developing a business plan takes time, effort, and a certain level of expertise. To make the job a good deal easier, I strongly encourage you to obtain a copy of the appropriate U.S. Small Business Administration Small Marketer's Aid on Business Planning. These are free of charge and are available for the asking from any field office of the U.S. Small Business Administration. The business plan for retailers is Small Marketer's Aid No. 150. The business plan for small service firms is no. 153. The business plan for small manufacturers is no. 218. Finally, the business plan for small construction firms is no. 221.

If you do not have a local field office of the Small Business Administration, you may request the appropriate business plan workbook by mail from the Small Business Administration, P.O. Box 15434, Fort Worth, Texas 76119.

This series on business plans is excellent, and the price is certainly right!

GOAL SETTING

Most small businesses fail. Most of the small businesses that fail do so because of a lack of management skill on the part of the owner, with the problems thus created magnified by undercapitalization. You know all that. And what has that to do with goal setting, anyway?

The answer is just about everything.

A tragically high percentage of all small businesses are opened with little or no marketing research, and the hardworking, well-intentioned owner and employees simply "do their best" each and every day, hoping that somehow, miraculously, enough income will be generated to handle the shop's fixed overhead and (even more miraculously!) leave a little something called profit for the owner to reinvest into the business, pay the kids' way through college, take a cruise around the world, or do whatever he or she might want to do with "all that money."

Too many small business owners operate in exactly this unplanned manner. Some might call it naiveté; I call it lunacy.

Not setting goals is just fine if you have no idea where you're going and couldn't care less when you get there, anyway. You need to be a cockeyed optimist to make it as an entrepreneur; you don't need to be an idiot. Forget the old "the Lord will provide" mentality. Take my word for it, God's busy with other things these days and hasn't any intention of providing monthly miracles so that you may meet your payroll.

Good intentions just won't cut it: You've got to set goals. A goal is simply an end toward which effort or ambition is directed. It gives aim and purpose to actions and activity. It delineates what state or condition is to be brought about and makes possible the planning of the course of action that will make the intention a reality.

All too few small firms even know what gross sales figures must be attained weekly, monthly, quarterly, and annually. Even fewer break this figure down so that each employee has goals or quotas they must reach. Little wonder few of them generate enough sales to stay in business.

But sales goals are only one kind of goal that can and should be set. Generally speaking, there are four kinds of goals. Regular work goals, problem-solving goals, innovative goals, and development goals.

The astute business owner sets goals that are both realistic and attainable. The goals require a little stretch; they can be met but only with concentrated effort.

The goals for your business will be unique. One of your goals might be to operate within the black within 18 months. Or you may want to open a second location within 5 years. Perhaps one of your goals will be to reduce complaints or to cut employee absenteeism by 50 percent over the next 12 months. Your goal could be to cut bad debts by 10 percent over the next quarter, or to get all accounts receivables in the 30-day column by the end of the year. You might establish as one of your goals that each of your sales staff will attend a special training course on product presentation within the next 2 years, or that you will reduce by 75 percent all industrial accidents at your firm this year.

Goals can be set and met in every area of your business. Until they are set, however, they cannot be met.

Setting goals for yourself and your staff cannot absolutely guarantee that yours will be one of the few small firms that will survive, grow, and prosper. But not setting goals will very definitely increase the odds in favor of failure.

Well, what are you waiting for? Set yourself some goals.

Management consists of planning, organizing, staffing, leading, and controlling. Management by objectives is a way of managing. It is both a system and a process.

A number of well-known clichés clearly express the need for a manager to be results-oriented. These include: "It's not what you do, but what you get done that counts." "You don't tell employees what they are supposed to do; you tell them what they are responsible for getting done." "The clearer the idea you have of what it is you are trying to accomplish, the greater are your chances of accomplishment." "If you know where you want to go, you increase your chances of getting there." Or the opposite, "If you don't know where you're going, any road will take you there."

These statements, truisms all, emphasize the fact that the most important consideration in a managerial situation is getting results. Equally important, results cannot be evaluated without some prior expectation or standard against which to measure them.

Management by objectives (MBO) concentrates first on setting objectives and determining the means to achieve them, and then seeing to it that results are forthcoming. The "father" of MBO, Peter Drucker, and others including George Morrisey, Anthony P. Raia, and George Odiorne have written books, designed courses, and produced a flurry of forms that define and outline the process and procedure. Some would argue rather effectively that this system is too confusing and too complex for any but the most devout and disciplined Harvard Business School graduate to implement.

But stripped to its essence, MBO makes excellent and productive sense for small business. Once you, the business owner, decide where you want to go and when you want to get there, you and your key employees should decide what steps will have to be taken to achieve these stated goals within the time frames given and how you will divide among you the various tasks that will have to be accomplished. You will then gather together regularly, say every month or two, to review your progress, make any necessary adjustments to the tasks and assignments, and carry on.

Again stripped to its essence, there are four basic components of the MBO system: setting objectives, developing action plans, conducting periodic reviews, and appraising the annual performance of each individual involved.

Under a well-conceived MBO system, the prevailing attitude is that an employee's job is to achieve his objectives, not change them. If for any reason it becomes difficult to achieve a given objective, the employee's job is to develop new plans—or modify existing ones—that take into consideration the difficulties encountered. The strategy is to change or modify plans, not objectives, unless market conditions have changed in a way that makes achieving the objectives unnecessary, impossible, or irrelevant.

Obviously, there is a whole batch of benefits to be accrued by your firm under the MBO system. At the top of the list is the fact that everyone knows where you're going, how you're going to get there, and when you intend to arrive. With your entire staff setting out at the same time for the same place with the same objectives, the journey should be pleasant and the destination profitable.

Management by objectives also will immeasurably assist you in evaluating your employees and assist you in determining just compensation for each. Under management by objectives, it's performance—not personalities—that counts. A clear understanding of what constitutes good performance is fundamental. When your firm practices MBO, objectives serve as standards against which the individuals can measure their own performance. Good performance is defined as the individuals' ability to get results, and they are evaluated on the basis of the progress being made.

Numerous studies have shown that there are a number of frequently encountered reasons for poor employee performance: Individuals may not know what is expected of them; they may not know how they are doing in terms of the results expected; they cannot do what is expected because of inadequate training and education; the employees may not do what is expected because they are not motivated to perform efficiently; they may lack the organizational support necessary for effective performance; and last but not least, they may have a poor relationship with "the boss."

A good MBO program is designed to greatly reduce—if not totally eliminate—most of these problems.

Under most systems (or nonsystems), good employees do what they think they should, and less-good employees do what they think they must. The problem is, neither group knows exactly what is expected of them by you—the employer. The overwhelming majority of employees also get caught in the 80/20 percent trap. That is to say, most of us spend 80 percent of our time doing what we want to do and 20 percent of our time doing what we ought to do. Just imagine how productivity and profitability could be affected if you and your employees spent more time on the important stuff.

Further confusing the issue is the fact that precious few employees know what *you* consider to be important stuff. You may feel the only important task for your salesperson to complete is the attainment of 100 percent of his or her sales quota for the month. Your salesperson, on the other hand, fusses about for 7 hours a day straightening stock, dusting shelves, and ensuring that everything looks neat and tidy at all times. He or she doesn't even know what the sales quota figure is and regards every customer as a necessary but very temporary interruption in stock maintenance activities. Obviously, you're going to be unhappy, the employee is never going to know what led up to the pink slip in his or her pay envelope, and the ultimate loser is your business. Management by objectives puts an end to all that nonsense.

Instead of a job description that lists tasks and functions, MBO provides your employees with an action plan and measurable, quantifiable goals and objectives that they are responsible for achieving. If what you really want from your salespeople is a 10 percent increase in sales over last year, say so. Let your staff know what last year's sales figures were; support their efforts with the necessary advertising, promotion, and public relations efforts; provide whatever staff support is necessary; review progress on a regular (probably monthly) basis. With all other things being equal, you will very likely have a 10 percent sales increase 1 year from now.

Management by objectives has been proved effective in getting results. If you are a results-oriented person and you want to operate a results-oriented business, start managing by objectives. And remember, if you don't plan for it, it'll happen anyway.

13

The Hand That Used to Rock the Cradle

Throughout history, women have always been producers. To them fell the tasks of producing and processing the majority of the family's foodstuffs and the manufacture of nearly everything the family wore; much of what passed for medicine was concocted by the woman of the house; and the family females were responsible for producing everything from bed linen to the lye soap with which to wash the linen. In past generations, men wrote books but women manufactured the candles by which those books were read.

Woman as consumer is a relatively recent phenomenon. And thanks to inflation, we've once again come full circle. No longer can woman be counted on by corporate America to consume its goods and services. She must now produce enough income to help pay for them.

Once again, we see woman as producer. She not only brings home much of the bacon, she is usually still the family member in charge of cooking it!

Many would blame the monumental numbers of women entering the work force on the sexual revolution, the women's movement, or a combination of a dozen other factors. While each has played its part, the move out of the kitchen and into the marketplace would likely have occurred no matter what. Our current inflationary spiral has made the two-paycheck family not just a reality but a necessity in most cases. Whatever the forces at work, women at work outside the home for pay is both a fact and a factor in everyday modern life.

The start of the eighties saw some historically significant statistical milestones: For the first time in history, more than half the adult female population worked for pay outside the home, and women comprised 42 percent of the total American labor force.

Just 10 years ago, women-owned businesses in the United States were estimated to number less than 500,000. In 1980, that estimate had soared to 1.8 million women-owned businesses in America.

This phenomenal increase is attributed to many causes: the new pool of experience and expertise created by the rapid rise in the total number of women in the work force; the increased numbers of women seeking gainful employment and being frustrated in that search; the hundreds of thousands of women being graduated from institutions of higher learning; the millions of women displaced from their traditional homemaker role by death or divorce; the new batch of role models that successful women entrepreneurs represent to other women.

There is also rising receptivity toward women-owned firms on the part of the financial community, government, and the private sector. New laws and new programs have considerably lessened the traditional chauvinistic resistence to woman as entrepreneur. Notice, I said lessened—not eradicated. Prejudice still exists and must be dealt with by any woman who seeks success as the owner-operator of her own firm.

SPECIAL PITFALLS AND PROBLEMS OF WOMEN IN BUSINESS

Generally speaking, female small business owners face the same problems as their male counterparts—only more so. While there are exceptions of both genders, those uniquely fortunate individuals who successfully run a small business tend to be more exceptional and more special when they also happen to be female.

Most small business owners suffer from a lack of adequate capital. Women tend to be even more undercapitalized for a number of reasons. If a woman has been working outside the home, odds are she's been earning considerably less than her male counterpart and consequently has had less of an opportunity to accumulate a personal net worth that's worth very much. Along this same line, the amount of credit available to her is likely to be limited.

While still on the subject of credit, a budding businesswoman is again much more likely to face discriminatory lending practices when she seeks her first or subsequent business loans. While the law grants women equal rights to credit, a banker or other lender can find dozens of perfectly legal reasons on which to base a "no" that are in reality expressions of sexual bias. When you add to individual prejudice most women's scanty-to-nonexistent credit history and little or nothing collateral by which to secure the loan, you have a pretty accurate (albeit grim) picture of what the average businesswoman faces when seeking to borrow money.

Outside investors also tend (for much the same reasons) to be less receptive to the woman business owner than to a man seeking a similar commitment. The only practical way to combat resistance on the part of a banker or an investor is to be so well-prepared, so businesslike, so knowledgeable you literally knock 'em dead with the facts. A well-written, well-documented business plan and loan proposal are musts. And you should understand every number and word they contain. It doesn't hurt to grow a thicker skin and to develop the female equivalent of Job's patience, either. One woman client got thirteen "nos" before a banker (a woman, by the way!) said "yes" to her loan request.

In an attempt to "equalize" the woman businessowner's access to start-up and expansion capital, the federal government has recently instituted several programs. The lead agency for most of them is the Small Business Administration. In 1979, for example, SBA was empowered to make special "mini-loans" to women. Amounts up to $20,000 were made avaible to qualified women borrowers direct from SBA, which meant much lower interest rates than when dealing with a private-sector financial institution. How long this program will continue is anyone's guess, given the vagaries of federal spending. But it's certainly worth checking with your SBA office to see if it's still in effect.

Women-owned firms are also (under certain circumstances) given preferential treatment by SBA-chartered and -funded small business investment corporations (SBICs) and their for-minorities-only counterpart, the MESBICs (minority enterprise small business investment corporation). Hard-to-get venture capital may be available to you through this program.

There is a new government mandate to buy more from, lend more to, and help more women-owned businesses, which will, it is hoped, raise significantly the number of women actively involved in the small business sector of our economy by increasing women's ownership of small, profitable companies.

Since government programs change constantly, a visit to your nearest Small Business Administration and/or Department of Commerce office is a trip worth taking. Ask to see their "women in business" specialist. The fact that such a position finally exists is progress in itself.

The lack of management skills is a universal problem among small business owners. A woman is much less likely to have occupied a middle- or top-management position prior to opening her own firm. This lack of practical supervisory and decision-making experience must be recognized and dealt with appropriately. On a more encouraging note, attendance by women at small business management workshops and seminars conducted by SBA and others is up significantly.

Women entrepreneurs also suffer from a lack of role models. Since there are far fewer successful existing women business owners than there are men in similar positions, the aspiring woman entrepreneur will find it much harder to locate a mentor to act as her guide or role model after which to pattern herself. Even with the enormous increases in women-owned businesses over the past decade, a woman seeking to own and operate her own firm is still very much in the minority; she may be viewed as a pioneer, an oddity, or both.

Most small businesses, regardless of the sex of their owners, are clustered in the service and retail categories—both high-risk, low-return-on-investment areas. Small businesses owned by women are almost exclusively service or retail in nature. Most women-owned businesses are very small; the majority have no employees, most are operated as sole proprietorships, and the overwhelming preponderance have gross annual sales of less than $100,000.

Added to all the other categorical small business problems, the woman entrepreneur is very likely to encounter some prejudice and discrimination on the part of her customers. Unfortunately, there is still also some resistance on the part of employees to working for a "woman boss."

While the woman business owner can take appropriate steps to ensure that her staff's attitudes are reasonably positive, she'll have to face customer resistance in whatever manner seems most appropriate at the time. Being human, your first inclination will very likely be to tell the bigoted "oink-oink" exactly where he or she can go. And I do mean "he or she." Resistance to doing business with a woman-owned firm can unfortunately be found on either side of the gender line.

My advice would be—unless your very honor is at stake—to hold your temper and your tongue. In business, bridges are for building—not burning. I have personally encountered situations where reluctance and resistance to doing business with a woman-owned firm (namely, my own) were overcome after additional work on my part and additional growth on "theirs." The ensuing business relationship was pleasant and profitable for both involved parties.

You can expect little or no customer resistance if your business activities are confined to the more "traditional" women-owned endeavors. Customer resistance increases dramatically when your business activities are in an area that could be termed nontraditional.

For example, a woman owning and operating a dress shop will encounter very little (if any) customer resistance. A woman-owned advertising and public relations firm will encounter some; such resistance will accelerate when her firm bids on male-oriented and -dominated accounts such as in automobile, technical, and heavy manufacturing areas. The resistance really gets heavy when the woman-owned business is itself an automobile dealership, highly technical in nature, or involved in manufacturing of any kind.

Women have wanted, needed, and deserved equality for a long time. Unfortunately, in the small business arena they are more than equal. They have the same multitudinous problems faced by the male of the species, only accentuated by archaic attitudes, misconceptions, and erroneous ideas that make making it a lot harder for the so-called weaker sex.

You can take heart from a slogan popularized by the current women's movement: "A woman has to work twice as hard and be twice as smart as a man to succeed in the same job. Fortunately, this isn't very difficult."

NOT-FOR-MEN-ONLY BUSINESS OPPORTUNITIES

Just as women are beginning to make some small progress as employees in jobs that offer upward mobility and career potential, so women entrepreneurs are waking up to the exciting prospects presented by small business ownership in areas that promise real growth and profit potential.

Women can no longer just drive cars or buy cars; they now sell cars. And while the ownership of new car dealerships is still very predominately a male domain, a number of women have broken the sex barrier and are doing very well, indeed, as automobile dealers. No longer do women simply keep house; they now design houses, construct houses, paint, plumb, wallpaper, reroof, and landscape the old homesteads of the world as business owners providing these services.

Women no longer just cook the family meals; there are women-owned firms growing food, commercially freezing and canning foodstuffs, hauling food and other products from one end of this country to the other, catering, and running restaurants ranging from fast-food to gourmet. Women own candy companies, the rights and recipes to patented bread and other specialty food items, fisheries, canneries, hatcheries, piggeries, dairies, chicken ranches, and everything in between.

Where women were once the primary target for all advertising messages, more and more women are owning and operating the agencies that create, produce, and place advertising and public relations material. Small and not-so-small fortunes have been made by Mary Wells Lawrence, Jane Trahey, Barbara Proctor, and any one of dozens more women I could name in the advertising business. While not yet numerous in the field, women are finally beginning to become owners of radio and television stations. And with a role model like Katherine Graham of the Washington Post, female ownership of print media is also growing by leaps and bounds.

Women now own banks, insurance companies, savings and loan associations, film studios, manufacturing plants, resorts, moving and storage companies, and dozens of other small and not-so-small businesses once considered the exclusive purview of those who wore blue booties as babies.

Until fairly recently, Olive Ann Beech was *the* guiding force behind Beech Aircraft and the Beechcraft's dramatic share of market increases. Ms. Beech had little academic or technical training; she started as the boss's secretary and made Beechcraft practically synonymous with private plane after her husband's illness and death put her in the pilot's seat. Mary Kay Ash has thousands of homemakers selling millions of dollars' worth of Mary Kay cosmetics each year. Beneath her almost-too-sweet exterior beats a businesslike heart that keeps her staff hopping and her banker happy. Her habit of handing out pink Cadillacs to top producers has paid off. Her company expects retail sales in excess of $150 million in fiscal year 1981. And Jean Nidetch turned the need to personally drop 70 pounds from her then-pudgy frame into Weight Watchers International, a multimillion dollar business that helps "fatties" slim down.

For any woman still wondering if the female of the species really has what it takes to make it in a "man's world," I would suggest two excellent and inspiring books: *Enterprising Women* by Carolyn Byrd and *Millionairess* by Lois Rich-McCoy. Ms. Byrd's book will give the reader an historical perspective of our enterprising foremothers. The second book will introduce you to a dozen remarkable self-made businesswomen. The most remarkable thing about this now-wealthy twelve is how much like *you* they really are. And if they can do it, so can you.

Women are also breaking into the lucrative area of federal contracts with something of a vengeance. Federal procurement from women-owned firms reached $200 million in fiscal year 1980. That figure should reach $600 million by the end of fiscal year 1982, with more to come.

Government literally does buy everything from soup to nuts. And an aggressive outreach effort is underway to identify woman-owned firms interested in and capable of contracting for the goods and services necessary to keep the federal bureaucracy well-supplied with weapons, printing, air-conditioning filters, toothbrushes, rubber bands, fried chicken, and any of several thousand other items it uses each year.

A bit of a caveat: Selling to the government can be complicated and costly for the uninitiated. If you are at all interested, see your friendly neighborhood Small Business Administration office for procurement assistance. Ask about registering your firm in SBA's Procurement Automated Source System (PASS). Once you're on the PASS system, your company's capabilities will be instantly available via computer when requests are made by federal purchasing offices seeking potential small business bidders on contracts. A couple of SBA publications that can give you more insight into federal procurement are "Selling to the U.S. Government," publication number PA-1, and "SBA's Procurement and Technical Assistance Programs," PA-3. Both are available free of charge through your nearest SBA office.

Also keep in mind that smaller units of government and almost all federal subcontractors of any significance are subject to the federal guidelines mandating that 10 percent of all procurement contracts utilizing federal funds must be awarded to small, minority, or woman-owned firms. While scrap iron, trucking, construction, or any of the other previously all-male avenues to financial independence may not personally appeal to you, just keep in mind that a lot of sexist walls are tumbling down these days. I must admit, it warms the cockles of my feminist heart every time I see my friend Lynn and her also-female partner exceeding everyone's expectations and projections in their microbiology laboratory business. And the mere thought of glamorous grandma Gilda Gjurich, a general contractor in Los Angeles, California, in her gold-plated hard hat directing her construction crews as they put the finishing touches on a new shopping center just absolutely makes my day!

WHAT CAN I DO FOR MONEY THAT I'VE ALWAYS DONE FOR FREE?

Many women who want to operate their own small businesses, need to generate additional income, or both find it difficult to determine what sort of business might be right for them. The majority of those who open and operate their own firms venture into small business ownership as a direct result of paid employment. In other words, they serve a sort of apprenticeship period working for someone else and then open a similar business of their own.

Especially if a woman has been a full-time homemaker to date, she can sometimes experience considerable difficulty identifying and assessing her marketable skills and talents. Funny that this should be a problem! The most recent statistics measuring the dollar value of the average homemaker's work in 1980 price her varied services at $41,000 per year. That is to say, it would cost that much money to replace her many chores, skills, and talents with outside paid labor.

Let's simply examine a few of the many products and services the "typical" homemaker produces or performs and see how these might translate into small business opportunities:

Cooking

While not everyone's mother produced meals by which the standard was set, most women learn to cook at an early age. We've already touched on a few of the obvious small business opportunities to which skills and talents in the kitchen can lead, but let's briefly explore a couple of unique "twists" that might spark your imagination. One enterprising woman got her family off to work and school each morning, made up a delicious assortment of sandwiches, and packed a large wicker hamper with her daily assortment. She augmented the sandwiches with delicious homebaked cookies and beautiful ripe fruit and headed for a nearby high-rise office complex. Between 10:00

A.M. and 12:00 noon she toured the various offices selling workers a veritable desk top banquet. It didn't take long before some offices were placing special orders with her and business was booming. She soon had to hire several friends to assist in the production, plus another twelve "lunch ladies" wearing frilly aprons to carry the huge wicker baskets full of goodies to all the major offices in the area. Another enterprising cook turned a family fruitcake recipe into a booming mail-order business. She uses the very finest in ingredients but still averages 50 percent profit on every $10 fruitcake she sells. And she sells a lot of fruitcakes!

Cleaning

The need for "dial-a-maid" and other types of janitorial and cleaning services is both obvious and growing. Most of these services are bonded and send in highly trained, efficient, competent teams of two or more workers. While the current price per hour sounds high ($10 and up), it's really a bargain when you know how these teams operate. I've seen two workers turn a room unfit for human habitation into a sparkling showplace ready for the most demanding inspection in 15 minutes! A good team can go through the average residence in 2 to 3 hours.

Errands and Chores

With the growth in the number of single heads of household, two-paycheck families, and one-parent families, the obvious need for someone to do odd jobs and errands becomes apparent. Based on the success of her "rent-a-wife" service, one enterprising woman is expanding to include "rent-a-husband" services. While nothing conjugal is implied or intended, the services do cover everything from hanging pictures to waiting for appliance repair people and deliveries. Requests have covered watering plants while the homeowner was off on vacation, assisting with Christmas shopping, and "helping a color-blind bachelor with no taste" move into his new home.

Child Care

This can range from taking a couple of kids in addition to your own into your home to operating a licensed day-care or preschool facility. To fill some of the unique and growing child-care needs, one enterprising woman offers 24-hour-a-day, 7-day-a-week care in her large, kid-proof home to the parent who travels on business or the couple which both needs and deserves a week or 2 of vacation away from their offspring. Another woman offers homework assistance, creative play, and storytelling to fill the hours between when school lets out and when mom and dad get home from work for a child too old for a day-care center but too young to be alone.

Entertaining

Two bright young women I know more than paid their ways through college by producing creative and easy-on-mom children's parties. They came up with several theme approaches including circus, magic, cowboys and Indians, and fairy princess parties. Another astute businesswoman turned her "Perle Mesta" tendencies into a going and growing concern specializing in business parties. She has planned everything from the boss's daughter's wedding to conventions for 7000. In addition to making a tidy profit, she goes to a lot of good parties!

Hobbies and Such

Amazing as it may seem, what you now do for fun you can also do for money. Sewing, knitting, macrame, jewelry making, furniture refinishing, doll houses and miniatures, typing, picture framing, pottery, painting, photography, bookkeeping, antiques, animals and pets, all these and many more can and have been turned into profitable home businesses, mail-order enterprises, or have served as the basis for the more traditional out-of-home shop.

Keep in mind that teaching other people how to do these things can also be a pleasant and profitable entrée into your own business.

While this list is certainly not all-inclusive, you can take it from here. An in-depth inventory of your individual skills, talents, and interests should produce several good potential profit-generating areas worthy of further analysis and exploration.

PROFIT IS NOT A FOUR-LETTER WORD

The major problems likely to be encountered by a woman entering the rarefied atmosphere of small business ownership will not come from outside sources and forces. They will be internal, self-generated, and stem from years of acculturation and conditioning, first as a girl-type child and then as a young woman.

To a greater or lesser degree, the attitudes and attributes infused into little girls from infancy on are going to have to be unlearned and overcome. One of the first you'll have to deal with is the idea of doing something for profit. That idea sounds pretty good to most men and some women. But the majority of females tend to have some rather strange notions regarding profit. Our society trains women to be loving, giving, caring, and sharing and inculcates them with the erroneous notion that money is not very important and that generating a profit is, at best, rather crass.

Women are usually also reared to be noncompetitive, but competition and a truly competitive spirit are both a reality and a necessity in the business world.

Much has been written in the recent past regarding women's fear of success. Not nearly enough attention has been paid to the even more paralyzing "fear of failure" syndrome shared by an inordinate and disproportionate number of women.

Since you obviously must risk failure to achieve success, you are going to have to deal with this one, like it or not. In workshops and seminars for women in business, many of my participants have found it helpful to recognize this personality pitfall. Especially when it comes to fear of failure, keep in mind that failing does not make *you* a failure. Not trying is the only thing that can do that. And becoming wildly successful or, conversely, attempting brave, new ventures with less than the expected outcomes does not make you any more or less lovable or loving—unless you allow either condition to change who you really are and how you react to the people you care about.

Women tend to view both success and failure as somehow "unfeminine." Obviously, given a choice, it's a lot more fun to succeed. But missing the mark—whether by a little or by a lot—can be a learning, growing experience. And the true entrepreneur, whether male or female, views what the rest of the world calls failure as a very temporary condition, subject to change at the first possible opportunity.

Women are reared with a lot of unproductive and downright dumb attitudes that the woman business owner will have to rid herself of, deal with, or work around. Trust me: Competition is fun, not unfeminine; being wildly successful or not quite making it does not in and of itself make you either lovable or unlovable; and profit is not a four-letter word.

WHAT HAVE YOU GOT TO LOSE?

In the work world, women earn 59 cents to every male dollar. While new numbers of women are moving into the ranks of middle management, top management is still pretty much a male-only locker room. And when you find a woman in the boardroom, it's still natural to assume she's someone's secretary. I didn't say "right," I said "natural."

I could continue this appalling litany, but I think my point has been made. Women are not exactly sitting on top of the work world. So when it comes right down to making the decision as to whether you should risk what you've got for what you want, why not go for it?

As a woman business owner, you face the same long hours, loneliness, frustration, fear, panic, worry, risk, potential for failure, and multitude of problems as does your male colleague. You also experience the same exhilaration of watching and guiding your fledgling firm as it progresses from an idea that keeps you awake nights to a reality that produces paychecks and profits.

You'll have the opportunity to make a lot more money than you've ever made before, and will run the awesome risk of losing everything you've managed to accumulate if it doesn't work out as planned. The pressure on your personal life will likely be much greater than that experienced by your male counterpart.

You'll be joining a pretty exclusive club: 1.8 million other women in the U.S.A. who own and operate their own shops. Club membership requires a lot—most of all, guts.

As my friend Barbara Gardner Proctor so eloquently put it: "Women are pretty much a flop collectively right now, so what have we got to lose? Besides, with the mess the world is in today we can't possibly do any worse than the men have already done!"

With all due respect to Marie Calendar, I don't really think women will ever completely stop baking pies (it is, after all, sort of fun). But most women also want a bigger piece of the economic pie than they've ever had before. For many, small business ownership is a viable way to get what they're after.

14

What to Do When All Else Has Failed

It is simply not possible to plan for every contingency. If it were, you could eliminate the possibility of failure entirely. While good planning and careful management will minimize the risk and improve your chance for success, there simply is no 100 percent fail-safe approach to small business ownership.

A business can fail for many reasons. A fire, flood, or other "act of God" could lead to the discovery that your insurance coverage is inadequate to the task at hand. A trusted employee could embezzle funds, leaving a financial hole so large the entire business falls into it. A key member of your staff could leave to form his or her own firm and take the lion's share of your clients along. A vital raw material or component might become unavailable, or too costly, or the country could experience an economic downturn so severe you simply cannot survive. Your firm's demise may come as a result of a large competitor underbidding you right out of the marketplace. You may simply find that not enough people want to buy what you have to sell.

Unpleasant though the thought may be, anyone going into business must face the possibility of having to go out of business on a negative note. What, then, can you do when everything else has failed?

DON'T JUMP

It was late afternoon. My secretary was off ill, the receptionist was down the hall at the copy center, and no one else on my staff even noticed the middle-aged man as he made his way to my office. I was a bit startled when I looked up as he entered my office unannounced, stated in a flat monotone, "If you can't help me, I'm going to kill myself," and lowered himself into the chair in front of my desk. His elbows on his knees, his head resting in his hands, he was the personification of abject depression.

Intuitively, I knew this fellow wasn't kidding. His was no idle threat. I didn't know what his problem was, but whatever it was, he felt it was big enough to end his life.

"Why don't you tell me about it," I said softly, hoping and praying I could say and do the right thing.

The man raised his head slowly, his eyes fixed on a spot on the carpet a few feet in front of his chair. In the same flat voice he told a classic small business horror story. He was an engineer by profession. A couple of years earlier, he mortgaged his home, cashed in his retirement plan, took a loan on his insurance policies, and shelled out $180,000, his entire net worth, as a down payment on a small manufacturing plant. He knew absolutely nothing about manufacturing, nothing about small business, nothing about accounting, precious little about supervision of personnel, had absolutely no sales experience, and had purchased an already failing business from a very good salesman.

After limping along for the toughest 2 years of his life, robbing Peter to pay Paul and borrowing heavily attempting to cover his losses, the man had finally reached the end of his rope. He had simply walked out of his office and had been wandering around aimlessly for almost 24 hours, trying to get up enough courage to go home and tell his wife that the business was bankrupt and they were about to lose everything they owned.

He completed his story by stating he had heard that our agency helped small businesses and repeated, "If you can't help me, I'm going to kill myself."

I took a deep breath, crossed my fingers, and began. "Mister, I don't know whether we can save your business or not. We'll sure give it a heck of a try. But a business failure certainly isn't anything to end your life! Suicide is a *terribly* permanent solution to a very temporary problem, no matter what the problem happens to be. And if the business can't be salvaged, we'll help you wind things down as painlessly as possible. And believe me, if that *is* what happens, you'll go on to do a lot of good and meaningful things."

I called in one of my staff, an absolute gem of a fiscal analyst, and together we spent the next hour with our troubled new friend asking questions and getting answers. It was soon very apparent that the business was long past saving. It probably couldn't have been saved if we'd been called in the day he'd bought the place, much less 2 years down a very bumpy road. We arranged for him to see one of our top legal advisers first thing the next morning. And somehow we convinced him that a failure in business, while certainly an unpleasant thing to have to go through, was not the end of the world.

This particular story has a very happy ending. Oh yes, the man did declare bankruptcy. There was absolutely no way around that. And he and his wife did suffer some rather severe financial setbacks. But he is once again gainfully employed in his chosen profession; his wife stood by him like the trooper she had always been, and they are living a full, happy, productive life.

Thousands upon thousands of corporations and individuals declare bankruptcy each year. While I'm sure none of them consider it fun, the vast majority do survive the experience rather nicely. Admitting that you failed in something you set out to do is never easy. But you *will* have another chance—unless you jump. So don't jump. Because everyone deserves a second chance—especially you.

BANKRUPTCY IN BRIEF

For hundreds of years, people who couldn't, wouldn't, or didn't pay their bills were subject to imprisonment, indentured service, or one of many other unpleasant punishments. As a matter of fact, being the son or daughter of a debtor could net you the same penalty even though you may have had absolutely nothing to do with getting your parents into debt. Then we got a little more humane. We started allowing individuals, married couples, and corporations to wipe the slate clean through a legal action called bankruptcy. Of course, in the process the bankrupt became a social pariah, incapable of utilizing credit for so many years it seemed like forever, I'm sure.

While it's still not considered the ideal way to endear yourself to either present or future creditors, bankruptcy is not necessarily the end of either your social standing or your ability to establish credit.

A significant number of bankruptcies are handled by individuals without benefit of significant legal counsel. In some judicial districts, this do-it-yourself group is running a sizable 30 to 40 percent of the total bankruptcy cases heard. It is possible to file for bankruptcy without benefit of an attorney. It is not the ideal, in my opinion.

To begin with, bankruptcy is a fairly complex legal action and should be handled on your behalf by competent legal counsel. The individual facing such an action has several legal options from which to choose, and these critical decisions can best be made with the help of a lawyer. There is also a great deal to be said for having someone whose mission is to look out for whatever is left of your interests. My advice is that, if at all possible, you scrape together the requisite legal fees and hire the best professional help you can afford. Be prepared to pay up front for these services. After all, your credit rating at the moment is a bit shakey, to say the very least.

While bankruptcy wipes your slate clean of most debts, alimony, taxes, and long-term mortgages cannot be discharged by declaring bankruptcy.

When you file a claim of bankruptcy, interest charges and legal actions against you (or your firm) stop automatically while a court-appointed trustee (who receives a fee paid by you out of assets) tries to untangle the mess you've gotten yourself into financially. I'm convinced that many individuals who declare bankruptcy would not do so if they were not being hounded and harassed by creditors. Many folks finally just reach the point where they absolutely cannot take one more nasty phone call, knock on the door, or threatening letter, so they quiet the creditors by filing a bankruptcy action. It does put an instantaneous stop to all this sort of thing! Once you inform a creditor you are declaring bankruptcy, they absolutely cannot (by law) continue to attempt to collect on your debt. It's a pretty heavy price to pay for peace and quiet, but one a lot of people every year are willing to pay.

Under the newly revamped Federal Bankruptcy Code, there are two types of bankruptcy available to individuals. If you have a regular income and some assets, you can take the so-called partial repayment bankruptcy. Under this action, you continue to work and own property while you pay off your debt under court supervision. This is also sometimes called a wage earner plan. The administrative office of the U.S. Courts Guidelines allows you to keep up to 75 percent of your take-home pay. The other 25 percent is used to repay your bills.

If you have a regular and stable income, you can take as long as 3 years to pay, and pay as little as a few cents on each dollar owed. The amount to be paid to each creditor is determined by the court. Under the revamped bankruptcy code which went into effect in October 1979, this partial payment is also available for the first time to self-employed individuals.

If you have no regular income, few assets, or cannot possibly spare one-quarter of your income to repay your bills (at least in part), straight bankruptcy is an option. This will mean listing and selling all of the assets and property that the court determines you don't need for survival. For example, your house and car would be exempt, your TV set and coin collection would not. The proceeds from the sale of your assets are then divided among all those you owe, and that's pretty much the end of it.

If you operated your business as a corporation, it is possible that only the assets of the corporation would be liquidated to pay off the company's debts. But corporate shields are neither bullet- nor bankruptcy-proof. You may consciously or unconsciously have stepped outside the corporate shield to pledge your own personal assets when obtaining an SBA loan or other funding for your firm. You may personally have guaranteed other purchase or lease agreements. It's not an open-and-shut, cut-and-dried situation. Which is another reason why I strongly encourage you to seek the assistance of a qualified attorney-at-law.

Before you file a petition for bankruptcy, you'll be asked to list your debts and assets in considerable detail. A hearing date will be set and you will be notified as to when you should appear in court. Following your day in court, during which you declare yourself bankrupt, the court's trustee will see to the liquidation of assets and distribution of same to your creditors. As I said, not fun—but not the end of the world, either. Do be advised that information about bankruptcy remains on your credit record for 14 years. While it used to be a black mark that made it virtually impossible to regain your credit reputation, this is no longer necessarily the case. I have assisted clients with two bankruptcies on their records to obtain small business financing in the healthy six-figure area. And since you can only declare bankruptcy once each 7 years as a maximum, many credit-granting organizations no longer view a past declaration of bankruptcy as automatic grounds for denial of your application for credit. But obviously, even given the new leniency, bankruptcy should be your last resort.

Probably the greatest testimonial to the entrepreneurial spirit that I've ever encountered is a fellow discussing his plans to incorporate a new business with his attorney as they left the courtroom following the gentleman's bankruptcy hearing.

"Good Lord, John. How can you be thinking of opening a business today? You're bankrupt!" said his attorney.

"It's my business that went broke, not me. I have at least a million ideas left!"

Now that's what I call an entrepreneur.

BATTERED BANKROLL, BRUISED EGO

Don't get me wrong: The events and decisions leading up to a declaration of bankruptcy are painful, traumatic, sometimes debilitating, and always difficult. Unfortunately, some people find a business failure so demoralizing, they do end the experience by suicide. Many others find the collective strain on marital relationships so overwhelming that the divorce court and the bankruptcy court follow each other in quick succession.

The exceptionally resilient entrepreneur I mentioned earlier is just that: exceptional. Your stress tolerance levels and coping skills will obviously be different from those of the man or woman seated next to you in bankruptcy court. Again, how battered your bankroll and bruised your ego are following a business failure will be unique to you and your situation.

Your bankroll will obviously be battered. The financial consequences of your business failure can range from a relatively mild inconvenience to a complete devastation of your financial resources.

If your bankruptcy involves your personal assets and liabilities, you may opt to reaffirm some or all of your personal debts. That is to say, you wi' sign a new contractual relationship agreement with those creditors you ' untarily choose to continue paying until the original debt is satisfied. If at all possible, I would certainly encourage you to do this. It makes obtaining credit in the future considerably easier when you have made whatever extraordinary efforts are called for to satisfy your past credit obligations.

If your credit history was pretty sloppy before the bankruptcy, you'll find it *much* more difficult to reestablish credit following your petition for bankruptcy.

If, on the other hand, you have always handled credit in a responsible manner, most lending institutions and credit-granting firms will take this into account when determining whether to extend your credit in the future.

Whether your personal situation finds you just a little bent or totally broke, your number one chore will be to find yourself gainful employment. Once you are generating some regular income, you'll begin to see a light at the end of the tunnel. And it's probably not a train coming in the other direction.

How battered you'll find your bankroll really depends on a number of variables. If the business was a strictly corporate affair, about all you'll need to do is find another job to replace the income from your business. Life keeps right on without much of a beat skipped. If, on the other hand, you operated your business as a sole proprietorship and the firm bore your name on the door, the consequences can be truly devastating. You might end up with a roof over your head if you can still make the mortgage payments, enough furniture to get by on, a car, and not much else. But things can be replaced, savings accounts can be rebuilt, and financial solvency can be reestablished.

The bankroll side of bankruptcy is usually the easiest to rebuild. The bruising that your ego takes in living through a business failure is something else again. It's tough, to say the least, to have to admit there was something you couldn't quite pull off—no matter what the reason behind the actual failure.

How bruised your ego and how permanent the damage will be a very individual thing. The variables here can include everything from your personal faith in God to your own positive self-concept, how the business failure affects your personal relationships, how visible you are in your community, and how public the knowledge of your business failure becomes. Obviously, every bankruptcy action is listed in the legal notices of the newspaper. There are folks (one might call them ghouls) who delight in reading legal notices and obituary columns. If their perception of you is important, you have a big problem on your hands. Of course, in my opinion, if their opinion of you was ever important, you've had a problem on your hands for some time.

If you're just setting up shop, you may want to consider how fragile your ego is when naming your firm. If you're John Jones and you make widgets, you may get some ego gratification out of naming your business John Jones Widgets, Inc. But you also may get considerably more lumps to your ego if the firm goes under one day than you would if you named your company the Widget Corporation of America. If W.C.A. goes belly up, John Jones doesn't personally take quite the ego battering.

There is, unavoidably, a lot of psychic pain involved in a business failure. After all, you have invested more of your personal time, energy, money, effort, love, personality, talent, plans, hopes, dreams, skills, and just plain hard work to your shop than in probably any other single effort or relationship you have ever undertaken in your life. Once you realize that it's OK to hurt, the healing process begins. Just as I am quick to refer small business owners to expert assistance in the fields of finance, law, insurance, etc., I am also quick to advise that anyone experiencing great emotional trauma and turmoil can and should seek assistance from a qualified expert. Whether you turn to a member of the clergy, a loving and trusted friend, a psychologist or psychiatrist, if the emotional pain of a business failure begins to be overwhelming, seek out someone with whom you can talk it out and gain a fresh perspective on the problem.

There is a cost, both financial and emotional, in a business failure. There are also some extraordinary rewards—both financial and emotional—in a business success. Ideally, you'll achieve the latter without ever having to experience the former. But always remember that you can experience the former, learn from the experience, and go on to achieve success beyond anything you previously imagined. Whether you find yourself on a high or at an all-time low, you'd be well-served to remember that nothing on this earth is forever.

PICK YOURSELF UP, DUST YOURSELF OFF, AND START ALL OVER AGAIN

OK, so you blew it. Your business failed. Like divorce, catastrophic illness, airplane crashes, and a child who grew up to be Jack the Ripper, you always thought it would never happen to you. But it did. So now what?

You have a choice. You're in the pits, down just about as low as you can get. You can stay there, or you can—as the song says—pick yourself up, dust yourself off, and start all over again. If you're weird enough to enjoy being at the bottom of the barrel, you'll probably opt to stay down. If that's your situation, I have nothing further to say. Except you probably should not have gone into business to begin with. If, on the other hand, you're not too thrilled with failure, then let's get going.

As I said earlier, nothing is forever. Not even the good stuff. But luckily this also means the bad stuff is temporary, too.

Rather than make a feeble attempt at "sermonizing" you into action, let me tell you about a remarkable woman I learned of not long ago—a Mexican-

American woman living in Texas that I'll call Maria Gallagos. About 10 years ago Mrs. Gallagos found herself newly widowed with five fast-growing adolescent children to care for. From her dead husband, she inherited a small family business she soon discovered was some $250,000 in debt and on the brink of bankruptcy.

This sweet but troubled woman could be considered a "bad risk" by any banker's yardstick. As a matter of fact, even the Small Business Administration refused to lend her money when she decided to open a Mexican food restaurant as a means of salvaging her rather meager inheritance and supporting her brood.

A lesser individual might have opted for defeat and subsistence as a welfare recipient. But Maria was tough, proud, and determined. Somehow she managed to scrape together $15,000 and opened her tiny ten-table restaurant against all odds. Three very long years later, SBA finally decided she might make it and granted her long-term financing. Today, Maria's restaurant chain encompasses six thriving restaurant outlets, a profitable Mexican food processing business, employs 700 people—including all five of her now-grown children—and grosses more than $12 million in annual sales.

You think you've got trouble? Here's a member of a minority group, a woman with little experience and five children to care for, the restaurant business with a failure rate higher than any other single category of small business, a mountain of debt to overcome; the odds seem almost insurmountable. But they weren't.

Maria Gallagos is a classic example of what to do when life gives you lemons: You make a great big pitcher of lemonade.

Vignettes and anecdotes about the triumph of the human spirit over adversity can—and do—fill volumes. If the day ever comes when you find yourself in dire emotional and financial straits, I sincerely hope you, too, will have the courage, the fortitude, the just plain guts to do what is both right and necessary: Pick yourself up, dust yourself off, and start all over again.

15

Parting Shots

Before actually starting your own business you would be well-advised to run through the following checklist. While it is certainly not all-inclusive (nor does every question apply to every individual business situation), most items covered will apply to you. The more "yes" answers you can check, the better off you and your business will be.

Now's your chance. Once you are actually swamped with the day-to-day details of operating your shop, you probably will not have time to thoughtfully and carefully consider each of these important questions.

Do yourself one further favor: Be truthful. Make a truly honest effort at candor. Consider carefully before deciding that a particular question doesn't really apply to you and your situation. The person most likely to be hurt if you "fudge" a bit on your answer is *you*.

NEW BUSINESS START UP CHECKLIST

	Check if Answer is "Yes"

Are You the Type?

Have you rated your personal qualifications using the questions and answers in Chapter 1 (Do You Have What It Takes?) or some similar personality characteristics test? _____

Have you carefully considered your weak points and taken steps to improve them or to find a partner or staff member whose strong points will compensate for them? _____

What Business Should You Choose?

Have you written a summary of your background and experience to help you in making this decision? _____

Have you considered your hobbies and what you would like to do? _____

Does anyone want the services you can perform? _____

Have you studied surveys and/or sought advice and counsel to find out what fields of business are expected to expand in the next few years? _____

Have you worked for someone else in a similar shop to gain more practical experience? _____

What Are Your Chances for Success?

Are general business and economic conditions good? _____

Are business conditions good in the city and neighborhood where you plan to locate? _____

Are current conditions good in the specific line of business you plan to start? _____

Is the competition in your particular line of business favorable for your success? _____

What Will Be Your Return on Investment?

Do you know the typical return on investment in the specific line of business you plan to start? _____

Have you determined how much money you will have to invest in your business? _____

Are you satisfied that the rate of return on the money you invest in your own business will be greater than the rate you would probably receive if you invested that money elsewhere? _____

How Much Money Will You Need?

Have you filled out work sheets similar to those shown in Figures 1 and 2 of this book? _____

In filling out the work sheets have you taken care not to overestimate income? _____

Have you obtained quoted prices for the equipment and supplies you will need? _____

Do you know the costs and quantity of goods which must be in your inventory? _____

Have you estimated expenses only after checking rents, wage scales, utilities, and other pertinent costs in the area where you plan to locate? _____

Have you found what percentage of your estimated sales your projected inventory and each expense line item is and compared each of these percentages with the typical percentage for your line of business? _____

Have you added a sufficient additional amount of money to your estimates to allow for unexpected contingencies? _____

Where Can You Get the Money?

Have you figured up how much money of your own you can put into the business? _____

Do you know how much credit you can get from suppliers (the people you will buy from)? _____

Do you know where you can borrow the rest of the money you need to start your business? _____

Have you selected a progressive and receptive bank with the credit and other services you may need now and in the future? _____

Is the bank of your choice physically located so as to provide both convenience and safety for your banking transactions? _____

Have you talked to a banker about your plans? _____

Does your banker have an interested, helpful attitude toward your plans and problems? _____

Should You Share Ownership with Others?

If you need a partner with money or know-how, do you know someone who will fill the bill—someone with whom you get along well? _____

Do you know the good and bad points about going it alone, having a partner, and incorporating your business? _____

Have you talked to a lawyer about it? _____

Where Should You Locate?

Have you studied the makeup of the population in the city or town where you plan to locate? _____

Do you know what kind of people will want to buy what you plan to sell? _____

Do people fitting that description live and/or work in the area where you plan to locate? _____

Have you checked the number, type, and size of competitors in the area? _____

Does the area honestly need another business like the one you plan to open? _____

Are employees available? _____

Have you selected the key members of your management team?   _____

Have you checked and found to be adequate the utilities, parking, police and fire protection, available housing, schools, and other cultural and community activities?   _____

Are the costs of the location reasonable in terms of taxes and average rents?   _____

Is there sufficient opportunity for growth and expansion?   _____

Have you checked the relative merits of the various shopping areas within the city, including shopping centers?   _____

Have you had a lawyer check the lease and zoning?   _____

Should You Buy an Existing Business?

Have you considered the advantages and disadvantages of buying an existing business? (See Chapter 8—Buying and Selling Existing Businesses.)   _____

Have you compared what it would cost to equip and stock a new business with the price asked for the business you are considering purchasing?   _____

Have you estimated future sales and profits of the existing business for the next few years?   _____

Are your estimated future profits satisfactory?   _____

Have you studied past financial statements of the business to determine the return on investment, sales, and profit trends?   _____

Have you verified the owner's claims about the firm with reports from an independent accountant's analysis of the books?   _____

Is the inventory you will purchase a good buy?   _____

Are equipment and fixtures fairly valued?   _____

If you plan to buy the accounts receivables, are they worth the asking price?   _____

Have you been careful in your appraisal of the company's goodwill?   _____

Are you prepared—if necessary—to assume the company's liabilities and are the creditors aggreeable?   _____

Have you learned the real reason why the present owner wants to sell?   _____

Have you found out what the present owner's reputation is with employees and suppliers?   _____

Have you consulted a lawyer to be sure that the title is good?   _____

Has your lawyer checked to find out if there is any lien against the assets you are buying?   _____

Has your lawyer drawn up an agreement covering all essential points including a seller's warranty for your protection against false statements?   _____

Should You Invest in a Franchise?

Have you considered how the many advantages and disadvantages of franchising apply to you?   _____

Have you made a thorough search to find the right franchise opportunity?   _____

Have you reread the section in Chapter 8 entitled Franchise Schemes and Things?   _____

Have you had a lawyer check out the franchise agreement to ensure adequate protections for you?   _____

Have You Worked Out Plans for Buying Stock?

Have you estimated what share of the market you think you can get?   _____

Do you know how much merchandise (or how many of each item) you will need to buy to open your business?   _____

Do you know what markup is utilized by similar businesses both locally and nationally?   _____

Do you know the average stock turnover in businesses similar to yours?   _____

Have you found suppliers who will sell you what you need at a good price?   _____

Do you have an ongoing plan for finding out what your customers want?   _____

Have you set up a model stock assessment to follow in your buying?   _____

Have you worked out stock control plans to avoid overstocks, understocks, and out-of-stocks; shoplifting and pilferage?   _____

Do you plan to buy most of your stock from a few suppliers rather than a little from many so that those from whom you buy will want to help you succeed?   _____

How Will You Price Your Products and Services?

Have you decided upon your price ranges?   _____

Do you know how to figure what you should charge to cover your costs? To make a profit?   _____

Do you know what your competitors charge?   _____

What Selling Methods Will You Use?

Have you studied the selling and sales promotion methods of your competitors?   _____

Have you studied why customers buy your type of product or service?   _____

Have you thought about why you like to buy from some salespeople while others turn you off?   _____

Have you decided what your methods of selling will be?   _____

Have you outlined your sales promotion policy?   _____

How Will You Select and Train Personnel?

If you need to hire someone to help you, do you know where to look?   _____

Do you know what specific skills and talents the people you hire should possess?   _____

Have you a written job description for each person you will hire?   _____

Do you know the prevailing wage scales?   _____

Do you have a plan for training new employees?   _____

Do you have a plan for providing good supervision and continuing training for your staff?   _____

What Other Management Problems Will You Face?

Do you plan to sell for credit?   _____

If you do, do you have the extra capital necessary to carry accounts receivable?   _____

Will you accept bank cards?   _____

If so, have you made the necessary arrangements for their use?   _____

Have you a policy for returned or defective goods?   _____

Have you planned how you will receive shipments and make deliveries?   _____

Have you considered other policies which must be made in your particular business?   _____

Have you made a written plan to guide yourself in making the best use of your time and effort?   _____

What Records Will You Keep?

Have you planned a system of records that will keep track of your income and expenses, what you owe other people, and what other people owe you?   _____

Have you worked out a way to keep track of your inventory so that you will always have enough on hand for your customers, but not more than you can sell?   _____

Have you planned how to keep your payroll records and take care of tax reporting and payments?   _____

Do you know what financial statements you should prepare?   _____

Do you know how to use these financial statements?   _____

Have you obtained standard operating ratios for your type of business which you plan to use as guides? _____

Do you have an accountant who will help you with your records and financial statements? _____

What Laws Will Affect You?

Have you checked with the proper authorities to find out what, if any, licenses are necessary for you to do business? _____

Do you know what police and health regulations apply to your business? _____

Will your business operations be subject to interstate commerce regulations? _____

If so, do you know to which ones they will be subject? _____

Have you received advice from your lawyer regarding your responsibilities under federal and state laws and local ordinances? _____

How Will You Handle Taxes and Insurance?

Have you worked out a system for handling the withholding tax for your employees? _____

Have you worked out a system for handling sales taxes? _____

Excise taxes? _____

Have you planned an adequate record-keeping system for the efficient preparation of income tax forms? _____

Have you prepared a work sheet for meeting tax obligations (see Figure 10)? _____

Have you talked with an insurance agent about what kinds of insurance you will need and how much it will cost? _____

Have You Set Measurable Goals for Yourself?

Have you set goals and subgoals for your business? _____

Have you specified dates when each goal is to be achieved? _____

Are these realistic goals, that is, will they challenge you but at the same time not call for unreasonable accomplishment? _____

Are the goals specific so that you can measure performance? _____

Have you developed a written plan—possibly using one of the SBA business plan aids to record your ideas, facts, and figures? _____

Have you allowed for obstacles (contingency planning)? _____

Will You Keep up to Date?

Have you made plans to keep up with improvements in your trade or industry? _____

Will you amend your written business plan as circumstances demand?   _____

Remember, the more "yes" answers you can truthfully come up with, the better off both you and your business are likely to be.

BUSINESS LOAN CHECKLIST

	Check if Answer is "Yes"
Can I show present or previous experience working in a business similar to the one I want to start?	_____
If there are gaps in my personal experience, can I present a well-rounded management team (two or three persons) or one or more partners so that we can collectively represent all the skills and talents necessary to manage the business?	_____
Can I demonstrate to the lending institution that I am a good money manager by showing how I have accumulated a good personal net worth and a savings account commensurate with my past income?	_____
Can I exhibit stability by (1) the time I have lived in local area, (2) the length of time at my present residence, (3) the length of time married, or (4) other factors?	_____
Can I show proper planning by (1) the length of time I have been planning to go into business, (2) the steps taken to prepare for going into business, and (3) a comprehensive written business plan, etc.?	_____
Can I demonstrate initiative by, perhaps, having taken a part-time job in a similar business to gain practical experience?	_____
Does my family (if applicable) approve and back my entry into small business ownership?	_____
Do I have in cash 10 to 30 percent of the total amount needed to start the business?	_____
Does my written loan proposal include the following: Personal data including résumé and personal financial statement?	_____
Tax returns for the past 3 years?	_____
All applicable legal documents such as lease agreements, partnership agreements, articles of incorporation, lease-purchase agreements, outstanding notes, etc.?	_____
Accurately completed loan application forms?	_____
A complete list of collateral to be used to secure the loan?	_____
Business financial statements (pro forma statements for a new firm, current financial statements for an existing business)?	_____

Have I included a break-even analysis and margin of safety analysis with my business statements?   _____

Have I included a 2-year cash flow analysis and profit forecast?   _____

Have I spelled out exactly how the proceeds from the loan will be used?   _____

Have I included a copy of my written business plan?   _____

Have I added any other miscellaneous information that might help the loan officer better understand my business?   _____

Am I negotiating the loan at the bank where I normally do business?   _____

If not, have I indicated my willingness to transfer my personal and business checking, savings, and other banking business to the bank with whom I am negotiating?   _____

Again, the list is not all-inclusive nor will each question necessarily apply to every funding request. But once again, the more "yes" answers you can come up with, the better your chances for getting a "yes" answer from your banker.

WHERE TO LOOK FOR HELP

If you are anything close to the norm, you'll need lots of help. Luckily, there are people and places ready, willing, and able to provide it. The following is a list of the more likely sources of assistance. Remember the old adage, "Ask and you shall receive."

One thing's for sure: If you don't ask, you sure won't. Receive, that is.

- The U.S. Small Business Administration (a list of SBA locations nationwide follows). Women can ask for the women's business specialist, a new service. Anyone can request an appointment with the small business development specialist.

- Business development organizations. Most major cities in the United States have one or more nonprofit federally or locally funded agencies providing free or low-cost assistance to small owners. Your nearest SBA office might be a good information and referral source regarding the services of these agencies in your area. If you're a minority group member, contact the Minority Business Development Agency (MBDA), U.S. Department of Commerce, Washington, D.C., for the location of the nearest MBDA.

- Your local college or university campus through their bureau of business research, small business institute, campus library, college of business, and/or individual course offerings.

- Major banks or other financial institutions. Check with their business development department, research unit, and/or commercial lending department.

- Your nearby public library. "Marian the Librarian" can be an excellent source of information on small business.

- The U.S. Bureau of the Census.

- The U.S. Department of Commerce.

- Your local and state chambers of commerce.

- Trade associations. If you cannot locate an association in your field, you can write for information to: Society of Association Executives, 1101 Sixteenth Street, NW, Washington, D.C. 20036.

- City hall. Of special help should be the office of the city clerk, the planning department, traffic engineering, and/or the economic development department.

- Your state's department of economic development. (You may also want to check with other state departments as applicable.)

- Local media including newspapers, billboard companies, radio and television stations. Most major media publish very useful data on business trends, local market conditions, population demographic characteristics, etc. Ask for the promotion department. They usually have what you're after.

- The United States Internal Revenue Service. The IRS has several good publications and conducts regularly scheduled workshops for small business people on subjects relating to taxation.

In addition to the above, watch your local media for announcements of small business management seminars and workshops conducted by government units, educational institutions, and trade associations. The SBA, IRS, and Department of Commerce all conduct such workshops at little or no cost to the participants.

Both specific and general information can often be obtained by contacting your banker, lawyer, accountant, insurance broker, advertising and/or public relations counselor, printer, graphic artist, architect, interior designer, and other professionals. Most major markets have a generous supply of management consultants. When dealing with these folks, proceed with caution. Some are great, some are god-awful.

In addition, you will often find assistance and information for the asking at the office of secretary of state, your state corporation commission, and your county clerk.

The following list of SBA field office addresses is provided for your convenience. Agencies have been known to move, however, so you may want to double-check the location nearest you before driving clear across town.

SBA FIELD OFFICES

Boston	Massachusetts 02114, 150 Causeway Street
Holyoke	Massachusetts 01040, 302 High Street
Augusta	Maine 04330, 40 Western Avenue, Room 512
Concord	New Hampshire 03301, 55 Pleasant Street
Hartford	Connecticut 06103, One Financial Plaza
Montpelier	Vermont 05602, 87 State Street, P.O. Box 605
Providence	Rhode Island 02903, 57 Eddy Street
New York	New York 10007, 26 Federal Plaza, Room 3214
Albany	New York 12207, Twin Towers Building, Room 922
Elmira	New York 14904, 180 State Street, Room 412
Hato Rey	Puerto Rico 00918, Federal Office Building, Carlos Chardon Avenue
Newark	New Jersey 07102, 970 Broad Street, Room 1635
Camden	New Jersey 08104, East Davis Street
Syracuse	New York 13202, 100 South Clinton Street, Room 1073
Buffalo	New York 14202, 111 West Huron Street
St. Thomas	Virgin Islands 00801, Franklin Building
Philadelphia	Bala Cynwyd, Pennsylvania 19004, One Bala Cynwyd Plaza
Harrisburg	Pennsylvania 17108, 1500 North Second Street
Wilkes-Barre	Pennsylvania 18702, 20 North Pennsylvania Avenue
Baltimore	Towson, Md. 21204, 7800 York Road
Wilmington	Delaware 19801, 844 King Street
Clarksburg	West Virginia 26301, 109 North 3d Street
Charleston	West Virginia 25301, Charleston National Plaza, Suite 628
Pittsburgh	Pennsylvania 15222, 1000 Liberty Avenue
Richmond	Virginia 23240, 400 North 8th Street, Room 3015
Washington	D.C. 20417, 1030 15th Street, NW, Suite 250
Atlanta	Georgia 30309, 1720 Peachtree Road, NW, Suite 600
Biloxi	Mississippi 39530, 111 Fred Haise Boulevard
Birmingham	Alabama 35205, 908 South 20th Street
Charlotte	North Carolina 28202, 230 South Tryon Street, Suite 700

Greenville	North Carolina 27834, 215 South Evans Street
Columbia	South Carolina 29201, 1801 Assembly Street
Coral Gables	Florida 33134, 2222 Ponce de Leon Boulevard
Jackson	Mississippi 39201, 200 East Pascagoula Street
Jacksonville	Florida 32202, 400 West Bay Street
West Palm Beach	Florida 33402, 701 Clematis Street
Tampa	Florida 33607, 1802 North Trask Street, Suite 203
Louisville	Kentucky 40202, 600 Federal Place, Room 188
Nashville	Tennessee 37219, 404 James Robertson Parkway, Suite 1012
Knoxville	Tennessee 37902, 502 South Gay Street, Room 307
Memphis	Tennessee 38103, 167 North Main Street
Chicago	Illinois 60604, 219 South Dearborn Street
Springfield	Illinois 62701, 1 North Old State Capitol Plaza
Cleveland	Ohio 44199, 1240 East 9th Street, Room 317
Columbus	Ohio 43215, 85 Marconi Boulevard
Cincinnati	Ohio 45202, 550 Main Street, Room 5524
Detroit	Michigan 48226, 477 Michigan Avenue
Marquette	Michigan 49885, 540 West Kaye Avenue
Indianapolis	Indiana 46204, 575 North Pennsylvania Street
Madison	Wisconsin 53703, 122 West Washington Avenue, Room 713
Milwaukee	Wisconsin 53233, 735 West Wisconsin Avenue
Eau Claire	Wisconsin 54701, 500 South Barstow Street, Room B9AA
Minneapolis	Minnesota 55402, 12 South Sixth Street
Dallas	Texas 75202, 1100 Commerce Street
Albuquerque	New Mexico 87110, 5000 Marble Avenue, NE
Houston	Texas 77002, 1 Allen Center, Suite 705
Little Rock	Arkansas 72201, 611 Gaines Street, P.O. Box 1401
Lubbock	Texas 79401, 1205 Texas Avenue
El Paso	Texas 79902, 4100 Rio Bravo, Suite 300
Lower Rio Grande Valley	Harlingen, Tx. 78550, 222 East Van Buren, Suite 500
Corpus Christi	Texas 78408, 3105 Leopard Street, P.O. Box 9253
Marshall	Texas 75670, 100 South Washington Street, Room G12
New Orleans	Louisiana 70113, 1001 Howard Avenue
Shreveport	Louisiana 71163, 500 Fannin Street
Oklahoma City	Oklahoma 73102, 200 NW 5th Street

San Antonio	Texas 78206, 727 East Durango, Room A-513
Kansas City	Missouri 64106, 1150 Grand Avenue
Des Moines	Iowa 50309, 210 Walnut Street
Omaha	Nebraska 68102, Nineteenth and Farnam Streets
St. Louis	Missouri 63101, Mercantile Tower, Suite 2500
Wichita	Kansas 67202, 110 East Waterman Street
Denver	Colorado 80202, 721 19th Street, Room 407
Casper	Wyoming 82601, 100 East B Street, Room 4001
Fargo	North Dakota 58102, 653 2d Avenue, North, Room 218
Helena	Montana 59601, 613 Helena Avenue, P.O. Box 1690
Salt Lake City	Utah 84138, 125 South State Street, Room 2237
Rapid City	South Dakota 57701, 515 9th Street
Sioux Falls	South Dakota 57102, 8th and Main Avenue
San Francisco	California 94105, 211 Main Street
Fresno	California 93721, 1229 N Street
Sacramento	California 95825, 2800 Cottage Way
Honolulu	Hawaii 96813, 1149 Bethel Street, Room 402
Agana	Guam 96910, Ada Plaza Center Building, P.O. Box 927
Los Angeles	California 90071, 350 South Figueroa Street
Las Vegas	Nevada 89101, 301 East Stewart
Reno	Nevada 89504, 300 Booth Street
Phoenix	Arizona 85012, 3030 North Central Avenue
San Diego	California 92188, 880 Front Street
Seattle	Washington 98174, 915 Second Avenue
Anchorage	Alaska 99501, 1016 West Sixth Avenue, Suite 200
Fairbanks	Alaska 99701, 501½ Second Avenue
Boise	Idaho 83701, 216 North 8th Street, P.O. Box 2618
Portland	Oregon 97204, 1220 South West Third Avenue
Spokane	Washington 99102, Courthouse Building, Room 651, P.O. Box 2167

TERMS AND EQUATIONS

When it comes to business terminology, many small business owners don't know their assets from their liabilities. There is absolutely nothing wrong with not knowing—as long as you don't permit this condition to continue. Unfortunately, all too many budding entrepreneurs are reluctant to admit they really don't know what their attorney, banker, or accountant is talking about. If this applies to you, the following brief listing of the most commonly used business terms and their meanings might prove helpful. If it's not for you, congratulations and skip this section.

After all, you can always return to it later, when no one is looking.

TERMS

Asset

An asset is something owned by the business and of use to the business.

Some assets are necessary so that there is a place for people to come together to work or to operate the business. Such assets include land, buildings, equipment, trucks, etc. These sorts of assets are generally kept for a fairly long time and are not sold to make a profit for the company.

Other kinds of assets may be kept for only a relatively short time and are sold to make a profit for the firm or are used to buy other assets or to pay off operating costs of the business. Such items would include inventories, which are sold for profit, or cash, which in turn is spent to buy other assets or to pay for other costs. Receivables are considered an asset because they represent money owed to you. As soon as the outstanding debt owed you is paid, you have more cash to use in the operation of your business.

Bad Debt

A bad debt is a receivable amount which you cannot collect.

A receivable arises when you sell something on credit—in other words, you do not collect cash immediately. If a customer never pays you that amount, you don't have a receivable—you have a bad debt. You have lost that amount of money which you expected to receive, and that's pretty bad. Most businesses assume that they will have a certain percentage of their total receivables which will become uncollectible—bad debts. They plan for them and price their services or products to compensate for them. I suggest you do likewise.

Balance Sheet

A balance sheet is a report which shows, on any particular day, what assets you own, what liabilities you owe, and the amount of your investment in your business. The report is called a balance sheet because of the way it is written; the amounts on the left and right sides of the report are equal, or are "in balance," as shown by the example on page 106.

Therefore, the total of the liabilities and investment in the business will always equal the total of the assets; also, to find the investment in the business, you would subtract the liabilities from the assets.

To further confuse things, a balance sheet is also called a financial statement since it shows the financial condition of the business on a particular day.

Buildings

Buildings refer to any factory, warehouse, office, store, or garage owned by the business. Any structure which is used for the operation of the business or to hold inventory or equipment owned by the business is considered a building.

Such buildings may be on land owned by the business or may be on rented land. The buildings themselves may be owned or rented. When owned, they will appear on the balance sheet; when rented, they usually do not appear there, since only assets owned by the business appear on its balance sheet. Buildings are an asset.

Cash

Cash is money belonging to the business which may be in your pocket, the cash register, or in the bank. If it's in your pocket, it should not be mixed with your personal cash. As a matter of fact, except in very rare cases, it shouldn't be in your pocket. Cash should not be spent—except in very specific cases—to buy things for your business. It also should not be used to pay bills the business may owe. The cash your business has in the bank is usually in a checking account. Since this money can be spent only by writing a check and since a check gives you a record, checks should be issued any time you are paying anything for your business. About the only exception to this no-cash rule is your petty cash fund (listed below). Cash is an asset.

Corporate Seal

A corporate seal is a notation made on certain legal documents and agreements in which one of the parties is a corporation.

An officer of the corporation will sign a document, and the seal of the corporation may then also be added. Generally, the seal is a metal disk about the size of a half-dollar which is mounted on the face of a handstamp. The document requiring the corporate seal is placed between the stamps of the tool, and the impression is squeezed onto the paper.

Should you choose to incorporate your business at any time, you will receive a corporate seal at the time your legal filing for corporate status is achieved.

Corporation

A corporation is one of the three basic forms of legal organization for your firm. The other two basic forms are sole proprietorship and partnership.

In order to be a legal "company" it is necessary to file certain forms with the state to obtain articles of incorporation, etc. In this form of organization, at least three persons are required to start the company as incorporators. A corporation sells shares of stock, which are certificates indicating ownership, to as many people as is desirable. The buyers are called shareholders. The shareholders then elect a board of directors who guide the company on an overall basis. The board of directors then elect a president and other officers who run the company on a day-to-day basis.

Cost of Sales

Cost of sales represents the cost of the particular products or services which are sold by your business.

When the product sold is merely purchased from another company for resale, the cost of sales is basically the price paid to the supplier. When the product is manufactured or assembled, the cost of sales includes the cost of the required parts in the product, labor required for manufacture or assembly, and other costs relating directly to the product.

If the firm sells services, the cost of sales includes mainly the wages for the people who provide the service plus certain other required costs which relate directly to the service. Cost of sales is subtracted from sales in finding net income figures.

Deposit Slip

A desposit slip is a form which is given to the bank along with the coins, currency, and checks which you deposit to your account. The deposit slip merely provides a listing of the items and dollar amounts put into the bank. The bank keeps a copy for their records and you keep one for yours.

Earnings Projection

An earnings projection is an estimate of how much money your business expects to earn in the future. This is often referred to as a pro forma statement. When completed, a statement of your earnings projection will look like an income statement. The difference is that an income statement reflects what happened in the past, while a projection (or pro forma) reflects what you expect to happen in the future. Such a projection may cover a month, a year, or several months or years to come.

Equipment

Equipment includes machinery, trucks, cars, tools, showcases, scales, two-wheeled hand trucks, lockers, air-conditioning units, and other such items which are owned by the business. Sometimes, pieces of equipment that are used for the same purpose are grouped together and called "delivery equipment," "factory equipment," "office equipment," etc. Equipment is an asset.

Income Statement

An income statement is a report which tells you how much your business made or lost over a specific period of time. The period of time might be a day, a week, a month, or a year or more. Generally, such a report covers not less than a month nor more than a year. An example of an income statement can be found on page 109.

Keep in mind that the net income figure shown at the bottom of your income statement does not necessarily mean there will be a cash increase of that amount during the period covered by the statement. Some of the income may very well have gone into purchasing equipment, inventory, etc., or toward reduction of liabilities.

Income Taxes

Income taxes are taxes which must be paid to the federal or state government and which are based on profits made by your business. Income taxes represent a cost to the business and therefore are shown on the income statement.

Income Taxes Payable

Income taxes payable represent taxes which are payable to the federal or to state or local governments by the business. They are usually paid four or five times a year, and, therefore, at certain times, you will owe the government for taxes which you have not yet paid. These amounts are just like any other payable except the amounts are owed for income taxes. Income taxes payable are liabilities.

Inventory

This item is of most importance to businesses which sell a product. For such firms, inventory includes the product items which you have purchased or manufactured but which you have not yet sold. In most businesses which sell a product, it is necessary to have a stock of these products on hand—that is the inventory.

In many cases, the products being sold are purchased in finished form from another company (your supplier) and merely sold to your customer as they are, perhaps after first repackaging the item. In other cases, the products being sold are manufactured or assembled in whole or in part within the company. If this is so, inventory includes both the completed products and the parts and pieces used to make the product.

Sometimes supply items such as envelopes, writing paper, and other printed forms might be included as inventory. Businesses which sell services typically do not have inventory, except for inventories of supply items.

Inventory is an asset.

Invoice

An invoice is a bill. You may send a bill to one of your customers, or you may receive a bill from one of your suppliers (often called vendors).

A bill which you sent to a customer is called a customer invoice; a bill received from a supplier is called a vendor or purchase invoice. Since the words "invoice," "bill," and "order" are all used for these two different things, it can be confusing. I would suggest you decide to call one a *customer* invoice and the other a *vendor* or *purchase* invoice and stick with the terms you decide upon.

Land

Land is any ground which is owned by your business. You may put parking lots, buildings, or other structures on the land or just leave it empty for later use. When land is owned, it appears on the balance sheet; when it is rented, it usually does not appear there. Land is an asset.

Landlord's Waiver

A landlord's waiver is a legal form which is signed by the landlord of the premises you rent for your business. This form is usually not necessary unless requested by one of your suppliers or your banker, etc.

When your landlord signs such a waiver, he or she is giving assurance that if you fail to pay the rent, the landlord will not try to hold any of your inventory, furniture, etc., in lieu of such payment.

Liability

A liability is something which is owed by your business to other people or other businesses. A liability includes such things as payables, income tax payables, and other obligations of the company.

Net Income

Net income is the amount that is left after subtracting all the costs of running the business from the sales generated by the business. Such costs include the cost of sales, other operating costs, and income taxes.

Other Operating Costs

Other operating costs include costs other than those relating directly to the product or service being sold by the business. Costs relating directly to the product or service are included in cost of sales.

Other operating costs include items such as salaries for salespeople, secretaries, and clerks; repairs to office furniture and equipment; hospitalization insurance for office employees, etc. Other operating costs are deducted from sales to determine net income.

Owner's Equity

Owner's equity represents the amount of cash or other assets which you have put in and have left in the business. The total amount of owner's equity is determined by subtracting the liabilities of the business from the assets of the business; the amount that is left represents your investment in the business.

The dollar amount of your investment in your business merely represents the difference between the assets and the liabilities of the business. That amount is not necessarily what the business is worth. If you sold the business for cash and paid off all your liabilities, the amount which you would have left might be more or less than what is called your investment in the business.

Partnership

A partnership is one of the three basic forms of legal organization for your company. The other two basic forms are sole proprietorship and corporation.

In a partnership form of organization there are two or more owners who organize the business, put in the owners' equity, and share in the profits or losses of the company. Before starting the firm, the owners (called partners) should agree on how much owner's equity each partner must contribute, the extent that each partner will work in the company, the share of the profits or losses to be received by each of them, etc. This partnership agreement should be in writing to avoid any further misunderstandings. It is advisable to have this partnership agreement prepared by an attorney. If the business is not successful and the partnership can't pay all it owes, the partners may be required to do so utilizing their personal assets.

Payables

Payables are the amounts of cash which your business owes to other people or businesses. The amount that your business owes is said to be "payable" since you have not yet paid the cash. The opposite of payables is receivables.

Payment on Account

Receivables are defined as the amounts of cash which other people or businesses owe you. Whenever they pay a part of that amount they are said to have made a "payment on account."

Petty Cash

Petty cash is a special kind of cash fund used to pay for minor items. Generally, you should pay all bills by writing checks. However, sometimes it is more convenient to pay small amounts such as delivery charges with cash. Therefore, it may be convenient to have a small amount of bills and coins kept in a safe place to use in this manner. These amounts should not be kept in the cash register, or at least if they are, they should be kept separate from the other cash in the register. It is also very advisable to keep a petty cash journal— a written account of the dates, amounts, and use to which petty cash is put.

Receivables

Receivables are the amounts of cash which other people or businesses owe to your business. When you sell things on credit, the amount that the buyer owes you is said to be "receivable" since it is owed to you and you will (you hope) receive it. The opposite of receivables is payables. Receivables are an asset.

Receiving Report

A receiving report is a form on which you or one of your employees has written down a description and quantity of merchandise which you have ordered from a supplier and which is being delivered. You do this so that you have a record of what you have received. Later, when you receive a vendor or purchase invoice for these items, you should compare the items shown on the bill with the receiving report to make sure you actually received everything for which you are being billed.

References

References are the names of people which you give to someone so that they can contact these people to ask questions about you or your business. They are normally utilized to provide other people's opinions about your character, personal habits, payment record, etc. The persons you use as references may be relatives, friends, business associates, teachers, etc. References are usually provided to vendors or suppliers, potential landlords, and bankers or other credit-granting individuals or businesses.

Sale

A sale occurs when a person or another business buys the product or service of your business.

Sales Discount

A sales discount is a reduction from the regular selling price you charge another person or a business when they buy something from you. A sales discount might be granted when the customer pays you cash immediately rather than charging a purchase; when the customer buys in large volume, thus saving you shipping and handling costs, etc.; when you have merchandise which is sold or damaged and which can only be sold by reducing the regular price.

Signature Card

A signature card is a card requested by a bank when you open a checking or savings account. On this card are placed the signatures of all persons who are allowed to sign checks for your company. The card ensures that the bank's personnel can identify those signatures and make sure they are the ones which should be appearing on the checks. If the signature on one of your business checks is different from that which appears on the signature card, the bank may not cash the check.

Sole Proprietorship

A sole proprietorship is one of the three basic forms of legal organization for your company. The other two basic forms are partnership and corporation.

In the sole proprietorship form of organization there is one owner (you), and if your company should get into a position of owing more to others than can be satisfied by the amount of cash and other assets of the business, your personal assets (home, car, etc.) may be required to be sold to pay the obligations of your business.

Trade-Style Registration

A trade-style registration results when you file a legal form with the state to keep anyone else from using the name of your company. This is not required if you operate your firm as a corporation. If you operate as a sole proprietorship or partnership, it is desirable to file a trade-style registration to avoid the confusion that would result between your company and someone else's if you both use the same business name. Since the state as a matter of course only lets one corporation use a particular name, such application is not necessary when you operate as a corporation.

Vendor

A vendor is a supplier to your company. The vendor may provide you with goods or services. A vendor is an outside firm or individual who sells you something.

EQUATIONS

The following brief list of equations should prove helpful if the formula for figuring any of these varied, but very important, factors ever slips your mind.

Assets

$$\text{Assets} = \text{liabilities} + \text{owner's equity (or investment)}$$

Owner's Equity or Investment

$$\text{Owner's investment} = \text{assets less liabilities}$$

Break-Even Point (BE)

$$\text{BE} = \text{total fixed costs} - \frac{\text{total variable costs}}{\text{corresponding sales volume}}$$

Cost Per 1000 (CPM)

$$\text{CPM} = \frac{\text{cost per spot}}{\text{total number of listeners}}$$

The CPM is used as a measure of effectiveness when purchasing advertising media.

Margin of Safety (Used to Determine the Difference between Break-Even and Projected Sales)

$$\text{Margin of safety} = \frac{\text{sales} - \text{break-even in sales}}{\text{break-even in sales}}$$

For more information on equations and ratios, I would suggest you obtain copies of the following booklets published by the Small Business Administration. They can be obtained from your nearest SBA office, or you can write to the Superintendent of Documents, Washington, D.C. 20402 for current price information:

A Handbook of Small Business Finance, SBMS no. 15
Ratio Analysis for Small Business, SBMS no. 20

CAVEAT EMPTOR!
CONSULTANTS AND OTHER BAD GUYS

I obviously have absolutely nothing against somebody making a buck. Unfortunately, lots of people try to make a buck or 2 or 5 off of existing or potential small business owners. Many of these people are called business consultants.

There are business consultants who more than earn their keep. But finding and separating the good from the bad is difficult, risky, and time-consuming. It can cost you a lot of money. If you really don't luck out, it can literally cost you your business.

Since there is no licensing, certification requirements, or competency examinations for individuals or firms who want to provide management consulting services to the small business community for a fee, literally anyone can purport to be such an expert, hang out a shingle, and solicit suckers from whom they can extract money for advice.

In addition to advice, some consulting firms will prepare loan proposals, feasibility studies, prospectus packages, and other such services and documents—always for a fee. The fee can range from reasonable to unreasonable; the service can range from terrible to terrific.

While there is absolutely no way to be absolutely sure you are dealing with a good—or a bad—small business consulting firm, one red flag should be any consultant who seeks to charge you a percentage of a loan. That is to say, the consultant will prepare a loan proposal for, say, $100,000 and receive, say, 10 percent, or $10,000, for this service. Please be advised that if the loan is granted or guaranteed by the Small Business Administration, this percent of the loan fee is totally unpermissible. As a matter of fact, the SBA demands disclosure of all fees paid by the borrower to any outside consultant for the preparation of the loan package. Also keep in mind that it takes no more time to prepare a good loan proposal for a $10,000 loan than it does for one of $10 million.

I am always a little more than leery of any consulting firm that attempts to guarantee they can secure investors or lenders for a small business owner.

To further muddy the waters, there are some very good small business management firms and consultants available. The problem is finding them. In short, caveat emptor. Let the buyer (that's you) beware.

OSHA AND OTHER SCARY STORIES

The intrusion of various pieces of legislation, the federal and local agencies who administer them, and the reams of regulations such agencies produce as a means of doing so are legendary. The problems they create for the small business owner can truly be the stuff of nightmares. The Occupational Safety and Health Administration (OSHA), a division of the U.S. Department of Labor, is just one of the many. It happens to be an exceptionally intrusive agency since it is responsible for ensuring that every worker in America has a safe working environment. Now this sounds like a pretty good premise from which to operate. Unfortunately, OSHA has gone a bit overboard, to the point where strict adherence to all of its rules and regulations has resulted in increased costs, decreased profits, and in some instances the failure and/or shutdown of individual businesses.

Unfortunately, OSHA is not the only agency likely to give you ulcers. In the Department of Labor alone you very well may have to deal with the Bureau of Apprenticeship and Training, and the Wage and Hour Division folks.

It's also likely that the Equal Employment Opportunity Commission (EEOC), the Social Security Administration, the U.S. Postal Service, the Consumer Product Safety Commission, and several other major federal departments will have something to say about the way you operate. It is a certainty that you will deal with the United States Internal Revenue Service. If you don't, you will certainly be dealing with the federal court system and, possibly, the federal penitentiary nearest your business.

Those agencies or regulations most likely to impact on your day-to-day operations are OSHA, EEOC, Wage and Hour (the Wage and Hour Division of the U.S. Department of Labor), and section 504 of the Handicapped regulations which will govern how problems of your employees and customers who are in any way handicapped must be addressed by you and your firm. In addition, you very well may be up for a bad time or two from a labor union or two.

And, of course, you absolutely will be impacted by the IRS and all tax-collecting agencies of local units of government.

To guide you through this maze of obstacles, look to your accountant and attorney to keep you honest. Comply fully with whatever regulations are applicable, from ensuring that your employees are paid at least the minimum wage to having a fire extinguisher and first-aid kit ready for emergencies and OSHA.

If you find all this discouraging, disheartening, and enraging, welcome to the club. Although you must comply, you do have a bit of recourse through your congressional representatives and other elected officials. While it's nice to work alone, you'll also find additional effectiveness by combining your efforts to minimize such governmental intrusion on your business's operation through joining forces with other interested small business people in your trade organizations and chamber of commerce.

SOMETHING SPECIAL (THAT'S YOU!)

Pardon me while I step on my soapbox for a few moments. What I'm about to say deserves to be said from that vantage point.

Small businesses—and the people who own and operate same—are the real backbone of the American economy. It's the sector within the private sector that provides the majority of our job opportunities, goods, and services. It's what really makes our system great.

To be a working part of that glorious whole is indeed something special. It takes men and women of real courage, vision, energy, creativity, ingenuity, fortitude, imagination, and just plain guts.

There is something almost indefinable about taking a raw idea and molding it into reality; creating an income from your own efforts for yourself—and possibly other people, too—that absolutely nothing else in life can match. To dare, to dream, to face failure so as to achieve success, to believe so strongly in yourself and your abilities that you leave behind the safe known for the risky unknown truly does take someone special.

If you opt to join the army of entrepreneurs that march to a drummer heard only by the relative few, I truly salute you. You know now it's not easy. But it is possible. And you are one of the special ones.

I wish you Godspeed, green lights, and blue skies. I hope that this book contributes in some small way to your success. And I sincerely hope you make it big.

Bibliography (A Little Bedtime Reading)

Brown, Diver, *The Entrepreneur's Guide*, Macmillan, New York, 1980.

Clark, Leta W., *How to Open Your Own Shop or Gallery*, St. Martin's Press, New York, 1978.

Crispi, Colleen Bickford, *Self Help for Beauty Salon Owners*, The Bickford Co., Phoenix, 1974.

Dible, Donald M., *Up Your Own Organization!*, The Entrepreneur Press, Santa Clara, Calif., 1971, 1974.

Drucker, Peter F., *Managing for Results*, Harper and Row, New York, 1964.

Fields, Lewis W. *Bookkeeping Made Simple*, Doubleday (Simple Books), Garden City, N.Y., 1956.

Greene, Gardiner G., *How to Start and Manage Your Own Business*, McGraw-Hill, New York, 1975.

Hailes, William D., Jr., and Raymond T. Hubbard, *Small Business Management*, Van Nostrand, New York, 1977.

Hewitt, Geof, *Working For Yourself*, Rodale Press, Emmaus, Pa., 1977.

Jessup, Claudia, and Genie Chipps, *The Woman's Guide to Starting a Business*, Holt, Rinehart and Winston, New York, 1976.

Mancuso, Joseph R., *How to Start, Finance, and Manage Your Own Small Business*, Prentice-Hall, Englewood Cliffs, N.J., 1978.

Metcalf, Wendell, *How to Make Money in Your Own Small Business*, The Entrepreneur Press, Vacaville, Calif., 1977.

Miller, Daniel, *Starting a Small Restaurant*, The Harvard Common Press, Boston, 1978.

Reddin, W. J., *Effective Management by Objectives*, McGraw-Hill, New York, 1971.

Stanton, William J., *Fundamentals of Marketing*, McGraw-Hill, New York, 1974.

Townsend, Robert, *Up The Organization*, Fawcett, Greenwich, Conn., 1971.

Index